SOCIAL WORK
AND THE COURTS

GARLAND REFERENCE LIBRARY OF SOCIAL SCIENCE
VOLUME 1046

Social Work
and the Courts
A Casebook

Daniel Pollack

Garland Publishing, Inc.
New York and London
1997

Library of Congress Cataloging-in-Publication Data

Pollack, Daniel.
    Social work and the courts : a casebook / by Daniel Pollack.
        p.   cm. — (Garland reference library of social science ; v. 1046)
    Includes bibliographical references and index.
    ISBN 0-8153-2069-8 (alk. paper) — ISBN 0-8153-2070-1 (paperback)
    1. Public welfare—Law and legislation—United States—Cases.   2. Social
workers—Legal status, laws, etc.—United States—Cases.   I. Title.   II. Series.
KF3721.A7P65   1997
344.73'0313—dc20
[347.304313]   96-44894
                                                                CIP

Paperback cover design by Mark Azzolina, Café Design.

Printed on acid-free, 250-year-life paper
Manufactured in the United States of America

With love, to my parents,
Leonard and Betty Pollack

Table of Contents

Detailed Table of Contents

D. Adoption

E. Child Abuse & Neglect

Chapter 2 SOCIAL WORKER LIABILITY & IMMUNITY

Chapter 6 INCOME SUPPORT

Chapter 7 SOCIAL WORKERS IN COURT

Chapter 8 SOCIAL WORKERS AS EMPLOYEES

ISSUES & DECISIONS

CHAPTER 1 CHILD WELFARE

A. CUSTODY

Bottoms v. Bottoms, **444 S.E.2d 276 (Va.App. 1994)**: As a matter of law, is a person who is involved in a sexually active lesbian relationship an unfit parent whose rights as a parent may be revoked and custody given to a third party? No.

In re Kirchner, **164 Ill. 2d 468 (1995)**: May a child be available for adoption if parental rights have not been properly terminated? No.

In re Marriage of Kovash, **858 P.2d 351 (Mont. 1993)**: May a court change the terms of a temporary custody order without definitely identifying a change in circumstances of the parties? Yes.

Sherman v. Sherman, **1994 Tenn. App. Lexis 660**: Where a parent lives with or has contact with an HIV positive person, can the court restrict visitation and require HIV testing in order to address the other parent's fear of the children's potential contact with the HIV positive person? No.

State ex rel. S.C. v. Chafin, **444 S.E.2d 62 (W.Va. 1994)**: Does a service plan filed by a department of human services constitute an adequate case plan for the placement of a child who is in the custody of the state? No.

Kingsley v. Kingsley, **623 So.2d 780 (Fla.App. 5 Dist. 1993)**: Do children have the right to initiate termination of their parents' rights and to petition for their own adoption proceedings? No.

Nance v. Arkansas Dept. of Human Services, **870 S.W.2d 721 (Ark. 1994)**: Does a juvenile court, having found a child to be dependent-neglected, have the authority to make a change of custody award? Yes.

In re Marriage of Carney, 598 P.2d 36 (Cal. 1979): Within the context of custody awards, does a disability necessarily imply an inability of a parent to serve in a child's best interest? No.

Brossoit v. Brossoit, 36 Cal.Rptr.2d 919 (Cal.App. 1 Dist. 1995): In a child custody dispute, what law controls in determining which state has jurisdiction? The Uniform Child Custody Jurisdiction Act is controlling.

Mezo v. Elmergawi, 855 F.Supp. 59 (E.D.N.Y. 1994): If a country does not participate in the Hague Convention on the Civil Aspects of Child Abduction, may there be a valid claim filed under the Convention? No.

B. FOSTER CARE

DeShaney v. Winnebago County DSS, 109 S.Ct. 998 (1989): Does the government have a constitutional duty to protect a child against physical abuse if it has not taken that child into custody? No.

Pfoltzer, et al. v. County of Fairfax, 775 F.Supp. 874 (E.D.Va. 1991): Does a department of social services have a duty to provide a foster home with a desired religious background of the biological parents so as to avoid any violation of the right to the free exercise of religion? No.

Artist M. v. Johnson, 917 F.2d 980 (7th Cir. 1990): Does the federal Adoption Assistance and Child Welfare Act of 1980 create a right under which a plaintiff may bring a claim that an organization bound under that legislation has violated such legislation and that the state is equally bound by such federal legislation under 42 U.S.C. § 1983? Yes.

Wildauer v. Frederick County, 993 F.2d 369 (4th Cir. 1993): Are a foster parent's rights violated by neglect investigations, searches, and removal of the foster children? No.

C. TERMINATION OF PARENTAL RIGHTS

Ferguson v. Stafford County DSS, 417 S.E.2d 1 (Va.App. 1992): Is incarceration in and of itself just cause for termination of parental rights? No.

Ybarra v. Texas Dept. of Human Services, **869 S.W.2d 574 (Tex.App.-Corpus Christi 1993)**: Absent clear and convincing evidence, may parental rights be terminated? No.

Helen W. v. Fairfax County, **407 S.E.2d 25 (Va.App. 1991)**: Can a court terminate residual parental rights of parents who refuse to comply with reasonable and appropriate efforts of social service, medical, and mental health agencies, if such termination is in the best interest of the child? Yes.

D. ADOPTION

Kennedy v. Children's Serv. Society of Wisconsin, **17 F.3d 980 (7th Cir. 1994)**: May adoptive parents successfully sue an adoption agency for withdrawing from services based on claims of defamation, breach of contract and intentional infliction of emotional distress when such charges involve adoptive parents who are members of a cult? No.

Engstrom v. State, **461 N.W.2d 309 (Iowa 1990)**: In the context of a preadoption agreement, can social workers be held liable for social worker malpractice, the infliction of emotional distress, breach of contract, and denial of due process rights when the cause of action is not specified in the applicable statute and administrative rules? No.

Michael J. v. County of Los Angeles, Dept. of Adoptions, **247 Cal.Rptr. 504 (Cal.App. 2 Dist. 1988)**: Should a county department of adoptions be immune from liability for intentional or negligent misrepresentation or concealment in relation to the health of a prospective adoptee? No.

Matter of Baby M, **537 A.2d 1227 (N.J. 1988)**: Regarding a contract for surrogate motherhood, are the best interests of the child the sole controlling question pertaining to termination of parental rights? No.

Meracle v. Children's Serv. Society of Wisconsin, **437 N.W.2d 532 (Wis. 1989)**: May adoptive parents successfully sue for emotional distress and extraordinary medical expenses when an adoption agency negligently misrepresents the health of a pre-adoptive child? No, as to the emotional distress; yes, as to the medical expenses.

In re Roger B., **418 N.E.2d 751 (Ill.App. 1981)**: By restricting the access to birth records of adopted children and their biological families, does a state violate a "fundamental" right, a privacy right, or a right to freedom of information? No.

E. CHILD ABUSE & NEGLECT

State v. Hosto-Worthy, **877 S.W.2d 150 (Mo.App.E.D. 1994)**: When acting jointly with a social worker, are law enforcement officers required to give *Miranda* warnings in a situation in which child abuse is suspected? Yes.

In Interest of M.A.V., **425 S.E.2d 377 (Ga.App. 1992)**: Is evidence from termination of parental rights for one child useable to support a decision to terminate a parent's rights with regard to another child of the same parent? No.

A.Y. v. Dept. of Public Welfare, **583 A.2d 515 (Pa.Cmwlth. 1990)**: Can the report of a small child regarding alleged sexual abuse be presented through heresay testimony by her mother? Can the testimony of a social worker be admitted into evidence when no videotape was made of the interview and no psychologist evaluated the child's credibility? Yes.

The People v. Cabral, **15 Cal.Rptr.2d 866 (Cal.App. 5 Dist. 1993)**: May a letter written to a psychotherapist, other than for the purpose of securing a diagnosis or treatment, be protected under the psychotherapist-patient privileged communication statute? No.

M.R.F. v. Dept. of Public Welfare, **595 A.2d 644 (Pa.Cmwlth 1991)**: In cases of expungement of a name from a child abuse registry, will "substantial evidence" be sufficient to keep a perpetrator's name on the registry? Yes.

Hildebrand v. Hildebrand, **736 F.Supp. 1512 (S.D.Ind. 1990)**: May a statute of limitations be a bar to a successful civil lawsuit regarding physical and sexual abuse? Yes.

CHAPTER 2 SOCIAL WORKER LIABILITY AND IMMUNITY

Tobias v. County of Racine, **507 N.W.2d 340 (Wis.App. 1993)**: May a department of social services be liable for damages caused by a superseding cause? No.

Gloria G. v. State DSRS, **833 P.2d 797 (Kan. 1992)**: May a state social services agency be liable for acts its employees commit which are "discretionary" under a Tort Claims Act? No.

Caldwell v. LeFaver, **928 F.2d 331 (9th Cir. 1991)**: Does a theory of absolute immunity or qualified immunity apply where a social worker removes children from one guardian to the care of another legal guardian in an emergency situation and the original guardian brings a civil suit? Absolute immunity.

Babcock v. Tyler, **884 F.2d 497 (9th Cir. 1989)**: Are social workers who perform investigative and placement services following child dependency proceedings entitled to absolute immunity? Yes.

Rowe v. Bennett, **514 A.2d 802 (Me. 1986)**: May a client successfully sue a social worker for negligent infliction of emotional distress if the client cannot show any physical injuries or if the client cannot show an underlying tort? Yes.

Franz v. Lytle, **997 F.2d 784 (10th Cir. 1993)**: Does a police officer have qualified immunity to conduct a warrantless search of a child's body for child abuse? No.

CHAPTER 3 MENTAL HEALTH ISSUES

In re Schouler, **723 P.2d 1103 (Wash. 1986)**: Can a court decide for an incompetent individual whether or not ECT treatment is an appropriate medical treatment? Yes.

Brookhouser v. State of California, **13 Cal.Rptr.2d 658 (Cal.App. 6 Dist. 1992)**: Can a social worker's and state's breach of duty to care, via a negligent act of omission, be construed as causing harm that might otherwise have been avoided? No, unless it can be determined that the injury would not have occurred *but for* the defendant's conduct, or, if the defendant's conduct was a *substantial* factor in causing the injury.

O'Connor v. Donaldson, **422 U.S. 563 (1975)**: Is it a violation of the Constitution's Fourteenth Amendment for a state to confine a non-dangerous individual who is capable of living safely in society? Yes.

Ricci v. Okin, **781 F.Supp. 826 (D.Mass. 1992)**: If there is a plan for the closing of an institution, does that institution remain responsible during the interim for adhering to previously agreed-upon rules and guidelines governing the care of the residents of the institution? Yes.

Lessard v. Schmidt, **349 F.Supp 1078 (1972)**: Does an involuntary civil commitment statute violate a person's right to due process by denying a timely fair hearing and by failing to provide an easily understandable standard for detainment and commitment? Yes.

Addington v. Texas, **441 U.S. 418 (1979)**: What standard of proof is required by the Fourteenth Amendment in a civil proceeding brought under state law to commit an individual involuntarily for an indefinite period of time to a state mental hospital? Clear and convincing evidence.

Grkman v. Dept. of Public Welfare, **637 A.2d 761 (Pa. Cmwlth. 1994)**: Must a hearing officer's decision confirming the transfer of a nursing home patient to domiciliary care be supported by substantial evidence? Yes.

CHAPTER 4 AGING

McKennon v. Nashville Banner Publishing Co., **115 S.Ct. 879 (1995)**: Is employee misconduct discovered after an employee has been unfairly discharged in violation of the Age Discrimination in Employment Act of 1967 a complete bar to recovery? No.

Billingslea v. State of Texas, **780 S.W.2d 271 (Tex.Cr.App. 1989)**: Does failure to care for and secure medical attention for an ailing, live-in parent constitute criminal negligence? No, unless there is an explicit statutory duty to act on behalf of the ailing individual.

In re Byrne, **402 So.2d 383 (Fla. 1981)**: Is an adult protective service statute constitutional which allows a department of social services to take emergency involuntary custody of an elderly person if sufficient probable cause and safeguards are evident? Yes.

Goldman v. Krane, 86 P.2d 437 (Colo.App. 1989): May a department of social services be liable for damages when a social worker uses a pre-signed petition for guardianship to take custody of and transport a person? Yes.

CHAPTER 5 WOMEN

The People v. Hudson, 6 Cal.Rptr.2d 690 (Cal.App. 2 Dist. 1992): May a state enact a stalking law which is sufficiently narrow to be constitutional? Yes.

Syndex Corp. v. Dean, 820 S.W.2d 869 (Tex.App. - Austin 1991): If an employer does not ratify or authorize a supervisor's sexually harassing conduct, can the employer still be liable under the state's Human Rights Act? Yes.

Thurman v. City of Torrington, 595 F.Supp. 1521 (1984): May a city police department be sued for failure to adequately enforce an order of protection? Yes.

Simmons v. State, 504 N.E.2d 575 (Ind. 1987): Is "rape trauma syndrome" admissible as evidence in a criminal proceeding? Yes, but only in some states.

Webster v. Reproductive Health Services, 109 S.Ct. 3040 (1989): Does a state statute regulating abortions in public facilities by public employees violate the Constitution? No.

CHAPTER 6 INCOME SUPPORT

Loper v. New York City Police Dept., 802 F.Supp. 1029 (S.D.N.Y. 1992): Is a statute which criminalizes all forms of begging in public constitutional? No.

State of Louisiana, Dept. of Social Srvs. v. Jones, 638 So.2d 699 (La.App. 3 Cir. 1994): Is DNA testing alone, sufficient proof of paternity? No.

Dexter v. Kirschner, **984 F.2d 979 (9th Cir. 1992)**: Do limitations of Medicaid statutes in state law signify a lack of constitutional-based rights for program participants? No.

King v. Smith, **88 S.Ct. 2128 (1968)**: Can a state disqualify an otherwise eligible needy child solely because the state wishes to discourage what it perceives to be parental immorality? No.

Goldberg v. Kelly, **90 S.Ct. 1011 (1970)**: Does the Due Process Clause of the Fourteenth Amendment require that a recipient of Aid to Families with Dependent Children (AFDC) be afforded an evidentiary hearing before the termination of benefits? Yes.

Wyman v. James, **400 U.S. 309 (1971)**: May a beneficiary of AFDC refuse a mandated home visit by a caseworker without risking the termination of benefits because of the beneficiary's rights protected by the Fourth and Fourteenth amendments? No.

Pickett v. Brown, **462 U.S. 1 (1983)**: Does a statute which imposes a two-year limitation on paternity and child support actions violate the Equal Protection Clause of the Fourteenth Amendment? Yes.

Siegal v. Kizer, **15 Cal.Rptr.2d 607 (Cal.App. 2 Dist. 1993)**: Are discretionary trust funds in which the beneficiary's access to the principal is restricted considered to be available property in determining Medicaid eligibility? No.

Anderson v. Edwards, **115 S.Ct. 1291 (1995)**: Does the federal family filing unit law prohibit California from removing the distinction between a "nuclear" family unit and a family consisting of an adult and various dependents not directly related, thereby decreasing benefits under the AFDC? No.

CHAPTER 7   SOCIAL WORKERS IN COURT

State v. Bush, **442 S.E.2d 437 (W.Va. 1994)**: Does expert testimony concerning a defendant's mental capacity from witnesses who had performed psychological evaluations on a defendant at the request of the state violate that defendant's right against self-incrimination? No.

Polotzola v. Missouri Pacific R. Co., 610 So.2d 903 (La.App. 1 Cir. 1992): Can client communications to a board-certified social worker lose their privileged status granted them under a state statute? Yes.

State v. Decker, 842 P.2d 500 (Wash.App.Div 1 1992): Absent a showing of special circumstances, do juvenile defendants in non-capital cases have a right to have an attorney present during a psychological examination for pre-sentencing purposes? No.

Gentry v. State, 443 S.E.2d 667 (Ga.App. 1994): Are results of a penile plethysmograph test admissible as scientific evidence? No.

CHAPTER 8   SOCIAL WORKERS AS EMPLOYEES

Birthisel v. Tri-Cities Health Services, 424 S.E.2d 606 (W.Va. 1992): Is a social worker protected against discharge by claiming that her employer's requests of her would constitute a violation of a state's public policy? No.

Doe v. City of Chicago, 883 F.Supp. 1126 (N.D.Ill. 1994): May a public employer test employment applicants for HIV? Yes.

Cunico v. Pueblo School District No. 60, 917 F.2d 431 (10th Cir. 1990): May a board of education rehire a black and an Hispanic social worker in keeping with its affirmative action plan, while its seniority policy, if followed, would have retained a white social worker with more seniority? No.

Murdock v. Higgins, 527 N.W.2d 1 (Mich.App. 1994): Does a supervisor have a duty to divulge an employee's sexual activities and suspected homosexuality? No.

Ross v. Denver Dept. of Health and Hospitals, 883 P.2d 516 (Colo.App. 1994): Does the language "immediate family" discriminate against same-sex partners under Colorado's Career Service Authority Rules, when family sick leave benefits are sought? No.

Belmont v. California State Personnel Board, 111 Cal.Rptr. 607 (1974): May a department of social welfare lawfully suspend its employees for refusing to obey an order? Yes.

Kilroy v. Lebanon Correctional Institution, 575 N.E.2d 903 (Ohio.Ct.Cl. 1991): If it is shown that defamatory remarks about a social worker are true, can a successful legal action be maintained? No.

Osborn v. Harrison School District No. 2, 844 P.2d 1283 (Colo.App. 1992): Must mental health professionals performing identical duties receive comparable salaries despite differences in training? No.

CHAPTER 9   MISCELLANEOUS

Matter of Guardianship of Matejski, 419 N.W.2d 576 (Iowa 1988): Does a district court have subject-matter jurisdiction to hear a case regarding the sterilization of a mentally retarded adult by her parents? Yes.

Wisconsin v. Mitchell, 113 S.Ct. 2194 (1993): Is a "hate crime" statute overbroad because it has a possible chilling effect on a person's First Amendment right to free speech? No.

Table of Cases

King v. Smith, 88 S.Ct. 2128 (1968)
Kingsley v. Kingsley, 623 So.2d 780 (Fla.App. 5 Dist. 1993)
Lessard v. Schmidt, 349 F.Supp. 1078 (1972)
Loper v. New York City Police Dept., 802 F.Supp. 1029 (S.D.N.Y. 1992)
Matter of Baby M, 537 A.2d 1227 (N.J. 1988)
Matter of Guardianship of Matejski, 419 N.W.2d 576 (Iowa 1988)
McKennon v. Nashville Banner Publishing Co., 115 S.Ct. 879 (1995)
Meracle v. Children's Serv. Society of Wisconsin, 437 N.W.2d 532 (Wis. 1989)
Mezo v. Elmergawi, 855 F.Supp. 59 (E.D.N.Y. 1994)
Michael J. v. County of Los Angeles, Dept. of Adoptions, 247 Cal.Rptr. 504 (Cal.App. 2 Dist. 1988)
M.R.F. v. Dept. of Public Welfare, 595 A.2d 644 (Pa. Cmwlth. 1991)
Murdock v. Higgins, 527 N.W.2d 1 (Mich.App. 1994)
Nance v. Arkansas Dept. of Human Services, 870 S.W.2d 721 (Ark.1994)
O'Connor v. Donaldson, 422 U.S. 563 (1975)
Osborn v. Harrison School Dist. No. 2, 844 P.2d 1283 (Colo.App. 1992)
The People v. Cabral, 15 Cal.Rptr.2d 866 (Cal.App. 5 Dist. 1993)
The People v. Hudson, 6 Cal.Rptr.2d 690 (Cal.App.2 Dist. 1992)
Pfoltzer, et al. v. County of Fairfax, 775 F.Supp. 874 (E.D.Va. 1991)
Pickett v. Brown, 462 U.S. 1 (1983)
Polotzola v. Missouri Pacific R. Co., 610 So.2d 903 (La.App. 1 Cir. 1992)
Ricci v. Okin, 781 F.Supp. 826 (D.Mass. 1992)
Ross v. Denver Dept. of Health & Hospitals, 883 P.2d 516 (Colo.App. 1994)
Rowe v. Bennett, 514 A.2d 802 (Me. 1986)
Sherman v. Sherman, 1994 Tenn. App. Lexis 660
Siegal v. Kizer, 15 Cal. Rptr.2d 607 (Cal.App. 2 Dist. 1993)
Simmons v. State, 504 N.E.2d 575 (Ind. 1987)
State ex rel. S.C. v. Chafin, 444 S.E.2d 62 (W.Va. 1994)
State of Louisiana, Dept. of Social Srvs. v. Jones, 638 So.2d 699 (La.App. 3 Cir. 1994)
State v. Bush, 442 S.E.2d 437 (W.Va. 1994)
State v. Decker, 842 P.2d 500 (Wash.App.Div. 1 1992)
State v. Hosto-Worthy, 877 S.W.2d 150 (Mo.App. E.D.1994)
Syndex Corp. v. Dean, 820 S.W.2d 869 (Tex.App. - Austin 1991)
Thurman v. City of Torrington, 595 F.Supp. 1521 (1984)
Tobias v. County of Racine, 507 N.W.2d 340 (Wis.App. 1993)

Acknowledgments

It is a pleasure to acknowledge the numerous people who have assisted in the writing of this book: David Estrin and Phyllis Korper of Garland Publishing, Inc., whose courtesy, professionalism and patience are always in abundant supply; Dean Sheldon Gelman for collegial support; students Lori Abramowitz, Diane Dougherty, Roni Loeb-Richter, Belinda Zylberman, Merritt McKeon, Carolyn Hittman, and Jade Docherty—research assistants par excellence; Tessie Spivey, whose typing and organization abilities are masterful; Rabbi Chaim Steinmetz and Lisa Steinmetz; Rafi and Chaya Lottner; and, Diana Kupershmit—your assistance was simply indispensable. Above all, I thank God for allowing me the opportunity to contribute to the repair of this wonderful world.

Daniel Pollack

January 1997
Wurzweiler School of Social Work
Yeshiva University
New York City

INTRODUCTION

We look to courts a lot these days. It seems that not a single day goes by when courts are not featured on the national newscast. By habit, and one hopes still with awe, we cling to courts as a last refuge for justice. Perhaps we grasp too tightly. Courts cannot solve our problems for us. Most often they mediate interpretations of our own indecisiveness. This is especially true regarding human services. We turn to courts to deal with one social problem after another: abortion, child and elder abuse, involuntary electroshock treatment, stalking, battered women, repressed memory, parental kidnapping. And the list goes on.

This book presents cutting-edge human services court decisions, mostly from the 1990s. Many different courts are represented, some of which arrive at contradictory decisions. These particular cases were selected because of their interest, timeliness, and relevance to social work practice.

It is the legal reasoning of each case which is intriguing and worthy of investigation. This is done by closely examining the facts, issues, decision, and reasoning of each case. This is followed by an "implications" section. Its purpose is to give you a point of reference, a place from which to begin a discussion, not to give you "the answer."

The language lawyers use is a major obstacle, keeping social workers and lawyers from understanding one another. This book attempts to bridge the language gap. While language may define our experiences for purposes of general thought and communication, law codifies our experiences for legal purposes. It assumes a complex set of relationships to which individuals must adjust. The nuances of law are explained and illuminated by each unique lawsuit. But the core meaning of law is derived from a previous consensus based upon generalizing, abstracting, and categorizing. Sadly, by dividing society into discrete statutes and court opinions, there is a loss of continuity. The stitching of legislative codes is not as seamless as a legislator, or a social worker, ever imagines.

Traditionally, law and social work do not have a common communications meeting ground. One leans toward arcane written exactitude, the other to speech that is emotional and intuitive. In law, the written word signals a meeting of the minds, resolution, finality. Words control and formalize relationships.

In social work, speech is paramount. When ambiguity occurs, it is discussed and contextualized but rarely documented with the

1

specificity which law thrives on and demands. Law distinguishes only between legal and illegal, not acceptable or unacceptable, better or best. It consciously does not make distinctions except where society wants a legal separation. The subject matter common to both professions—social justice—is forcing them to work together on behalf of the same clients. To do this effectively, the professionals of each discipline must quickly learn to understand the language of the other.

Perhaps we don't realize how much law affects social work and social workers. As social work becomes more complex, law is inevitably implicated. The importance of social workers being acquainted with legal concepts cannot be understated. The more you understand how critical legal reasoning works, the better equipped you will be to distinguish between policy and practice considerations, and the less often lawyers will make decisions for social workers that could readily be made by social workers themselves. Prior to being able to communicate effectively with lawyers and legislators, it is necessary to have some knowledge and appreciation of how the legal system works. This book introduces you to the fascinating world of critical legal thinking and how that thinking has recently been applied to real-life social work situations. It is a book ideally suited for students and teachers of social work and law.

Perhaps we think of law as very orderly and social work as not-so-orderly. The merits of this hypothesis will not be debated here. What does seem to be clear is that law is bringing an orderliness of language to certain areas of social work, welcome or not. At a time when social work is being greatly influenced by law and the lines between them may be blurring, the imprint of a more rigorous language may be beneficial for social workers, and the realization that legal categories which exist on paper but not in reality may help lawyers realize that achieving social order and social justice is not so easily done.

Our disciplines are not as insular as they once were. Pride of profession may lead to a perception of the client as fitting into either law or social work. This is a mistake. If the disciplines are perceived as too discrete from each other, the gap between them is apt to be exaggerated for the sake of self-definition, and distrust and suspicion will only grow.

Law is likely seen by social workers as a sense of elaborate statutes, saturated with directives pertaining to the minutest aspects of life—all written in a foreign language. In fact, law is a process, just like social work. There is a blending and overlap between law and social work that should be celebrated, not disdained. For the sake of our mutual clients, we need to work flexibly with each other. Far from losing the unique identity of each profession, it is likely that each will grow richer, and a deeper appreciation of ourselves and our clients will follow.

How to Use This Book

Written court opinions are the way in which the judicial branch of government communicates to legislators, lawyers, social policy makers, and the public. When reading each case, try to focus on the broad principles the court is addressing. For example, let's look carefully at the very first case in the book, *Bottoms v. Bottoms.*

(1) The two parties who are involved in the lawsuit are a mother and her daughter. The daughter is appealing a lower court decision to grant custody of her son to her mother. The daughter is the appellant (1a), and her mother is the appellee (1b).

(2) This case can be found in volume number 444 of a series of books called "Southeastern 2d" on page 276. The first number always tells you the volume number (2a); the page number where the case begins is noted (2b), and the date the case was decided (2c).

(3) Enough facts are given so that you understand the context and background of the case.

(4) The key issue facing the court is identified. Notice that the issue is not particular *only* to this case. Rather, it is an issue that could come up again in future, similar cases.

(5) The decision of the court is noted, followed by a very brief explanation of the court's thinking.

(6) A more in-depth explanation of the court's reasoning is offered.

(7) The implications for social work practice and policy making are suggested. Especially noted are recent social work perspectives found in the recent professional literature (7a). Lastly, a full reference citation is given (7b).

As you read each case, be aware that the court is focusing only on the narrow issue before it. Tangential issues and implications are left for another time.

2b   2c

Bottoms v. Bottoms
444 S.E.2d 276 (Va.App. 1994)

1a

FACTS: Sharon Lynne Bottoms appealed a circuit court decision granting custody of her son to her mother, Kay Bottoms. Between the years 1989 and 1993, Sharon Bottoms married and divorced her husband, during which time she had a son. She moved frequently and dated both men and women. In 1992, she moved in with April Wade who was and remains her lesbian companion. Also during this time, Sharon was in continuous contact with her mother, who frequently cared for her grandson at Sharon's request.

In January of 1993, Sharon Bottoms approached her mother regarding her son, stating that due to her mother's relationship with Tommy Conley, her mother's live-in male companion, her son would discontinue his visits. Sharon Bottoms revealed that Conley had sexually abused her as a child and she was therefore uncomfortable leaving her son around Conley. Soon after this conversation, Kay Bottoms filed a petition with the juvenile and domestic relations court seeking custody of her grandson. The court granted custody to Kay Bottoms and Sharon Bottoms appealed.

ISSUE: As a matter of law, is a person who is involved in a sexually active lesbian relationship an unfit parent whose rights as a parent may be revoked and custody given to a third party?

DECISION: No. While the Court conceded that "sexual indiscretions in a child's presence is conduct which may render a parent unfit to have custody of a child" (p. 282), it stated that an open lesbian relationship does not make the parent unfit as a matter of law.

REASONING: The Court steadfastly supported the relationship of parent and child. Generally there is a presumption that a child's best interests will be served under the care of his/her parents and that the child will be removed from the parents only if there are "compelling reasons to do so" (p. 280). To award custody to a third party, there must be "clear and convincing evidence" of inappropriate parenting.

While Virginia law regards homosexual relationships negatively and lesbian "sexual conduct" is illegal, this court said it was not enough to remove the child from its mother. "A court will not remove a child from the custody of a parent, based on proof that the parent is engaged in private, illegal sexual conduct or conduct

based only on compelling reasons, such as concern
for the life, physical safety, and mental health of the
child, certainly not on a parent's sexual orientation
(p. 3). *7a*

On recent appeal, this decision was reversed and remanded. That court looked to the trial court's factual findings and determined that Sharon Bottoms was in fact unfit to be a mother. Among the factors that court considered were her lesbian relations. This translated into an issue of neglect, and custody was granted to the grandmother. This reversal exhibits the judiciary's conflict with gay parenthood and this new area of law (Pershing, 1994; Cox, 1994). Since the illegality of *7a* homosexuality in Virginia played a major part in the reversal, this might indicate that this state policy has a greater influence on the rights of homosexuals than the lower court had postulated. Thus, the extremely divergent views displayed in this case by different courts, exemplifies society's range of perspectives regarding this issue.

REFERENCES

Cox, J. (Summer 1994). Judicial enforcement of moral imperatives: Is the best interest of the child being sacrificed to maintain societal homogeneity? *Missouri Law Review, 59*, 775-805.

Laird, J. (1993). Lesbians and lesbian families: Multiple reflections. *Smith College Studies in Social Work, 63*(3), entire issue.

Leonard, A. (Summer 1994). Lesbian and gay families and the law: A progress report. *Fordham Urban Law Journal, 21*, 927-972.

Pershing, S. (Summer 1994). Defining family: Gays, lesbians, and the meaning of family: "Entreat me not to leave thee": *Bottoms v. Bottoms* and the custody rights of gay and lesbian parents. *William & Mary Bill of Rights Journal, 3*, 289-325.

7b

considered by some to be deviant, in the absence of proof that such behavior or activity poses a substantial threat of harm to a child's emotional, psychological, or physical well-being" (p. 282).

7 — (**IMPLICATIONS:**) A natural parent is assumed to have a right to custody of his or her child. That right may be overcome by a showing of clear and convincing evidence which serves the child's best interest. While this would seem to be a beneficial decision for the gay community in terms of parenting rights, the court seemed to imply that had there been an available responsible father, the mother's parental rights in this case would have been revoked. With the rising number of gay parents, this decision brings attention to issues that courts will examine when deciding a parent's fitness (Laird, 1993). While this 7a court deemed the "illegal sexual conduct" insufficient to remove the child from the home, a parent's homosexual relations will be scrutinized and most certainly be at issue in a child custody suit.

> Of course, courts must not delay in granting a remedy until a parent's conduct or behavior has harmed the child; the rule of law does not require that the damage sought to be avoided must occur before a court may act to prevent injury or to remedy a harmful situation. However, before courts may deprive a parent and child of their fundamental rights to be together and to associate with one another, the evidence must show that the parent is unfit and that the child is subjected to conduct and behavior that will harm the child. A court may not simply surmise, speculate, or take notice that because a parent engages in private, sexual conduct, even that which is illegal or conduct that is perceived by some as immoral and antisocial and to which the child is not subjected and which does not affect the child, the parent is unfit or the child is being harmed (p. 281-82).

The National Association of Social Workers filed an amicus brief along with several other national and state organizations. The brief states, in part, that NASW believes

> that parent-child bonding, especially during the early months and years of life, is crucial to a child's de- } 7a
> velopment and well-being. Disruption . . . should be

CHAPTER 1
Child Welfare

Bottoms v. Bottoms
444 S.E.2d 276 (Va.App. 1994)

FACTS: Sharon Lynne Bottoms appealed a circuit court decision granting custody of her son to her mother, Kay Bottoms. Between the years 1989 and 1993, Sharon Bottoms married and divorced her husband, during which time she had a son. She moved frequently and dated both men and women. In 1992, she moved in with April Wade who was and remains her lesbian companion. Also during this time, Sharon was in continuous contact with her mother, who frequently cared for her grandson at Sharon's request.

In January of 1993, Sharon Bottoms approached her mother regarding her son, stating that due to her mother's relationship with Tommy Conley, her mother's live-in male companion, her son would discontinue his visits. Sharon Bottoms revealed that Conley had sexually abused her as a child and she was therefore uncomfortable leaving her son around Conley. Soon after this conversation, Kay Bottoms filed a petition with the juvenile and domestic relations court seeking custody of her grandson. The court granted custody to Kay Bottoms and Sharon Bottoms appealed.

ISSUE: As a matter of law, is a person who is involved in a sexually active lesbian relationship an unfit parent whose rights as a parent may be revoked and custody given to a third party?

DECISION: No. While the Court conceded that "sexual indiscretions in a child's presence is conduct which may render a parent unfit to have custody of a child" (p. 282), it stated that an open lesbian relationship does not make the parent unfit as a matter of law.

REASONING: The Court steadfastly supported the relationship of parent and child. Generally there is a presumption that a child's best interests will be served under the care of his/her parents and that the child will be removed from the parents only if there are "compelling reasons to do so" (p. 280). To award custody to a third party, there must be "clear and convincing evidence" of inappropriate parenting.

While Virginia law regards homosexual relationships negatively and lesbian "sexual conduct" is illegal, this court said it was not enough to remove the child from its mother. "A court will not remove a child from the custody of a parent, based on proof that the parent is engaged in private, illegal sexual conduct or conduct considered by some to be deviant, in the absence of proof that such behavior or activity poses a substantial threat of harm to a child's emotional, psychological, or physical well-being" (p. 282).

IMPLICATIONS: A natural parent is assumed to have a right to custody of his or her child. That right may be overcome by a showing of clear and convincing evidence which serves the child's best interest. While this would seem to be a beneficial decision for the gay community in terms of parenting rights, the court seemed to imply that had there been an available responsible father, the mother's parental rights in this case would have been revoked. With the rising number of gay parents, this decision brings attention to issues that courts will examine when deciding a parent's fitness (Laird, 1993). While this court deemed the "illegal sexual conduct" insufficient to remove the child from the home, a parent's homosexual relations will be scrutinized and most certainly be at issue in a child custody suit.

> Of course, courts must not delay in granting a remedy until a parent's conduct or behavior has harmed the child; the rule of law does not require that the damage sought to be avoided must occur before a court may act to prevent injury or to remedy a harmful situation. However, before courts may deprive a parent and child of their fundamental rights to be together and to associate with one another, the evidence must show that the parent is unfit and that the child is subjected to conduct and behavior that will harm the child. A court may not simply surmise, speculate, or take notice that because a parent engages in private, sexual conduct, even that which is illegal or conduct that is perceived by some as immoral and antisocial and to which the child is not subjected and which does not affect the child, the parent is unfit or the child is being harmed (p. 281-82).

The National Association of Social Workers filed an amicus brief along with several other national and state organizations. The brief states, in part, that NASW believes

> that parent-child bonding, especially during the early months and years of life, is crucial to a child's de-velopment and well-being. Disruption . . . should be

based only on compelling reasons, such as concern
for the life, physical safety, and mental health of the
child, certainly not on a parent's sexual orientation
(p. 3).

On recent appeal, this decision was reversed and remanded. That
court looked to the trial court's factual findings and determined that
Sharon Bottoms was in fact unfit to be a mother. Among the factors
that court considered were her lesbian relations. This translated into an
issue of neglect, and custody was granted to the grandmother. This
reversal exhibits the judiciary's conflict with gay parenthood and this
new area of law (Pershing, 1994; Cox, 1994). Since the illegality of
homosexuality in Virginia played a major part in the reversal, this
might indicate that this state policy has a greater influence on the rights
of homosexuals than the lower court had postulated. Thus, the
extremely divergent views displayed in this case by different courts,
exemplifies society's range of perspectives regarding this issue.

REFERENCES

Cox, J. (Summer 1994). Judicial enforcement of moral imperatives: Is
the best interest of the child being sacrificed to maintain societal
homogeneity? *Missouri Law Review, 59*, 775-805.

Laird, J. (1993). Lesbians and lesbian families: Multiple reflections.
Smith College Studies in Social Work, 63(3), entire issue.

Leonard, A. (Summer 1994). Lesbian and gay families and the law: A
progress report. *Fordham Urban Law Journal, 21*, 927-972.

Pershing, S. (Summer 1994). Defining family: Gays, lesbians, and the
meaning of family: "Entreat me not to leave thee": *Bottoms v. Bottoms*
and the custody rights of gay and lesbian parents. *William & Mary Bill
of Rights Journal, 3*, 289-325.

In re Kirchner
164 Ill. 2d 468 (1995)

FACTS: Otakar Kirchner and Daniella Janikova were involved in an intimate relationship over a period of about two years. During that time, Daniella became pregnant, and sometime later the couple began to make plans to marry. Shortly before the birth of their child, and still not married, Otakar returned to his native country for two weeks to care for a dying relative. Daniella, believing Otakar had left her for another woman, gave up any hope of marriage and through the advice of a friend, decided to put her child up for adoption. Within a matter of days, the adoption proceeding was underway, and the "Does" were ready and willing to adopt Daniella's unborn child.

Meanwhile, Daniella, knowing that Otakar would not consent to the adoption, planned a scheme with the Does and their attorney to pretend that the baby had died at birth so as not to raise suspicion in Otakar. No attempt by any of the parties involved was made to contact Otakar or to inquire as to his whereabouts.

Before the birth of the child, Otakar returned to Chicago. Sometime thereafter, the couple reconciled and in September 1991 married. Prior to the marriage, on March 16, 1991, Daniella gave birth and proceeded with the scheme to keep Otakar in the dark about the adoption, giving him the false impression that the child had died.

Otakar, suspicious of the circumstances surrounding the baby, began an immediate investigation by inquiring at the original hospital where the birth was to have taken place. Almost two months later, Daniella finally confessed to having given up the baby, Baby Richard, for adoption and lying about the baby's "death." At hearing this news, Otakar immediately took steps to get custody of his child. On June 6, 1991, Otakar's lawyer entered an appearance at the adoption proceeding at which time the Does should have legally turned over the child to his father. From this point on, the Does fought for the custody of the child over a period of several years, claiming that Otakar's parental rights were terminated as he was an unfit father. Four years later, the Illinois Supreme court heard Otakar's petition asking the Does to turn over his son.

ISSUE: May a child be available for adoption if parental rights have not been properly terminated?

DECISION: No.

REASONING: The "best interest of the child" standard is not used until parental rights have been properly terminated. The court voted that "parents may be divested of parental rights either through their voluntary consent or involuntarily due to a finding of abuse, abandonment, neglect, or unfitness by clear and convincing evidence" (p. 476). The court unanimously agreed that during the first 30 days of Baby Richard's life, Otakar had demonstrated sufficient interest in his child, and therefore he should not have been found to be "unfit." In a series of U.S. Supreme Court decisions [*Lehr v. Robertson*, 103 S.Ct. 2985 (1983); *Michael H. v. Gerald D.*, 109 S.Ct. 2333 (1989)], the principle has been firmly established that unwed fathers enjoy all constitutional rights if they face and claim their responsibilities of parenthood.

Consequently, the writ of *habeas corpus* sought by Otakar was granted.

IMPLICATIONS: This case indicates that, "It would be a grave injustice not only to Otakar Kirchner, but to all mothers, fathers and children, to allow deceit, subterfuge . . ., together with the passage of time . . . to inure to the Does' benefit at the expense of Otakar and Richard." Courts demand that plaintiffs must come into court with "clean hands." The best interest of a child will not substitute for due process of law.

BARNES & NOBLE
STORE #2769
BRADLEY, IL 60914
(815) 935-2209

REG#03   BOOKSELLER#056
RECEIPT# 31653 12/03/98   3:31 PM

S 0815320701   SOCIAL WORK & THE COURTS
                  1 @ 17.95   17.95

SUBTOTAL   17.95
SALES TAX - 6.25%   1.12
TOTAL   19.07
CHECK PAYMENT   19.07

BOOKSELLERS SINCE 1873

6 and separated in boys. Among the e between Myron porary restraining onth in a battered included strictly etween Myron and conversations with ns, the supervising olved in the case ction between the ct until Myron had , the court granted August 1992, the District Court terminated all contact between Myron and his children contingent upon certain conditions. It is this decision that Myron appeals.

ISSUE: May a court change the terms of a temporary custody order without definitely identifying a change in circumstances of the parties?

DECISION: Yes. When a court finds circumstances to grant a temporary order, it is looking at the specific circumstances "determining the best interest of the child with regard to temporary custody pending resolution of the action" (p. 355). Thus, a permanent order can be issued and will be issued in cases where circumstances have not changed or have worsened.

REASONING: The court, citing the earlier case of *In re Marriage of Allen* [771 P.2d 578, Mont. (1989)], stated that temporary custody acts only as an "initial determination" from which further findings can be made. Myron's actions were found to be dangerous, both before the temporary order and at the time of the permanent order. The court referred to the best interests of the children throughout the process, and it is for this reason alone that the temporary order was issued without a formal hearing.

If changed circumstances are required to be proven before modifying temporary custody orders, parents would be forced to litigate temporary custody. This result would be contrary to the purpose of the statute. Therefore, we hold that the District Court was not required to find a change in circumstances before modifying the temporary custody order (p. 355).

Thus, Myron's argument that a change of circumstances had to occur before the final custody order was issued is not a valid argument. As for custody of the children, the court stated that its standard of review "is whether substantial credible evidence supports the court's determination" [p. 356, citing *In re Marriage of Fesolowitz*, 852 P.2d. 658 (Mont.1993)]. While joint custody is normally preferred, the testimonies of several persons involved in the case were substantial enough as credible witnesses to show that Myron was dangerous and that the welfare of the children would be jeopardized if he were to be permitted unlimited unsupervised visitation and joint custody.

IMPLICATIONS: This ruling is important for two reasons. In many, if not most situations, where a temporary order is sought out, the situation is grave. Acts of violence are in the process of being perpetrated, and the victim needs to get to safety immediately. If the courts were to institute a lengthy period of discovery in order to ascertain the specifics of the situation, many women and children could be severely harmed. Furthermore, once the temporary order has been issued, courts and social workers have a period of time in which to determine the facts and at that point ascertain if the temporary order was necessary and remains so (therefore providing a reason for a permanent order) or if the circumstances have changed such that the order can be lifted.

Social workers are faced with this type of situation frequently. They are called upon to use their best judgement in predicting future behavior based upon present actions.

Sherman v. Sherman
1994 Tenn. App. Lexis 660

FACTS: This case concerns visitation rights between a father and his children. Patrick and Hazel were married in August 1980 and during their seven-year marriage gave birth to two daughters. Throughout, the family had contact with appellant's homosexual brother and his companion.

When the couple divorced in February of 1988, Hazel was awarded custody, and Patrick had visitation rights on alternate weekends and holidays.

In May of 1991 Hazel remarried and made plans to move out of state with the children and her new husband. During visitation negotiations, she moved before any terms could be finalized. A few months later she learned of the death of Patrick's brother's companion due to AIDS. While Patrick and his family had known of the companion's condition and the brother's HIV positive status since 1987, Hazel had never been told. Concerned for her children's welfare and disturbed by the news that her children could have been exposed to the disease during their visits with their father, Hazel filed a petition in June 1992 in order to modify visitation to visits only within a 100-mile radius of her new residence. A hearing was held in November 1992. Patrick argued that this was restrictive, unreasonable, and financially unfeasible.

The trial court found the geographical restrictions unreasonable but did establish a visitation schedule which included mandatory periodic HIV testing, supervised visits by the children's grandmother, and living arrangements with the grandparents when the children were visiting their father. Patrick Sherman appealed.

ISSUE: Where a parent lives with or has contact with an HIV positive person, can the court restrict visitation and require HIV testing in order to address the other parent's fear of the children's potential contact with the HIV positive person?

DECISION: No. While the children are the court's main concern in custody and visitation disputes, mandatory HIV testing and unreasonable restrictions on visitations are remedies only when reasonable cause can be proven and the protection and best interests of the children are at stake.

REASONING: While the court had various issues to deal with, it considered this mainly a dispute over visitation rights. Therefore, it was bound by precedents set regarding visitation proceedings. The court's principal concern was to provide for visitation with both parents as "a court-imposed custody and visitation arrangement should interfere as little as possible with each parent's interests in maintaining a relationship with the child[ren]" [*Rust v. Rust*, 864 S.W.2d. 52, 56 (Tenn. Ct. App. 1993)].

Regarding visitation where the HIV positive brother resides, the court discussed at length what is known about contemporary HIV and AIDS research. It concluded that current research shows that "household contact" is clearly not enough to pose a risk of transmission.

The most significant issue, however, was the mandatory AIDS testing that Hazel requested. This concerned the court, as it stated: " . . . requiring an individual to undergo involuntary AIDS testing raises significant issues concerning the State's authority to intrude into the constitutionally protected realm of personal privacy. These issues become even more delicate when the results of these involuntary tests will be made available to persons other than the person being tested" (pp. 15-16). The court concluded that while the parent's rights are secondary to those of the children, for mandatory AIDS testing, there needs to be reasonable grounds, and it must be conclusive that the testing would in fact protect the children. The court could not find reasonable grounds, and therefore the value of testing did not outweigh the potential harm to those who would be tested.

IMPLICATIONS: With the fear of AIDS spreading more quickly than the disease itself, decisions such as this are imperative if persons living with HIV or AIDS or persons who have contact with such people are to be treated fairly and consistently both in the public and private sectors. This is especially true in minority communities where HIV/AIDS is spreading more rapidly than in the general population and where foster care rates are high (Marder & Linsk, 1995; Taylor-Brown & Garcia, 1995; Groze, et al., 1994).

REFERENCES

Groze, V., Haines-Simeon, M., & Barth, R. (1994). Barriers in permanency planning for medically fragile children: Drug affected children and HIV infected children. *Child and Adolescent Social Work Journal, 11*(1), 63-85.

Marder, R., & Linsk, N. (1995). Addressing long-term care issues through education and advocacy. *Health and Social Work, 20*(1), 75-80.

Taylor-Brown, S., & Garcia, A. (1995). Social workers and HIV-affected families: Is the profession prepared? *Social Work, 40*(1), 14-15.

State ex rel. S.C. v. Chafin
444 S.E.2d 62 (W.Va. 1994)

FACTS: In August 1991, thirteen-year-old S.C. was put into the temporary custody of the Department of Health and Human Resources (DHHR). This action was taken after a determination that her mother's boyfriend and his son were sexually abusing S.C. It was also determined that S.C. was being physically and emotionally abused by her mother. Later, psychological and medical evaluations showed that S.C. used drugs and alcohol and had been raped.

A day after being taken into custody, S.C. was moved from one county emergency shelter to another. Approximately two months later, S.C. was placed in the trial custody of her grandmother. However, this was unsuccessful because S.C. was not attending school. As a result, a month thereafter S.C. was placed in a youth crisis shelter. Three days later, S.C. was returned to a second county shelter where she had been placed.

A month after being placed in a county shelter for the second time, S.C. took an overdose of drugs in a suicide attempt. She was hospitalized and later transferred to another hospital for follow-up evaluation and treatment. A month after her suicide attempt, S.C was placed in county youth services. In the following two months, S.C. was placed in five more facilities. These included a private foster home from which S.C. requested a transfer. Finally, S.C. ended up in a group home for girls.

At the group home, the site supervisor filed an Unusual Incident Report regarding S.C.'s behavior. The report stated that an argument developed between a child protective services (CPS) worker and S.C. during a meeting with group home staff. A staff member present in the meeting wrote that the CPS worker told S.C. that, "she dressed like a whore, that her actions were going to result in pregnancy and that she was going to end up like her mother" (p. 67).

Eleven months after S.C. was removed from her home, the Circuit County Court found her to be a delinquent child based on the Unusual Incident Report. The court also directed S.C to remain in the temporary "care, custody and control" of DHHR. The court indicated that "the parties hereto are in agreement" with its determination (p. 67). Consequently, a hearing was not held on the matter and S.C. was not represented by counsel. As a result of the court finding, it was directed that S.C. be moved to a DHHR facility. She was transferred to the facility the day following the court order.

Two weeks later, the executive director of the group home where the Unusual Incident Report was filed contacted S.C.'s guardian *ad litem*. The executive director questioned the court order and the fact that S.C. received neither a delinquency hearing nor representation by an attorney.

The executive director questioned the accuracy of the site supervisor's portrayal of S.C., noting that there had been improvements in S.C.'s behavior. The executive director stated that S.C.'s case "should be reviewed for accuracy and due process" (p. 67). Subsequently, the Juvenile Justice Committee unsuccessfully attempted to contact the guardian *ad litem* regarding S.C.'s situation.

Six months later, a petition was filed against the Secretary of DHHR and the director of staff of the secure residential facility, seeking S.C.'s release from the DHHR facility and DHHR's compliance with requirements to develop a case plan. After the petition was filed, S.C. was released from the DHHR facility and returned to the group home where she formerly resided.

ISSUE: Does a service plan filed by a department of human services constitute an adequate case plan for the placement of a child who has come into the custody of the state?

DECISION: No. Documents filed by the department did not constitute a state-required case plan according to the decision of the Supreme Court of Appeals of West Virginia. The court also found that the department did not comply with several other statutorily required procedures including the requirement of a court hearing in the event a child is subject to three or more placements in one year.

REASONING: The purpose of requiring the formation of a case plan within 60 days of a child being transferred into the custody of DHHR is to ensure that logical steps are set forth to identify, resolve, or lessen the child's problems.

The court found that DHHR failed to fulfill its responsibility to file a case plan within 60 days after S.C. was placed in its temporary custody due to abuse or neglect. The court noted that the "service plan" documents submitted by DHHR did not constitute a case plan since they had been developed only days after S.C. was removed from her mother's home. They included only general and superficial information regarding S.C. and did not include a physician's evaluation. Likewise, weekly progress reports prepared on S.C. were not found by the court to meet with statutory requirements for a case plan.

The court pointed out that lengthy procedural histories are common in abuse and neglect cases, and that "child abuse and neglect cases must be recognized as being among the highest priority for the court's attention. Unjustified procedural delays wreak havoc on a child's development, stability and security" (p. 69).

In this case the court found that the system failed S.C., and in order to ensure that such failures do not occur in the future, it ordered a commission to review West Virginia's procedures.

IMPLICATIONS: Children of abusive or neglectful parents not provided with the necessities of life risk an unsuccessful future. When those same children then become wards of the state, it is imperative that, at a minimum, the state provide conditions that do not hinder the child's continued growth.

How the state chooses to work with a child who has come into its custody can have lifelong implications for that child. For instance, it has been found that children who are placed in temporary foster care for an extended period of time develop many difficulties (Herring, 1992). Consequently, these children spend more time in temporary foster care due to emotional difficulties and become increasingly less attractive to potential adoptive parents. As a result, it is more likely that they will remain in foster care and continue to develop even more emotional difficulties (Herring, 1992).

With the many possible pitfalls that exist for a child who is in the care of the state, the federally required case plan becomes an integral part of protecting that child's welfare. By laying out the steps that will be taken by the state on the child's behalf, the case plan can be the cornerstone that ensures a child's well-being. A case plan requires an outline of the reasons for the child's separation from his/her parents, efforts taken to improve the circumstances that led to the separation, and a projected time when the child and parents may be reunited (Sudia, 1989). In addition, it is necessary that the case be reviewed to ensure progress and needed refinements of goals. The result is a well-formed case plan through which society is better able to protect children not only from abuse and neglect but also from becoming a victim of the state's child welfare bureaucracy.

REFERENCES

Herring, D. (1992). Inclusion of the reasonable efforts requirement in termination of parental rights statutes: Punishing the child for the failures of the state child welfare system. *University of Pittsburgh Law Review, 54*(139), 139-209.

Sudia, C. (1989). "Reasonable Efforts" under P.L. 96-272. *Children Today, 1*(3), 9.

Kingsley v. Kingsley
623 So.2d 780 (Fla.App. 5 Dist. 1993)

FACTS: With permission from the court, eleven-year-old Gregory Kingsley filed for termination of the parental rights of his natural parents and for his adoption by his foster parents. Termination of parental rights was also petitioned by each of the following parties: George Russ and Elizabeth Russ (Gregory's foster parents), the guardian *ad litem*, and by the Department of Health and Rehabilitative Services. Gregory's request for adoption by his foster parents was supplemented by the Russes' petition for adoption.

Despite objections from Rachel Kingsley, Gregory's natural mother, the court tried both the termination and adoption proceedings simultaneously. Pursuant to the trial, Rachel's parental rights were terminated, and the Russes were granted petition for adoption.

George Russ appealed the denial of summary judgement. He asserted that a preponderance of evidence was a sufficient burden of proof for termination proceedings, the necessity of clear and convincing evidence being unwarranted.

Rachel Kingsley appealed the termination of her parental rights and the adoption of Gregory by his foster parents. Specifically, she claimed that Gregory, as a minor, had no legal basis upon which to file termination proceedings. Moreover, the trial court's decision to hear both the issue of termination and adoption at the same time violated Rachel's due process rights.

ISSUE: Do children have the right to initiate termination of their parents' rights and to petition for their own adoption proceedings?

DECISION: No. Minors cannot bring suit; only a guardian *ad litem* or next friend can do so for the child.

REASONING: While the court maintains its protection of the child, the law has historically deemed it illegal for minors to initiate legal proceedings. Instead, a guardian *ad litem* or next friend is appointed to protect the child's welfare. As required by the court, the *ad litem* or next friend must have substantial knowledge of the child's situation, even though "the child is the real party in interest" (p. 184).

IMPLICATIONS: Despite the news media's characterization, Gregory Kingsley didn't divorce his parents. The significance of this case is that

Kingsley attempted to initiate proceedings to have parental rights terminated. Permission to sue in one's own name is referred to as "standing to sue," i.e., the right and authority to bring a lawsuit. The right to access to the courts was held by the U.S. Supreme Court to be a fundamental right guaranteed by the Constitution [*Chambers v. Baltimore & O.R.R.*, 207 U.S. 142 (1907)], but not for children. This case generated debate in legal and social welfare circles regarding the wisdom of allowing children direct access to courts. Would such access be a positive reform of child protection laws or would it open the way for intra-family lawsuits that would prove destructive? Our attitudes toward children have been an amalgam of property and contract rights. Only recently have we begun to see children less as chattel and more as citizens with rights to constitutional protection. As child abuse and neglect increases, the likelihood of greater legal rights for children also increases. As one of the co-counsels of Gregory Kingsley wrote, "There is no justifiable reason to assume that family relationships are any less important to a child than to a parent. Indeed, because of a child's unique vulnerability such relationship should be presumed to be of far greater significance to a child."

The implication is that there are times when children, not their parents or the social services department, may know what is in their own best interest. Certainly there is a need for continuous reform of the child welfare system. Does giving children enhanced legal rights, apart from their parents and *in loco parentis* agencies, go too far?

At issue in this case is a question which raises many concerns within the professions of law and social work: What unique rights does a child have when he or she is removed from the parental home? If he or she does indeed have certain rights, how do these rights impact upon the civil liberties of parents? And what is the effect on the family (Kaslow, 1990)?

Children by their nature are vulnerable and in need of protection, yet at the same time they are immature and not yet knowledgeable of their own needs and rights. While there is no question that the physical and emotional safety of children must be guarded, it is not always possible to make accurate and reliable assessments about what are considered to be the best and most appropriate options for children at risk.

Further complicating this issue is the acknowledgement that parental fitness is highly subjective. Much of what is judged to be in a child's best interest is based on preconceived value judgements of lawyers and social workers. Because of this, "it is not easy to separate personal values from professional knowledge and to distinguish both of these in turn from the societal values embedded in law" (Goldstein, 1986, p. 10).

Although the United States Constitution guarantees that families generally are entitled to privacy in raising their children, at times these rights are called into question. In situations of child abuse or neglect, the civil liberties of parents are compromised in favor of their children. On the other hand, any unnecessary disruption or even examination of the parent-child relationship can be detrimental to the child and infringe on the parents' right to family privacy.

Unlike criminal or delinquency proceedings, which require one to prove beyond a reasonable doubt that a crime has been committed, abuse and neglect cases require a less rigorous standard of proof. Standards of evidence have also been relaxed in some states to allow children to testify in court with a minimum of trauma. Due to their subjective nature, child protection laws are vague and ambiguous. Additionally, parents are rarely informed of their right to counsel following the removal of a child from the home. Because much of what is considered to be identified as abuse occurs behind closed doors, there is a high possibility of misinterpretation. As a result, parents risk being implicated on false charges of child abuse (Huxtable, 1994).

Advocates for children have stressed the need for courts to take more decisive action in proceedings of parents who are either abusive or neglectful. As the incidence of child abuse continues to rise, more and more children are being placed in foster care. Moreover, the system of foster care is fraught with serious difficulties. Legal decision-makers often erroneously think that children are relatively safe in foster care, and as a result judges do not make swift and decisive determinations regarding more permanent placements (Herring, 1995; Fine, 1992). Foster placements tend to be poorly planned, resulting in a situation in which children live in long-term and open-ended placements. Most judges, as well as attorneys, do not have a background in child development and are unable to comprehend the developmental hazards that are evident in temporary foster care (Herring, 1995). Additionally, lawyers are often wary of interventions made by social workers in the courtroom (Hill et al., 1992).

Caseworkers also tend to neglect the civil liberties of parents in favor of the children they represent. In most cases, the threat of litigation against caseworkers is significantly higher if a child who is not removed from the home is harmed, than if services to keep a family together are not provided. Recently, however, cases supporting the rights and civil liberties of parents have become more prominent, and as a result, child welfare personnel have been sued for making judgements that neglect the rights of parents (Huxtable, 1994).

Further exacerbating this problem is the fact that few child welfare workers are certified as social workers (Huxtable, 1994; Lieberman, Hornby & Russell, 1988). Because many clients served by welfare agencies are involuntary, there is a high level of mistrust of caseworkers (Diorio, 1992). Trained social workers can provide needed help in the assessment process of families involved in termination hearings, specifically in areas of ethnicity, economic status, social relationships, and prevention strategies (Hill et al., 1992). Likewise, attorneys and judges would benefit from receiving guidance in the areas of child development and abuse. It is hoped that both professions working together will be able to provide more appropriate and beneficial interventions for the people they serve.

REFERENCES

Diorio, W. (April, 1992). Parental perceptions of the authority of public child welfare caseworkers. *Families in Society*, 222-235.

Fine, M. (1992). Where have all the children gone? Due process and judicial criteria for removing children from their parents' homes in California. *Southwestern University Law Review, 21*, 125-153.

Goldstein, J. (1986). *In the best interest of the child.* New York: Free Press.

Herring, D. (1995). Exploring the political justifications for permanency planning for children. *Loyola University of Chicago Law Journal, 26*(2), 183-258.

Hill, M., Lambert, L., Triseliotis, J., & Buist, M. (1992). Making judgements about parenting; The example of filing for adoption. *British Journal of Social Work, 22*, 373-389.

Huxtable, M. (1994). Child protection: With liberty and justice for all. *Social Work, 39*(1), 60-65,

Kaslow, F. (1990). Children who sue parents: A new form of family homicide? *Journal of Marital and Family Therapy, 16*(2), 151-163.

Lieberman, A., Hornby, H. B. & Russell, M. (1988). Analysing the educational background and work experiences of child welfare personnel. *Social Work, 33,* 485-489.

Nance v. Arkansas Depart. of Human Services
870 S.W.2d 721 (Ark. 1994)

FACTS: At the time of Roy David and Vicki Nance's divorce in 1982, Ms. Nance was awarded custody of their two children. In the summer of 1992, the older daughter, fourteen-year-old Mary Lila, visited her father in Texas. While with the father, Mary Lila allegedly stated that she did not want to return home to her mother in Fayetteville. Mr. Nance did not return Mary Lila to her mother. Consequently, a custody battle ensued.

Each party took steps to gain custody of Mary Lila in their local court, but both courts dismissed the case for lack of jurisdiction. However, the Texas court finally ordered Mary Lila returned to her mother pursuant to Ms. Nance's petition for a writ of *habeas corpus*.

Ms. Nance enrolled Mary Lila in a boarding school for the 1992-93 school year. However, soon after the beginning of school Mary Lila began to have psychological problems and became incoherent. Ms. Nance then took Mary Lila out of the school and returned with her to Fayetteville.

On August 27, 1992 when Ms. Nance was taking Mary Lila to a doctor in Oklahoma, they were involved in a serious car accident. Ms. Nance and Mary Lila were both taken to a hospital. At the hospital, Mary Lila was at times catatonic and at times hallucinating that a serpent was in her throat. Consequently, a psychological examination was ordered. The psychological examination was delayed when Ms. Nance demanded that her daughter be evaluated by a Christian psychiatrist. By September 1, 1992, Mary Lila had not yet been evaluated because the hospital and Ms. Nance could not agree upon an appropriate doctor to examine her. Ms. Nance then allegedly attempted to remove Mary Lila from the hospital contrary to medical advice. As a result, a supervisor from the Washington County Department of Children and Family Services ordered a 72-hour protective hold on Mary Lila and ordered that she be given a psychological examination.

The doctors who performed the examination concluded that Mary Lila was suffering from "acute adjustment disorder with psychotic thinking" and recommended in-patient psychiatric treatment (p. 722). The Brookhaven psychiatric facility in Tulsa was chosen in keeping with Ms. Nance's request for a Christian-affiliated institution. However, Brookhaven refused to admit Mary Lila due to her lack of Medicaid or insurance coverage.

After Ms. Nance failed to find another religiously affiliated psychiatric institution, Harborview in Fort Smith, was suggested. By this time doctors had become doubtful about whether Ms. Nance would be willing to take Mary Lila to Harborview or, if she did, whether Ms. Nance would leave Mary Lila at the facility for the duration of the treatment. Consequently, the Department of Human Services (DHS) petitioned for emergency custody of Mary Lila, arguing that she was dependent-neglected as defined by the Juvenile Code, i.e. " . . . one who as a result of abandonment, abuse, sexual abuse, sexual exploitation, neglect, or parental unfitness is at substantial risk of serious harm" (p. 724). Neglect is further defined as, "an act or omission by a parent which constitutes failure or refusal to provide medical treatment necessary for a juvenile's well being, except when the failure or refusal is caused primarily by the financial inability of the person legally responsible and no services for relief have been offered or rejected" (p. 724).

The Washington County Juvenile Court granted custody of Mary Lila to DHS. Mr. and Ms. Nance were both notified of their right to counsel, and Mary Lila was placed in Harborview, where she began to receive psychiatric treatment.

After the DHS gained custody of Mary Lila, Mr. Nance petitioned the Washington County Chancery Court to change the custody aspect of his divorce decree. He then asked the Juvenile Court to transfer the petition and consolidate it with the DHS case. However, the Juvenile court refused to transfer the petition.

At the first of several Juvenile Court hearings, it was held that probable cause existed that Mary Lila's family was unable to provide her with needed medical care. Accordingly, the court ordered continued DHS custody of Mary Lila. In two subsequent Juvenile Court hearings, the court held that although both Mr. and Mrs. Nance were fit to raise Mary Lila, she was temporarily placed with her father upon release from Harborview. After monitoring Mary Lila's progress, the Juvenile Court ruled that it was in Mary Lila's best interest to be placed with her father and the proceedings were dismissed.

Ms. Nance appealed the decision.

ISSUE: Does a juvenile court, having found a child to be dependent-neglected, have the authority to make a change of custody award?

DECISION: Yes. Since the child was deemed dependent-neglected by sufficient evidence, the court had the authority to change custody arrangements for the child.

REASONING: In dependent-neglected hearings, a juvenile court requires a preponderance of evidence to prove neglect. Even if the motives of the parent are not characterized as intending to harm or not care for the child, a determination of neglect can be made. Moreover, the findings of the court are not set aside unless it is shown that the decision was clearly erroneous. In this case, the determination of dependent-neglect was made because Ms. Nance and Mary Lila's doctors were not in agreement as to how Mary Lila's treatment should proceed. If treatment did begin, the record suggested that some involved doctors and social workers questioned whether Ms. Nance would allow Mary Lila to remain in the psychiatric facility for the duration of the doctor-recommended treatment. In addition, with respect to the jurisdiction question, the court held that whereas custody is often decided during a divorce proceeding, a juvenile court custody order supersedes any existing custody order. Thus, when a juvenile is found to be dependent-neglected, a juvenile court may transfer custody to the DHS, a relative, or other individual (p. 723).

IMPLICATIONS: Most cases of reported child maltreatment involve suspected neglect. Jenny and Roesler (1993) define neglect as, " . . . the inability of parents to provide for the basic needs of the child, including nutrition, shelter, clothing, hygiene, medical care, and supervision, all of which children require to grow and develop" (p. 112).

With the concept of neglect arises the conflict between parents' desire to retain control over the upbringing of their children and the government's interest in ensuring that children are not harmed by a parent's life choices. State governments were propelled into taking responsibility for the well-being of children when the federal government enacted the Child Abuse and Prevention Act in 1974. The Act required states to enact child abuse reporting laws with specific federally mandated guidelines in order to be eligible for federal funds. The federal government's stance on child care was further strengthened in 1987 when the Department of Health and Human Services redefined neglect to include failure to provide medical care (Wadlington, 1994). Recently, courts have widened the interpretation of neglect due to failure to provide medical care beyond only life-threatening cases and are using the broader consideration of whether the "child's welfare and . . . best interest will be served by the medical treatment" (Wadlington, 1994, p. 331).

With increased government involvement in neglect prevention and the broadened definition of neglect, there arises a growing need to find alternative living situations for children who have been determined to be neglected or abused. Accordingly, fathers are increasingly being considered as a suitable placement resource, and children's desires are being taken into account (Ganong, Coleman, & Mistina, 1995; Johnson, Yoken, & Voss, 1995). Most often, fathers gain custody of children when the mother wants to give up custody, a child protective service agency seeks out the father after maltreatment has occurred, or when the child chooses to be with the father. However, many studies have shown that children of abusive or neglected mothers are frequently maltreated when placed with their fathers (Greif & Zuravin, 1989).

As the well-being of children becomes an increasingly important consideration to governmental authorities, the need for alternative living environments for maltreated children grows. Since there have been ongoing difficulties in the foster care system, fathers are more often considered a placement resource.

REFERENCES

Ganong, L., Coleman, M., & Mistina, D. (1995). Home is where they have to let you in: Beliefs regarding physical custody changes of children following divorce. *Journal of Family Issues, 16*(4), 466-487.

Greif, G., & Zuravin, S. (1989). Fathers: A placement resource for abused and neglected children. *Child Welfare, 38*(5), 479-490.

Jenny, C., & Roesler, T. (1993). Medical evaluation of children in custody disputes. *American Journal of Family Law, 7,* 111-116.

Johnson, P., Yoken, C., & Voss, R. (1995). Family foster care placement: The child's perspective. *Child Welfare, 74*(5), 959-974.

Wadlington, W. (1994). Medical decision making for and by children: Tensions between parent, state, and child. *University of Illinois Law Review, 2,* 311-336.

In re Marriage of Carney
598 P.2d 36 (Cal. 1979)

FACTS: In 1971, William and Ellen Carney moved for a separation agreement to end their three-year marriage. With Ellen's written consent, sole custody of their two sons was granted to William in November 1972. Lori Rivera, William's girlfriend, acted as stepmother to the boys, and the four took up residence together in California while Ellen remained in New York. Limited contact with Ellen ensued. A jeep accident in August 1976 left William paralyzed from the waist down and with impaired use of his arms and hands.

William filed for divorce in May 1977. Ellen then demanded immediate custody of both children, despite her absence from the boys since the November 1972 separation. As stated by Ellen at the initial hearing, her main reason for requesting this change was William's paralysis. She felt he would no longer be able to adequately care for their children given his handicap. The trial judge sanctioned her reasoning and ordered an immediate removal of the boys from William's custody. Despite testimony to the contrary, the judge rested sole consideration for custody on William's physical condition and subsequent inability to participate in physical activities with the boys. William appealed the ruling, citing indiscretion on the part of the trial court in its custody decision. He felt that the court did not properly weigh all relevant factors.

ISSUE: Within the context of custody awards, does a disability necessarily imply an inability of a parent to serve in a child's best interest?

DECISION: No. Total integration of handicapped persons into society includes functions of family life. The crux of parent-child relationships does not depend solely on participation in physical activities. A physical disability alone is not sufficiently pertinent to warrant an immediate change in custody.

REASONING: Custody awards are dependent on various factors and policy considerations. No change of custody can take place "unless the material facts and circumstances occurring subsequently are of a kind to render it essential or expedient for the welfare of the child that there be a change" [*Washburn v. Washburn*, 122 P.2d 96, 100 (1942)]. William's disability was not "essential or expedient" to necessitate uprooting the children from their current home to a new environment 3,000 miles away. The best interests of the children would not be served. Courts may no longer presumptively favor custody to the mother.

Assuming that a parent's handicap inevitably handicaps the child ignores the function of the family system and what will best serve the child. William's relationship with his sons was described as interactive, positive, and stable. A healthy environment was provided for the children, as told to the court by a psychologist. The stereotype surrounding physically disabled persons undermines social policy to accept people with disabilities into the mainstream of society. Handicapped adults can be effective parents and provide a suitable environment in which to promote the optimum development of their children.

IMPLICATIONS: Because custody decisions most heavily affect children, their best interests become the focus in such cases. However, the definition of "best interests" remains murky despite significant unanimity among legal and mental health professionals regarding its use. Miller (1993), in attempting to define the psychological best interests of the child, maintains that "it is implicit in the literature that the clinician's chief tasks are to determine who of the competing adults will form the most favorable intimate and affectionate relationship with the child and who will provide an environment enabling the child to make satisfactory relationships with others" (Miller, 1993, p. 27).

Recent studies in the area of divorce outline the most reliable predictors of healthy child development. Pearson and Thoennes (1990) compared various types of sole and joint custody only to find that children's adjustment was unrelated to custody type. Rather, "family function was the greater predictor." Sorensen and Goldman (1990) agree that "unique benefits were shown to arise from the individual relationships of the child with each parent after divorce; neither parent was more important in general for the development of children" (p. 66). Overall, children's adjustment under the circumstances of divorce has been found to be greatly influenced by the emotional equilibrium between parent and child (Tschann, et al. 1990). The implication of these findings is clear: content and quality of the parent-child relationship are determining factors in healthy child development in divorced families.

Custody determinations are better served when dependent on psychosocial factors rather than physical disabilities. As courts advance to more specific guidelines delineating the best interests of the child, greater consideration of psychological components is a necessary component in deciding a child's future.

REFERENCES

Miller, G. (1993). The psychological best interest of the child. *Journal of Divorce and Remarriage, 19*(1/2), 21-36.

Pearson, J., & Thoennes, N. (1990). Custody after divorce: Demographic and attitudinal patterns. *American Journal of Orthopsychiatry, 60*(2), 233-249.

Sorensen, E., & Goldman, J. (1990). Custody determinations and child development: A review of the current literature. *Journal of Divorce, 13*(4), 53-67.

Tschann, J., Johnston, J., Kline, M., & Wallerstein, J. (1990). Conflict, loss, change and parent-child relationships: Predicting children's adjustment during divorce. *Journal of Divorce, 13*(4), 1-22.

Brossoit v. Brossoit
36 Cal.Rptr.2d 919 (Cal.App. 1 Dist. 1995)

FACTS: Dee Anna M. Brossoit, the mother of the two children who are the subjects of this proceeding, appealed an order declining to exercise jurisdiction over her motion to modify child custody. Dee Anna and Lawrence Brossoit divorced in 1987. The divorce court ordered joint legal custody of the couple's two minor sons, with primary physical custody to the husband and reasonable visitation rights to appellant Dee Anna. Since 1987, the children have lived with their paternal grandmother, Marion Brossoit. In 1991, Dee Anna filed an application for modification of child custody, seeking to obtain physical custody of the children, and obtained a temporary restraining order prohibiting the grandmother from removing the children from the state.

In 1993, appellant Dee Anna filed another application to get custody and again obtained a temporary restraining order prohibiting the grandmother from removing the children from the state. At the time the court ordered primary physical custody to the children's father, Dee Anna did not have sufficient earning capacity to provide a home for her children. Since that time, Dee Anna continued her education and obtained the skills necessary to provide a stable home for the children. The children's father had not lived with them since 1987 or provided for their support, had several criminal convictions, was on probation, had not held a steady job for over five years, had no permanent residence, and had a history of violence against Dee Anna. The children had been on Aid to Families with Dependent Children since July 1989. The grandmother told Dee Anna she was moving to Tennessee on March 19, 1993 and that the children would remain on state aid if they moved with her.

Dee Anna had maintained constant contact with her children while they lived with the grandmother. She was earning approximately $40,000 annually and was ready and willing to support and care for the children. Dee Anna was concerned about her children being raised by the grandmother whose own children had grown up to have histories of criminal behavior, alcoholism, and drug abuse.

Dee Anna told the grandmother, on the day she filed her petition for custody in 1993, that a temporary restraining order had been issued. The grandmother left for Tennessee with the children shortly after this conversation. For several months Dee Anna was unable to find the grandmother or the children and filed another application to change child custody. The hearing date was set for December 21, 1993. On December 20, 1993, the grandmother filed a petition for guardianship of the children in Tennessee. The petition did not mention the California custody case. Also on December 20, 1993, the grandmother signed a declaration in the California case stating that the children had lived with her since January 1987 and in Tennessee since March 1993. The declaration alleged that Dee Anna had known in advance that the children were moving to Tennessee, had the ability to telephone them, and that Dee Anna did not want to pay support for the children.

At the December 21, 1993 hearing in California, appellant's former husband informed the court of the Tennessee guardianship proceeding, and the case was continued until the following day so that the California court could contact the Tennessee court. On December 22, 1993, after speaking with the Tennessee judge and learning that the guardianship proceeding was set for hearing on January 13, 1994, the judge hearing the California case held off hearing the case until January 20, 1994, and set a briefing schedule, instructing the parties to file their briefs in both courts simultaneously.

On January 13, 1994, the Tennessee court granted the grandmother's guardianship petition, finding that the petition was unopposed after notice to the parent. It also held that Tennessee had subject matter jurisdiction and that guardianship by the grandmother was in the best interest of the children.

On January 20, 1994, the California judge read into the record a letter to the Tennessee judge confirming a conversation of the previous day. The Tennessee court had indicated its decision that Tennessee was the children's home state was based on the belief that California had declined to exercise its continuing custody jurisdiction and the fact that the parents had not filed opposition to the petition. The California judge had explained that she had not previously reached a decision on the jurisdictional question. The California court concluded that (1) California had continuing jurisdiction over the custody issue; (2) this continuing jurisdiction was exclusive; (3) under Tennessee law California appeared to have home state jurisdiction as there were ongoing proceedings in California when the Tennessee guardianship petition was filed; (4) California was the more convenient forum because the children had lived continuously with the grandparents in California from January 1987 to March 1993; and (5) California should decline to exercise its continuing jurisdiction because it was in the children's best interest for Tennessee to assume jurisdiction. The court noted that its decision to decline to exercise jurisdiction was also based upon the Tennessee judge's assurance that Dee Anna would be able to make an appearance in the Tennessee action and that if she requested reconsideration of the custody issue, the Tennessee court would grant a rehearing and order a home study of the children, grandparents, and parents. The court's findings were filed on February 1, 1994.

ISSUE: In a child custody dispute, what law controls in determining which state has jurisdiction?

DECISION: The Uniform Child Custody Jurisdiction Act is controlling. In this case, California had continuing jurisdiction over the children but relinquished it to Tennessee.

REASONING: The determination of which state can and should exercise jurisdiction to determine the custody of the children in the present case is governed by the Uniform Child Custody Jurisdiction Act (UCCJA) (Fam.Code, § 3400 et seq.) (Civ.Code, former § 5174 et seq.); Tennessee Code Annotated (T.C.A. § 36-6-201 et seq.) and the Parental Kidnapping Prevention Act (PKPA) 28 U.S.C.A. § 1738A. The purpose of the UCCJA includes avoiding competition and conflict for jurisdiction between courts of different states; promoting cooperation with courts of other states so that a custody decree is rendered in the state that can best decide the case in the interest of the child; assuring that litigation concerning child custody takes place in the state with the closest connection to the child and child's family; discouraging continuing controversies over child custody; deterring abduction and other unilateral removals of children undertaken to obtain custody awards; avoiding relitigation of custody decisions of other states; facilitating enforcement of other states' custody decrees; and promoting exchange of information and mutual assistance between courts concerned with the same child (California Fam.Code, § 3401). The PKPA was enacted in 1980 to resolve problems that remained even after most states had adopted the UCCJA.

Under the UCCJA as adopted in both California and Tennessee, "[a] court of this state shall not exercise its jurisdiction under this part if at the time of filing the petition a proceeding concerning the custody of the child was pending in a court of another state exercising jurisdiction substantially in conformity with this part, unless the proceeding is stayed by the court of the other state because this state is a more appropriate forum or for other reasons" (Fam.Code, § 3406, subd. [a]). "If a court of another state has made a custody decree, a court of this state shall not modify that decree unless (1) it appears to the court of this state that the court which rendered the decree does not now have jurisdiction under jurisdiction prerequisites substantially in accordance with this part or has declined to assume jurisdiction to modify the decree and (2) the court of this state has jurisdiction" (Fam.Code, § 3414, subd. [a]).

Under the UCCJA as adopted in California, a court has jurisdiction to make a child-custody determination by initial or modification decree if one of a number of conditions is met, including "(1) This state . . . is the home state of the child at the time of commencement of the proceeding, or . . . had been the child's home state within six months before commencement of the proceeding and the child is absent from this state because of removal or retention by a person claiming custody of the child or for other reasons, and a parent or person acting as parent continues to live in this state . . . 'Home state' is defined as 'the state in which the child immediately preceding the time involved lived with the child's parents, a parent, or a person acting as parent, for at least six consecutive months, and in the case of a child less than six months old the state in which the child lived from birth with any of the persons mentioned'" (Fam.Code, § 3402, subd. [e]).

IMPLICATIONS: Interstate parental kidnapping is a very common problem. It is devastating to the left-behind parent as well as the child. Parents can protect themselves and their children by securing a court order giving them custody in the home state and by documenting the child's substantial ties to the state, including school records and medical reports. If the child is removed from the state by the other parent, the left-behind parent should seek a court order immediately so that another state cannot exercise control of jurisdiction over the custody action. The police should be contacted, even if it is only a misdemeanor and not a felony in the home state.

A social worker can help a client to contact support groups and manage the stress of coping with legal problems and the pain of losing a child to a parental kidnapping. Support can be as practical as helping to sort paperwork or simply being caring and supportive, while encouraging the left-behind parent to seek out legal assistance and court orders promptly.

Time is of the essence in an interstate parental abduction, as in many cases, after six months, the abduction parent can simply seek a new court order in the new state. If there has been no order issued by the home state in the meantime, the left-behind parent may be unable to return the children to the "home state."

Mezo v. Elmergawi
855 F.Supp. 59 (E.D.N.Y. 1994)

FACTS: Plaintiff Barbara Mezo, a social worker, started this action under the Child Abduction Act to obtain an injunction ordering the Secretary of State, Warren Christopher, to perform his duties under the Hague Convention on the Civil Aspects of International Child Abduction, an international treaty (the "Hague Convention"). Mezo also wanted the court to order the return of her two children, who were living in Libya with her husband, Abdelaziz Mohammed Elmergawi, another defendant in this action.

After Mezo and her husband separated on June 13, 1986, both children lived with her. After the divorce proceedings were commenced, but before final custody was decided, Elmergawi abducted both children on May 10, 1988, and went to Egypt. On August 17, 1988, Mezo was granted legal custody of both children. She traveled to Egypt and was eventually awarded custody of both children under Egyptian law in an Egyptian court. However, after this award of custody, Elmergawi fled with both children to Libya, where they remain.

Mezo started this action to have the court order the Secretary of State to use the Child Abduction Act to obtain the return of her two children. It was the position of the Secretary of State that neither the Child Abduction Act, nor the Hague Convention, apply to this case because neither Egypt nor Libya are members of the Hague Convention and are not bound by it. Secretary Christopher moved to dismiss the complaint for failure to state a claim.

ISSUE: If a country does not participate in the Hague Convention on the Civil Aspects of International Child Abduction, may there be a valid claim filed under the Convention?

DECISION: No. Countries not participants in the Convention are not bound by it.

REASONING: The stated objective of the Convention is to "secure the prompt return of children wrongfully removed to or retained in any Contracting State" (Hague Convention, Article 1). The Convention does not apply to a child "removed to" or "retained in" a country which is not a "Contracting State." The provisions of the Convention only apply to a "child who was habitually a resident in a Contracting

State immediately before any breach of custody or access rights" [Hague Convention, Article 4; see also *Mohsen v. Mohsen*, 715 F.Supp. 1063, (D.Wyo.1989)]. When these limitations are examined together, they show that the Hague Convention only applies in a situation in which a child: (1) is "habitually resident" in a Contracting State prior to removal; and (2) is removed to another Contracting State [See Hague Convention, Article 1 & 3; see also *Application of Ponath*, 829 F.Supp. 363, 364 (D.Utah 1993)].

The Child Abduction Act required the President to designate a Federal Agency to serve as the "Central Authority for the United States under the Convention" (42 U.S.C. § 11606[a]). This "Central Authority" appears to act as a mediator between countries in an attempt to obtain the safe return of an abducted child. One of the regulations of the Department of State requires that when a child is abducted from the United States, the left-behind parent must send the Department of State "an application requesting access to a child or return of a child abducted from the United States and taken to another country party to the Convention . . ." (22 C.F.R. § 94.7). If a child is taken from the United States and is taken to another member country, the only way the Department of State can respond is if the child can be found in a member country or has been taken from a member country to the United States. The Department of State, which interprets and implements the Child Abduction Act, can only assist in situations involving two countries that signed the Hague Convention. If a child is taken from a member country and is retained in a non-member country, there is no remedy under either the Child Abduction Act or the Hague Convention. Likewise, if a child is taken from a non-member country and is retained in a member country, there is no remedy.

The children were taken from the United States to Egypt and then from Egypt to Libya. Although the United States is a member country to the Hague Convention, Egypt and Libya are not. As a result, the Convention and the Act do not apply in this situation.

IMPLICATIONS: The court commented that "it is a tragic circumstance when, despite two valid court orders, a mother is unable to regain the lawful custody of her two minor children, or to even see her children, by reason of the unlawful conduct of their father. However, since the Federal Court is a court of limited jurisdiction and the Child Abduction Act is only applicable between countries that signed the Hague Convention, this Court does not have jurisdiction under the statute and must therefore dismiss the complaint."

Approximately 100,000 children annually experience an attempted non-family abduction (Finklehor, Hotaling, & Asdigian,

1995). For parents whose children have been taken to non-member countries, there are other ways of returning them. Those alternatives involve the use of the criminal justice system. Either a warrant for the arrest of the abducting parent is issued by a state and then a federal warrant for "unlawful flight" is obtained, or the left-behind parent can seek a federal arrest warrant under the International Parental Kidnapping Crime Act of 1993, 18 U.S.C., Section 1204. This law makes it a federal felony for a parent to remove or retain a child in violation of the other parent's right of custody, including the right of visitation. Before this law was enacted, it was not a federal felony for a parent to kidnap his or her own child from the United States. The law requires that parents use the Hague Convention when the child is taken to a member country.

In an abduction, the Department of State should be contacted immediately, and a petition under the Hague Convention should be made for the return of the children. The Department has consular officials who can mail packages of information and forms to parents, attorneys, and social workers who request them. Even if the children have been taken to non-Hague countries, it is a good idea to request a packet of materials, since they have useful suggestions for left-behind parents.

The Department of State is limited in what it can do for a left-behind parent. A social worker can be helpful to a left-behind parent by referring the parent to the consular officers and helping that parent remain calm while he or she talks to officials and law enforcement officials. It can be deeply frustrating for the left-behind parent. He or she may feel isolated and powerless at trying to make the machinery of government work to find the child. The materials provided by the government can be extremely helpful, but support and guidance is needed for the adult victims of these crimes. Helping a client to organize a plan of action can be of great assistance for the left-behind parent's success in returning a child. And, in the many cases where the return is impossible, the help of a social worker can be essential.

REFERENCES

Finklehor, D., Hotaling, G., & Asdigian, N. (1995). Attempted non-family abductions. *Child Welfare, 74*(5), 941-955.

DeShaney v. Winnebago County DSS
109 S.Ct. 998 (1989)

FACTS: On March 8, 1984, four-year-old Joshua DeShaney was severely beaten by his father. While it was not his first beating, this beating left Joshua brain damaged, retarded, and partially paralyzed. Joshua first came to the attention of the Winnebago County Department of Social Services (DSS) in 1982 when allegations of abuse were reported. The following year he was admitted to the hospital with bruises and abrasions and put in temporary custody of the hospital. Based on the recommendation of the hospital's Child Protection Team, the juvenile court dismissed the child abuse allegations and returned him to the custody of his father. For the next six months, the Winnebago County DSS social worker noted in her files after each monthly visit that Joshua had a number of suspicious head injuries and that someone was physically abusing Joshua. However, she did nothing other than make notations. Randy DeShaney, Joshua's father, was eventually convicted of child abuse as a result of Joshua's last beating.

Also sued by Joshua's mother was the Winnebago County DSS. She alleged that Joshua was deprived of his Fourteenth Amendment "Due Process" rights because the Winnebago DSS failed to intervene to protect Joshua against the violence of his father, about which the social worker knew or should have known.

ISSUE: Does the government have a constitutional duty to protect a child against physical abuse if it has not taken that child into custody?

DECISION: No. Custody is the sole determinant in deciding whether the government may be constitutionally liable under the Fourteenth Amendment for child abuse caused by a parent or guardian in a case in which a child welfare agency is involved.

REASONING: The Fourteenth Amendment "does not require a state or local government entity to protect its citizens from private violence or other mishaps not attributable to the conduct of its employee" (p. 1002). The Supreme Court specifically rejected a finding that a "special relationship" exists between the government and the child simply because the government undertakes to protect the child from abuse. The Fourteenth Amendment is "a limitation on the State's power to act, not a guarantee of certain minimal levels of safety and security . . . Its purpose was to protect the people from the State, not to ensure that the

State protected them from each other" (p. 1003). Because the government did not physically take Joshua into its custody as it does in cases of incarceration or involuntary mental health, there is no corresponding duty to assume responsibility for his general well-being. A most important question was purposely not addressed by the Court:

> Had the State by the affirmative exercise of its power removed Joshua from free society and placed him in a foster home operated by its agents, we might have a situation sufficiently analogous to incarceration or institutionalization to give rise to an affirmative duty to protect (p. 1006).

In fact, the court has not revisited this issue since this case was decided.

IMPLICATIONS: Every state has a law designating social service agencies as the government entities responsible for investigating and interceding on behalf or "at risk" children. Three major directives are given to social workers involved in child protection. First, social workers are instructed to provide services to abusing or neglectful parents in the parents' own home. Removal of the child is a last resort; it is disruptive to the child and family and costly for the state. Second, social workers are told to make sure that children do not wind up in foster care "drift," i.e., remaining indefinitely in the foster care system and being constantly moved from one home to another. Third, there is a legitimate privacy right which families have. The unwarranted or premature intrusion of the government into the homes of non-abusive families is improper and unconstitutional.

This case points out the difficulty of a government social service agency wanting to be a sanctuary for at-risk, abused, and neglected children, while not being the guarantor for every child who may potentially be abused (Bullis, 1990; Pollack, 1993).

There has been a steady increase in the past thirty years of the number of children reported to the child protection agencies as suspected victims of neglect or abuse. This has put pressure on individual caseworkers. If the worker fails to remove the child in time, there is the danger of that child becoming another "Joshua." Alternatively, premature removal results in emotional trauma which may rival the physical abuse that might have been sustained. How can social service agencies be held accountable for the employee's most egregious and negligent errors while not sending them a message to remove a child preemptively? This case leaves the social worker with the knowledge that, at least for constitutional purposes, custody of the child is the key factor to focus upon. If the child is not in the custody of the state, there is no constitutional liability. There may, however, be liability under state law.

REFERENCES

Bullis, R. (1990). Cold comfort from the Supreme Court: Limited liability protection for social workers. *Social Work, 35*(4), 364-366.

Pollack, D. (1993). Liability insurance for foster parents and agencies: The role of commercial insurers. *Journal of Law and Social Work, 4*(1), 33-40.

Pfoltzer, et al. v. County of Fairfax
775 F.Supp. 874 (E.D.Va.1991)

FACTS: Gloria Pfoltzer, along with three of her minor children, brought a claim asserting that their First Amendment rights to religious freedom had been violated when the children were removed from the home and placed in foster care. Among the defendants were the director of the Department of Human Development, two social workers, and their supervisor.

On May 27, 1988, an emergency order was issued to remove four of Pfoltzer's children. Legal custody was given to the Fairfax County Department of Social Services. Based on sworn allegations, the Juvenile and Domestic Relations District Court found that Daniel Pfoltzer (their stepfather), had "subjected the children to violent and unduly embarrassing disciplinary methods and that Gloria Pfoltzer either contributed to or acquiesced in the use of these methods" (p. 878). On June 3, 1988, a preliminary removal hearing was held, and the court ordered that custody remain with the Department.

Trial was set for August 5, 1988, but soon before, a consent order was signed by both plaintiffs and defendants. It provided: "(i) that the parties agreed that Daniel Pfoltzer's methods of discipline were 'inappropriate' and that Gloria Pfoltzer had been aware of them but did not intervene; (ii) that it was the parties' intention to make a determination to return the three plaintiff children home, contingent on certain factors; (iii) that temporary legal custody of [the children] shall continue in the Department until further order of the court; and (iv) that Gloria and Daniel Pfoltzer would cooperate with Home Based Services, actively participate in therapy with a Dr. Broars, and have the children participate in therapy with a Dr. Federici" (p. 879). Upon signing, the children were returned to their home.

In the following weeks, several of the defendants became concerned that the order was not being complied with. A meeting was held to assess the situation, and a letter of removal was sent on January 13, 1989, stating that since the Pfoltzers had not followed the terms of the order, they could not be responsible for their children, and therefore the children needed to be removed from the home. Two months later a three-day hearing was held regarding the abuse and neglect alleged in the May 1988 petitions. The court found "clear and convincing evidence" that the Department had established that the children "were in need of services" (p. 879) which the parents had failed to supply and that continued custody with the Department was necessary. The Pfoltzers did not appeal this order.

During the following year and a half, various motions were filed by the Pfoltzers, attempting to have custody returned to them. The motions were denied, but in May 1990, upon the Department's consent, the children were returned to the home, and in December 1990, custody of the children was returned to Gloria Pfoltzer. The Pfoltzers brought suit claiming their First Amendment religious rights were violated during the time the children were in foster care.

ISSUE: Does a department of social services have a duty to provide a foster home with a desired religious background of the biological parents so as to avoid any violation of the right to the free exercise of religion?

DECISION: No. The social services division only has a duty to make a reasonable effort in providing a desired religious environment and opportunities. "So long as the state makes reasonable efforts to assure that the religious needs of the children are met during the interval in which the state assumes parental responsibilities, the free exercise rights of the parents and their children are adequately observed" [*Wilder v. Bernstein,* 848 F.2d 1338 (1988)].

REASONING: The integrity of the family unit and the raising of children are values and rights upon which our society places great emphasis. However, as the court stated, "liberty interests are not absolute" (p. 881) and therefore may be taken away when extreme circumstances mandate. Regarding the plaintiff's due process rights, the court found that not only could the children be removed under state law but that they were removed in accordance with the Department's customary procedure. Furthermore, once the Pfoltzers signed the consent order, the court held that they, in effect, waived their rights. "If one voluntarily surrenders a liberty interest to the State, there has been no 'deprivation' of that interest by the State, and no due process violation" [*Stone v. University of Maryland Medical System Corp.,* 855 F.2d 167, 172-73 (4th Cir.1988)].

Furthermore, when the Pfoltzers did not appeal the January 1988 order, they did not take advantage of a right accorded to them. Later, when they decided to petition for custody, they decided to take advantage of their right to do so, but the fact that they were not victorious does not signify inadequate due process.

Regarding the plaintiff's First Amendment claim, the Pfoltzers argued that their children's right to practice their religion while in foster care was hampered as they did not have access to their mother's guidance, their church, or a Catholic school. The court articulated its standard when it stated that parents' rights to "select religious experiences and opportunities for their children" is not absolute (p. 884). In this case, the court urges that the plaintiffs voluntarily gave custody of their children to the state and it would be unreasonable to expect the state to duplicate the parents' religious standards. The court quoted *Wilder v. Bernstein*, 848 F.2d 1338 (1988) which states

> . . . it is one thing to recognize the right of parents to choose a religious school for their children as a private alternative to meeting state-imposed educational requirements in public schools. It is quite another matter, however, to suggest that parents who are unable to fulfill their parental obligations, thereby obliging the state to act in their stead, at their request or involuntarily, nonetheless retain a constitutional right to insist that their children receive state-sponsored parenting under the religious auspices preferred by the parents (pp. 1346-47).

The court, in its analysis, determined that the state had made a reasonable effort, and therefore no constitutional rights had been violated.

IMPLICATIONS: While courts are often hesitant to enter into "private family issues," this case stands as one of a group of cases creating a standard in which the state may intervene. The court reiterated the importance of the maintenance of the family unit yet emphasized the broad discretion possessed by trial judges in custody proceedings. While this opinion may seem to strike against "family," its intention is to protect children and ensure against child abuse and neglect.

The court recognized the burdens placed on social services and the limited availability of foster homes with specific qualifications in many situations. Courts are not willing to make rulings regarding freedom of religion in such cases because the first priority is a safe and healthy environment for the children.

Freedom of religion, like freedom of speech, is not absolute. While both constitutional rights are clearly set out in the First Amendment, the courts have historically allowed for exceptions and flexibility within this fundamental right. As this court stated, "It is beyond dispute that the right to the free exercise of religion is of signal constitutional importance and that parents exercise this right when they

select religious experiences and opportunities for their children . . . .
Equally well-established is that this parental right is not absolute"
[*Wisconsin v. Yoder*, 406 U.S. 205, 233-234 (1972)]. Therefore, while a
court should consider a child's religious welfare as part of a custody
proceeding, its final decision should not be based on this factor alone.
A proscribed inquiry into the spiritual practices, desires, and needs of a
child and its parents is permissible so long as the purpose of the inquiry
is pertinent to the health and well-being of the child.

Artist M. v. Johnson
917 F.2d 980 (7th Cir. 1990)

FACTS: The plaintiffs are wards of the Juvenile Court in Cook County, Illinois. They brought this action in 1988, alleging that the Department of Children and Family Services (hereinafter "DCFS") failed "to assign caseworkers to members of their class in a timely manner and that this violates the federal Adoption Assistance and Child Welfare Act of 1980" (p. 982). This claim was based on DCFS procedures. DCFS, in conjunction with the State's Attorney's Office, investigates suspected cases of abuse or neglect. The cases are screened and then some of them are petitioned in juvenile court. At that point, after a hearing, some of the children might become wards of the state and in so doing become wards of DCFS, which serves as a custodian. Meanwhile, others will be returned to their families under protective orders.

This class action has its plaintiffs divided into two classes. Class A consists of "all children who are or will be subjects of Juvenile Court petitions, who are or will be in the custody of DCFS (or in a home under DCFS supervision) by an order of the Juvenile Court, and who are or will be without a DCFS caseworker for a significant period of time. Class B, the subclass, is identical to Class A except that Class B does not include children who are in a home under DCFS supervision by order of the Juvenile Court" (p. 983). The plaintiffs claim that DCFS fails to assign them caseworkers in a reasonable amount of time and that it fails to reassign caseworkers in a timely manner when a caseworker can no longer be responsible for a particular case.

ISSUE: Does the federal Adoption Assistance and Child Welfare Act of 1980 (hereinafter "AAA") create a right under which the plaintiffs or any individual may bring a claim that an organization bound under that legislation has violated such legislation and that the state is equally bound by such federal legislation under 42 U.S.C. § 1983?

DECISION: Yes. Section 1983 provides plaintiffs with a cause of action where they have been deprived of a right, privilege, or immunity protected by the Constitution and the laws of the United States (42 U.S.C. § 1983). Thus, plaintiffs have a valid claim against DCFS alleging their rights under AAA have been violated.

REASONING: The court, citing *Wilder v. Virginia Hospital Ass'n* [110 S.Ct. 2510 (1990)], notes that "a statute will not be found to have created an enforceable right unless the provision in question is intended to benefit the plaintiff, the provision imposes a binding obligation on the state, and the right is not so amorphous that courts are unable to adequately enforce it" (*Wilder,* 110 S.Ct., p. 2517).

The court further reasoned that to find a statute indicating direct and enforceable rights, the legislative history and context of the statute must be examined. The court, in so doing, found in fact that because of the explicit provisions of the statute, plaintiffs had a claim.

IMPLICATIONS: The AAA was enacted by Congress in 1980 as an amendment to the Social Security Act in order to "lessen the emphasis on foster care placement and . . . encourage greater efforts to find permanent homes for children either by making it possible for them to return to their own families or by placing them in adoptive homes" [S.Rep. No. 96-336, reprinted in 1980 U.S. Code Cong. & Admin. News 1448, 1450 (96th Cong., 2d sess.)]. While this case did not decide the fate of the children bringing the claim, it did give them a voice in court and validated that their rights are of great societal concern. The idea that "reasonable efforts" could therefore be verified in a judicial setting and not simply left to the good faith efforts of social service agencies was short lived. The U.S. Supreme Court, in 1992, declared that an individual had no standing to enforce the AAA (see Carlo, 1993; Kopels & Rycraft, 1993; O'Donnell, 1992).

REFERENCES

Carlo, P. (1993). Parent education vs. parent involvement: Which type of efforts work best to reunify families? *Journal of Social Service Research, 17*(1/2), 135-150.

Kopels, S., & Rycraft, J. (1993). The U.S. Supreme Court rules on reasonable efforts: A blow to child advocacy. *Child Welfare, 72*(4), 397-406.

O'Donnell, S. (1992). Rethinking accountability in child welfare. *Child and Adolescent Social Work Journal, 9*(3), 261-270.

Wildauer v. Frederick County
993 F.2d 369 (4th Cir. 1993)

FACTS: The plaintiff-appellant, Ann Wildauer, was a foster mother responsible for fifteen children, most of whom were disabled. Two sets of parents who had placed their children with her complained to the Frederick County Department of Social Services (FDSS) that Wildauer refused to release their children to them. The parents alleged Wildauer claimed she had adopted the children, though she did not have legal custody over the four children involved in the FDSS complaint. Wildauer alleged the children had been abused by their parents, who had made the complaint to FDSS.

After an investigation by an FDSS social worker, Wildauer willingly released the two youngest children to their parents but claimed the two older children had disappeared. She invited the social worker and deputy sheriff to help her search the house for the children. They were eventually discovered in a neighbor's home.

As a result of the social worker's observation that Wildauer's home was unhygienic and unsuitable for disabled children, the social worker opened a neglect investigation for the eleven children remaining in Wildauer's care, one of whom was Wildauer's son and another who was her adopted child. The other nine children were living without any formal, legal arrangement. The social worker visited Wildauer's home with health department nurses. At the time Wildauer did not object. She later claimed she was threatened into cooperation.

The investigation concluded that the children were being neglected. FDSS prepared a petition for custody of the children by way of a Child in Need of Assistance (CINA) petition. Before FDSS filed the petition, it learned that Wildauer had moved to another county. FDSS filed the petition there, but the other county refused to give her department custody.

Wildauer filed this action alleging violation of her civil rights. She protested (1) the unreasonable entry and search of her home in violation of the Fourth Amendment, (2) the medical exams of children in her home in violation of the Fourth and Fourteenth Amendments, (3) the removal of children from her care in violation of the Fourteenth Amendment and the Adoption Assistance and Child Welfare Act, (4) the neglect investigation in violation of the Fourteenth Amendment. The complaint named Frederick County, the social worker, and various other employees of Frederick County. Summary judgement was granted to the defendants. The Court of Appeals affirmed.

ISSUE: Are foster parents' rights violated by neglect investigations, searches, and removal of foster children?

DECISION: No.

REASONING: Wildauer characterized the visit to her home as an unconstitutional search in violation of the Fourth Amendment. Investigative home visits by social workers are not subject to the same scrutiny as searches in a criminal context. Since she did not have custody of the four children, she voluntarily released two of them to their parents, and after alleging the other two were missing, she invited the social worker to help her look for them. The entry of the deputy sheriff under these circumstances was therefore not unreasonable.

Since Wildauer did not have legal custody of the four children, she could not claim her privacy rights were violated by their removal from her home. Nor did she have the right to a hearing in connection with the removal of the children from her home. As far as the other alleged constitutional violations, the state's interest in examining the neglected children outweighed any privacy interest of Wildauer.

IMPLICATIONS: There is immunity from liability because the social worker never stepped outside of her role as a social worker in looking for the children who were not in the legal custody of the plaintiff. Since everyone agreed on the essential facts, summary judgement was granted. Summary judgement is a decision of law based on facts which are not disputed by either side, which create enough evidence for a judge to apply the law to those facts without a trial.

The social worker acted not as a police officer but as a social worker who was accompanied by a police officer. The social worker was invited by the plaintiff to look for the children with her. There was no "seizure" of the children, who were not even in Wildauer's legal custody.

Ferguson v. Stafford County DSS
417 S.E.2d 1 (Va.App. 1992)

FACTS: In this Virginia case, Richard Wayne Ferguson appealed the trial court's order terminating his residual parental rights to his son, Richard A. Gochenour.

Ferguson alleged that following his sentence to serve life in prison, the Department of Social Services disregarded his rights and took no actions to support him in an attempt to strengthen his relationship with his son, as specified by state regulation.

Evidence supporting the termination of Ferguson's parental rights pointed to the absence of any history of a relationship between the father and son. The social work supervisor for the Department, Jane Namoit, testified that Richard Jr. would not have benefitted by contacts with his father during his father's incarceration and that no services could have strengthened the parent-child relationship. The Department denied that it disregarded its obligation to make "reasonable and appropriate" efforts in the direction of rendering the necessary services to eventually reunite Richard Jr. with his father.

ISSUE: Is incarceration in and of itself just cause for termination of parental rights?

DECISION: No. Incarceration *per se* does not justify termination of parental rights. However, incarceration combined with the proper circumstance as well as other indications relating to the parent-child relationship, may lead the court to conclude that termination of parental rights would ultimately be in the best interest of the child.

REASONING: The Department cited Virginia Code § 16.1-283(C):

> C. The residual parental rights of a parent or parents of a child placed in foster care as a result of court commitment, an entrustment agreement entered into by the parent or parents, or other voluntary relinquishment by the parent or parents may be terminated if the court finds, based upon clear and convincing evidence, that it is in the best interest of the child, and that:
> 1. The parent or parents have, without good cause, failed to maintain contact with and to provide or

> substantially plan for the future of the child for a
> period of twelve months after the child's placement
> in foster care, notwithstanding the reasonable and
> appropriate efforts of social, medical, mental health
> or other rehabilitative agencies to communicate with
> the parent or parents and to strengthen the parent-
> child relationship . . . .

In response to Ferguson's claim that the Department "wrote him
off" after he was incarcerated, the Department referred to its first
service plan after Ferguson's initial, brief incarceration, which plainly
evidenced Richard Jr.'s planned return to his parents. It was only
following the knowledge of Ferguson's long-term incarceration that the
goal was changed to seek a termination of Richard Sr.'s rights.

In determining what constituted reasonable and appropriate efforts,
the court heard the testimony of a licensed clinical social worker who
testified:

> Q. In your expert opinion, based upon what you know
> about Mr. Ferguson and his son, would the
> Department's offering contacts . . . have strengthened
> the parent/child relationship in this case?
>
> A. It's difficult for me to see anything positive that
> could have come out of contact between Richard and
> his father during his incarceration. We are talking
> about a child with whom there is no history of a
> relationship.
>
> Q. Would the contacts have benefitted the child at all
> in your opinion?
>
> A. I don't see how it could have benefitted him.
>
> Q. If the Department of Social Services had . . . for
> the past three years encouraged contacts and arranged
> for visitation . . . what, in your expert opinion, would
> have been the likely effect on the boy?
>
> A. . . . Richard . . . would probably find these kind of
> contacts in the context of incarceration very

confusing, very anxiety-provoking, and that in and of itself would not be very good for him.

Q. Are you aware of any counseling services which could have been offered . . . which would have strengthened the parent/child relationship, in your opinion?

A. I know of no services that could have been offered that would undo and remedy the damage that has been done to this child.

IMPLICATIONS: The rights of an incarcerated parent are not superior to or subordinate to those of the child. Customarily, a statute providing for the termination of parental rights must allow for parents to have a reasonable opportunity to mitigate the circumstances which led to a child protection service agency recommending that those rights be terminated. Efforts to ameliorate the adverse conditions must result in substantial progress as demonstrated by consistent and active behavior; reasonable efforts alone are insufficient. Neither the social worker nor the parent may impose his or her definition of progress on the other. Ultimately, it is a court, based largely upon the social worker's recommendation, which has the authority to terminate parental rights. Undisputed evidence that a parent has failed to establish normal relations with his or her child will be sufficient to make out a presumptive case to terminate parental rights. Courts are cognizant that although incarceration does not in and of itself establish a basis for termination of parental rights, they place great emphasis on evidence that the parent/child relationship may have deteriorated sufficiently to make reunification an unrealistic goal.

Numerous obstacles can hinder an effective parent-child relationship when a parent is incarcerated: distance of the prison facility; restrictive visiting hours; lack of cooperation by prison authorities; and communication and transportation problems (Beckerman, 1994; Hairston, 1991). The more severely the relationship is strained, the greater the possibility that a judge will be prompted to terminate parental rights. Conditions for children of incarcerated persons will improve only when there is an increased understanding that children of incarcerated parents are "sentenced" along with the parents.

REFERENCES

Beckerman, A. (1994). Mothers in prison: Meeting the prerequisite conditions for permanency planning. *Social Work, 39*(1), 9-13.

Hairston, C. (1991). Mothers in jail: Parent-child separation and jail visitation. *Affilia, 6*(2), 9-27.

Ybarra v. Texas Depart. of Human Services
869 S.W.2d 574 (Tex.App.-Corpus Christi 1993)

FACTS: Elida Ybarra separated from her husband, the father of her five children, in 1984. In May 1989, when the five children ranged in age from ten to five, the Department of Human Services (DHS) received a complaint about the children's condition. While investigating the complaint, a DHS worker found the children alone at home in a squalid condition. The substandard housing included holes in the floor covering and roof. As a result of the investigation, caseworkers helped the mother to improve the children's living conditions, including a move into public housing and the suggestion that Ms. Ybarra apply for food stamps and day-care services. Ms. Ybarra was also directed to attend Alcoholics Anonymous (AA) meetings. Ybarra did attend AA meetings but did not apply for food stamps although she probably would not have qualified due to her income level.

When a caseworker visited the family in June 1990, the home was found to be fairly clean by one caseworker and not clean enough by a second caseworker. The children were alone, and there was little food in the home. A caseworker went to the bar where the mother worked. Ybarra smelled of alcohol and was brought home. Later that same night, the children were removed from the home and placed in foster care.

A month later, " . . . DHS was named temporary managing conservator of the children, and that conservatorship was renewed on several occasions" (p. 577). After a January filing, the motion to terminate parental rights was tried in October 1992. As a result, the District Court terminated Ybarra's parental rights and she appealed.

ISSUE: Absent clear and convincing evidence, may parental rights be terminated?

DECISION: No. The Court of Appeals held that there was insufficient clear and convincing evidence to demonstrate that termination of parental rights was in the best interest of the children. This judgement was further supported by inadequate evidence that the children were endangered by remaining with their mother.

REASONING: The court noted that since the termination of the parent-child relationship severs rights treasured by the law, strict standards apply and evidence to meet those standards must be clear and convincing (p. 576). The best interests of the child are determined by considering several factors. These include the child's desires, emotional and physical needs of the child, the parental abilities of those seeking custody, parental assistance programs available to those seeking custody, the plans for the child by the agency or individual seeking custody, the acts or omissions of the parent which indicate that the parental relationship with the child is inappropriate, and any excuse for the acts or omissions of the parent.

The DHS did not present any evidence regarding the impact on the children of the alleged endangering conditions. Neither medical nor psychological reports were presented. Moreover, Ybarra attended AA meetings and was employed. Thus, there was no clear and convincing evidence that the children were endangered on the evening they were removed from Ybarra's home nor that they would be in danger if they were returned to Ybarra.

The desires of the child must be considered when determining the best interest of the child. The two oldest children " . . .strongly opposed the termination of their mother's parental rights" (p. 579). The wishes of the three younger children were not known.

IMPLICATIONS: Social workers are among the professionals required by every state to report suspected child abuse or neglect. Often the language which guides the social worker is vague and broad. For instance, terms such as "severe," "suspected," and "accidental" are undefined in laws and guidelines (Huxtable, 1994).

The potential for bias in child abuse and neglect cases exists and must be recognized. For instance, the adequateness of a parent's care may be considered when there is a question of child neglect. Since a social worker's own conception of "adequate parent" is influenced by the worker's own culture and ethnicity, there is the possibility that the worker will report a parent for neglect or abuse simply due to a lack of understanding.

An inability to recognize cultural or ethnic differences must be considered since a disproportionately high number of parental termination cases due to child abuse or neglect occur among racial and ethnic minorities (Azar & Benjet, 1994). In the effort against child abuse and neglect, social workers are in an exceptional position. They must use their understanding of the impact of ethnic and cultural differences on the family to ensure that civil liberties are respected while confronting the child abuse and neglect that affects millions of children in the United States.

REFERENCES

Azar, S.T., & Benjet, C.L. (1994). A cognitive perspective on ethnicity, race and termination of parental rights. *Law and Human Behavior, 18*(3), 249-268.

Huxtable, M. (1994). Child protection: With liberty and justice for all. *Social Work, 39*(1), 60-66.

Helen W. v. Fairfax County
407 S.E.2d 25 (Va.App. 1991)

FACTS: Sarah W. was a seventeen-year-old multi-handicapped adolescent who suffered from severe mental retardation, was hearing impaired, and had a number of physical disabilities that required medical intervention. She was enrolled in a special education program but was frequently absent. Due to her parents' neglect, the Fairfax County Department of Human Development obtained an emergency removal order and took custody of Sarah. Subsequently, it was determined that Sarah's parents should both undergo mental health evaluation and treatment. The mother was diagnosed as suffering from paranoid schizophrenia, and the father from a paranoid personality. Both were deemed incapable of parenting Sarah. Accordingly, the juvenile court terminated their residual parental rights and approved a plan for Sarah to be available for adoption. The parents sued to prevent this action.

ISSUE: Can a court terminate residual parental rights of parents who refuse to comply with reasonable and appropriate efforts of social service, medical, and mental health agencies if such termination is in the best interest of the child?

DECISION: Yes. Termination of parental rights means that a parent has no rights whatsoever to participate in decisions affecting their child's life. The court concluded that the Virginia statute was determinative:

> The residual parental rights of a parent or parents of a child placed in foster care as a result of a court commitment . . . may be terminated if the court finds, based upon clear and convincing evidence, that it is in the best interest of the child and that the parent or parents, without good cause, have been unwilling or unable within a reasonable period of time . . . to remedy substantially the conditions which led to the child's foster care placement. [§16.1-283(C)]

REASONING: The Department of Human Development asserted that sufficient evidence was presented demonstrating that termination of parental rights was in Sarah's best interest and that the requirements of the statute had been met. While the court recognized that termination of parental rights is a grave and irreversible action, it found that sufficient warning was given to Sarah's parents. The department's records showed that supervised visits between Sarah and her parents, when they did occur, were detrimental to Sarah. The visits frequently left Sarah agitated and upset, and unsupervised visits were not done in accordance with department procedures. Finally, the parents refused to participate in mental health treatment for themselves.

IMPLICATIONS: Courts generally are loathe to terminate all parental rights. When no less drastic measures are available, and when statutory procedures have been complied with, courts will take this action. Frequently, statutes regarding termination of parental rights are vaguely worded. They are broadly written to allow courts to intervene when necessary, yet not so vague as to be unconstitutional. To terminate parental rights many states use a multi-pronged test: a trial court must find the child to be dependent, and then the court must determine that there are no other viable social service alternatives available. In addition, the parents must demonstrate incapacity or misconduct. If a social service agency does not have a readily available alternative placement, should parental rights be terminated? Child protection workers advocate for termination. Placement workers advocate caution. Each is mindful of the child's immediate needs, yet neither wants the child to go from one unacceptable environment to another.

Kennedy v. Children's Serv. Society of Wisconsin
17 F.3d 980 (7th Cir. 1994)

FACTS: In this Wisconsin case, Children's Service Society of Wisconsin (CSS), a private adoption agency, was found by the trial court to have acted appropriately by withdrawing an adoption opportunity to adoptive parents whom they believed were members of a cult. The adoptive parents, Michelle and Dale Kennedy, filed suit against the adoption agency, its director and its insurers, making claims of defamation, breach of contract, and intentional infliction of emotional distress.

When Mary Shelby was five months pregnant, she applied to CSS for pregnancy counseling and to facilitate the termination of her parental rights. CSS agreed to assume guardianship of the child in the interim period before finalization of the adoption by the Kennedys.

A home study of the Kennedys was arranged and conducted by social worker Norma Spoonemore of Lutheran Social Services of Seattle. In her report, Spoonemore noted the Kennedys' religion as "The Way International" ("TWI"). Upon further investigation, it was learned that TWI appeared to be a cult——that members were known to use mind control and kept themselves sheltered and isolated from the rest of society. Shortly thereafter, CSS withdrew from the Shelby-Kennedy adoption because of its concerns about the Kennedys' involvement with TWI.

ISSUE: May adoptive parents successfully sue an adoption agency for withdrawing from services based on claims of defamation, breach of contract, and intentional infliction of emotional distress when such charges involve adoptive parents who are members of a cult?

DECISION: No.

REASONING: The court concluded that the plaintiffs in this case failed to allege special damages necessary to make a defamation claim and that the statements in question between the birth mother, her lawyer and the social worker, were privileged. The Kennedys alleged that in all three communications, the director of CSS characterized them as unsuitable adoptive parents because they belonged to a cult. Regarding defamation, the Kennedys failed to prove that: (1) a false statement was made; (2) there was communication by speech, conduct, or in writing to a person other than the person defamed, and (3) that the statements were harmful to their reputation so as to lower their standing in the community [*Munson v. Milwaukee Bd. of School Directors,* 969 F.2d 266, (7th Cir.1992)]. Ultimately, the Kennedys' defamation claim failed because they failed to plead or prove special damages. The Kennedys' allegations of resulting stress and harm to their reputation were deemed too general. Although additional costs were accrued by the adoptive parents, the costs were found not to be directly caused by the alleged defamatory remarks.

Regarding the alleged breach of contract, the court found that no contract ever existed between the two parties, and therefore no breach took place. Finally, the plaintiffs failed to state a claim of intentional infliction of emotional distress based on sufficient evidence.

IMPLICATIONS: What distinguishes a cult from a bona fide religion, organization, or group is not easy to define. One way to try to define a cult is by its characteristics. These may include: leadership that is messianic; use of deception and misrepresentation to recruit and retain members; secretiveness; purposeful separation of members from family and friends; financial exploitation of members; and the use of manipulation, or mind control. On an individual psychological basis, Spero (1983) has found that cult members may share the following symptoms: deteriorated or neglected health, inability to converse without resorting to cultic language, paranoia, defensive tendencies of denial, projection, and externalization.

Identifying and working with individuals influenced by cults is difficult and sometimes dangerous. Ultimately, experts agree that a meaningful family life and positive community atmosphere is the best defense against individuals being attracted to cults. Social workers are presently involved in deprogramming and exploring ways to lessen the impact of recruitment efforts by cult members (Goldberg & Goldberg, 1982; Zweig & Abrams, 1991).

REFERENCES

Goldberg, L., & Goldberg, W. (1982). Group work with former cultists. *Social Work, 27,* 234-251.

Spero, M. (1983). Individual psychodynamic intervention with the cult devotee: Diagnostic and treatment procedure with a dysautonomous religious personality. In D. Halprin (Ed.), *Psychodynamic perspectives on religion, sect, and cult.* Boston, MA: John Wright PSG.

Zweig, C., & Abrams, J. (1991). *Meeting the shadow: The hidden power of the dark side of human nature.* Los Angeles, CA: Jeremy P. Tarcher, Inc.

Engstrom v. State
461 N.W.2d 309 (Iowa 1990)

FACTS: Howard and Dorothy Engstrom filed suit against the State of Iowa and five state-employed social workers for damages resulting from a failed adoption. In July 1974 Melody was born to Denise and Michael Ehmke. Denise and Michael later separated, and Denise began a relationship with Terry Dochterman. Terry, Denise, and Melody moved to Iowa in 1977 or 1978.

In 1980, Denise was an inmate in a women's reformatory, and the Iowa Department of Human Services began a "child in need of assistance" action in juvenile court. The petition was granted, and the department gained custody of Melody. In 1984, a termination of parental rights hearing was held. At the hearing a social worker testified that the files indicated that Melody's father was dead and therefore Melody was adoptable. Information concerning Michael's death had earlier been given to social workers by Denise and Terry. Although the files indicated that the social workers had doubts about Michael's death, they did not investigate the issue. In fact, Michael was located in California when Denise applied for welfare benefits. However, this information was never conveyed to the social workers involved in Melody's case.

The Engstroms were accepted as potential adoptive parents, and Melody was placed with them in 1984. At that time, they were informed that Melody's mother no longer had parental rights and her father was deceased. In 1985, Michael requested custody of his daughter, and the State attempted to terminate his parental rights. The termination request was denied, and the juvenile court began to take steps to reunite Melody with her father. Consequently, the department changed Melody's status with the Engstroms from preadoptive to foster care. In 1986, Melody expressed a desire to live with her father, and in January 1987, custody of Melody was transferred from the department to Michael.

Following the state district court's dismissal, the Engstroms filed an appeal with the Supreme Court of Iowa.

ISSUE: In the context of a preadoption agreement, can social workers be held liable for social worker malpractice, the infliction of emotional distress, breach of contract, and denial of due process rights when the cause of action is not specified in the applicable statute and administrative rules?

DECISION: No. Since the placement agreement did not detail duties and obligations owed by the state and the social workers to the Engstroms and no applicable law provided a basis for recovery, the claim was denied.

REASONING: The Supreme Court of Iowa explained that in order to obtain restitution, the plaintiff must establish a violation of a statutorily protected legal right. The court noted that the applicable Iowa statute places the welfare of the adoptive person as the paramount goal. Thus, while the interests of the adoptive parents are considered, they are secondary (p. 316). The interests of the adoptive parents are subordinate to those of the natural parents.

The court found that the State and its social workers were not compelled by implied contractual duties of reasonable care and good faith to determine the status of a natural father before establishing a preadoptive association between a custodial child and potential parents. Consequently, the preadoptive parents had neither a claim of deprivation of protected liberty, property, nor an actionable malpractice claim.

IMPLICATIONS: In 1980, Congress passed the Adoption Assistance and Child Welfare Act. This Act emphasizes permanency planning for foster children including family reunification and adoption. The focus on permanency placement is based on the belief that multiple placements cause risk for a child (Mica & Vosler, 1990). The goal is to move children through the foster care system and back home or into adoptive placements as quickly as possible.

This approach is based on an underlying objective to create a system that most benefits the child. Social workers are confronted with a foster child in a pre-adoption situation when unresolved custodial issues still exist. The social worker must attempt to limit the threat to the placement while maintaining a cooperative relationship between the agency and the family. This may require the social worker to balance the welfare of the child with the concerns and interests of the prospective adoptive parents. This balancing may be facilitated by developing a "common means of evaluating the degree of uncertainty associated with a particular foster-adoptive placement, so that prospective foster-adoptive parents have a clear basis for making an informed decision about accepting a particular child" (Mica & Vosler, 1990, p. 437).

Included in the 1980 Act is a call for "reasonable efforts" to be exercised in attempting to return children to their biological families. This emphasis is based on the belief that parents have a right to care for their biological children and those children have a right to receive care from their natural parents. Although the Act does not precisely define "reasonable efforts," establishing paternity and locating biological parents is understood to be part of that effort. However, if a duty is imposed on agencies to definitively establish the location of biological parents, the possibility of punishment due to breaching that duty or the actual punishment itself could cripple the entire adoption system (Dapolitano, 1993, p.1016). Consequently, foster care social workers must maintain their focus on acting in what is believed to be the best interest of the child while balancing the child's interests with the other, sometimes competing, interests of prospective adoptive and biological parents.

REFERENCES

Chou, C. (1993). Renewing the good intentions of foster care: Enforcement of the Adoption Assistance and Child Welfare Act of 1980 and the substantive due process right to safety. *Vanderbilt University Law Review, 46*, 683-713.

Dapolitano, A. (1993). The failure to notify putative fathers of adoption proceedings: Balancing the adoption equation. *Catholic University Law Review, 42*, 979-1026.

Mica, M., & Vosler, N. (1990). Foster-adoptive programs in public social service agencies: Toward flexible family resources. *Child Welfare, 69*, 433-445.

Michael J. v. County of Los Angeles, Depart. of Adoptions
247 Cal.Rptr. 504 (Cal.App. 2 Dist. 1988)

FACTS: On March 30, 1970, Michael J. was born with a port wine stain on his upper torso and face. The examining doctor failed to indicate a prognosis for Michael despite the fact that medical knowledge at that time would have enabled him to do so. Mary Trout, the potential adoptive parent, was told by the agency social worker that the stain was merely a birthmark. Trout says that she would not have proceeded with the adoption had she known the child was sick. After suffering from an epileptic seizure in 1981, Michael was diagnosed with Sturge-Weber Syndrome, a diagnosis that should have been made at birth. Trout is seeking damages for negligence, fraud, emotional distress, and current and future medical expenses incurred as a result of Michael's illness.

The County Department of Adoptions filed for summary judgement, claiming that at the time of adoption Michael was believed to be in good health. Summary judgement was granted by the trial court on the basis of immunity.

ISSUE: Should a county department of adoptions be immune from liability for intentional or negligent misrepresentation or concealment in relation to the health of a prospective adoptee?

DECISION: No. California law does not shield its counties from liability for negligent or intentional misrepresentations regarding the health of a prospective adoptee.

REASONING: The Court of Appeals outlined numerous triable issues. Governmental liabilities are addressed by that state's Tort Claim Act: "Liability is the rule, immunity the exception" (p. 507). Prior cases indicate financial and commercial interest to be the main focus of immunity. Adoption does not fall within the purview of commercial transactions. While the court did not expect "the adoption agency [to be] a guarantor of the infant's future good health" (p. 512), failure to divulge all known information was unjustifiable.

IMPLICATIONS: Absolute immunity from prosecution means that persons cannot be sued in their professional capacity. Only courts have absolute immunity. Qualified immunity means that a person is immune from prosecution only under certain circumstances. Some courts have recognized qualified immunity for social workers, while others have done so only for those employees whose investigative or administrative duties encompass specific functions. The more a social worker's duties appear quasi-judicial, the greater the likelihood that qualified immunity will be recognized. The defense of qualified immunity applies only to government-like functions. Generally, social workers performing discretionary functions are immune from liability unless their actions violate clearly established or constitutional rights of which they should have known. Some courts have instituted a two-part test to determine if qualified immunity should be recognized: first, whether the alleged behavior specifies a clear constitutional violation; and second, whether the constitutional standard was applicable at the time of the alleged violation. The burden is on the plaintiff to show that qualified immunity should be granted.

Matter of Baby M
537 A.2d 1227 (N.J. 1988)

FACTS: In February 1985, William Stern and Mary Beth Whitehead entered into a surrogacy contract. The details of the contract stipulated that Whitehead would be artificially inseminated with Stern's sperm, bear their child, and relinquish the child to Stern. Whitehead would then terminate her rights as the mother, thereby allowing the adoption of the child by Stern. In turn, William Stern agreed to pay $10,000 to Whitehead upon delivery of the child and $7,500 to the agency that orchestrated the surrogacy arrangements.

On March 27, 1986, Baby M was born. From the moment of birth, Ms. Whitehead was aware that she would not be able to separate from her child. As such, it was with great reluctance and difficulty that Whitehead turned the baby over to the Sterns. Whitehead subsequently experienced great emotional unrest stemming from her severe doubts at having given up her baby. Her depression led her back to the Sterns, and they agreed to give Mary Beth the baby for one week. What ensued was Ms. Whitehead's abduction of the baby to Florida and a four-month search by the Sterns for the child. Baby M was ultimately removed from the possession of Whitehead by force and transferred back to the Sterns. Baby M remained with the Sterns throughout the ensuing trial pursuant to the court order.

The Sterns sought enforcement of the surrogacy contract. They claimed a right of procreation under constitutional law. Custody of Baby M, termination of Whitehead's maternal rights, and the Sterns' adoption of the child were included in the court proceedings. The trial court upheld the legality of the surrogacy contract. In the best interest of the child, the judge terminated Whitehead's parental rights, granted sole custody to the Sterns, and allowed the adoption of Baby M by Mrs. Stern.

Mary Beth Whitehead appealed. She sought to have the surrogacy contract declared null and void because it deprived the child of contact with both natural parents, denied the mother companionship of her child under constitutional law, and conflicted with well-established adoption legislation. The best interests of the child as well as discouragement of future surrogacy arrangements served as the basis for her arguments.

ISSUE: Regarding a contract for surrogate motherhood, are the best interests of a child the sole controlling question pertaining to termination of parental rights?

DECISION: No.

REASONING: The surrogacy contract was invalid: it was in direct conflict with both existing statutes and public policies of New Jersey. Applicable to this case are laws forbidding monetary exchange in conjunction with adoption, laws preventing termination of parental rights without proof of parental unfitness or abandonment, and laws that grant revocability in private placement adoptions.

Contracts for baby-selling disregard the interests of the child and the natural mother. Public policy prefers that "adoption statutes seek to further humanitarian goals, foremost among them the best interest of the child" (p. 1242). The use of monetary arrangement does not allow for the attainment of this goal.

Statutes pertaining to termination of parental rights set out very specific guidelines under which a court can terminate the rights of a parent. Private placement adoption does not differ. Unless there is clear proof that parents have neglected or abandoned their responsibilities, parental rights remain intact. Without a valid termination, adoption cannot take place. A contractual provision stipulating the termination of the mother's rights and allowing for the subsequent adoption of the child is insufficient ground for such severe action.

Irrevocability is another aspect of adoption that is dealt with explicitly by this New Jersey law:

> The surrender must be in writing, must be in such form as is required for the recording of a deed, and, must be such as to declare that the person executing the same desires to relinquish the custody of the child, acknowledge the termination of parental rights as to such custody in favor of the approved agency, and acknowledge full understanding of the effect of such surrender as provided by this act (p. 1244).

Without these strict prerequisites, revocability prevails. Contrary to the requirements of the law, the surrogacy contract between Mary Beth Whitehead and William Stern provides no provision enabling Mary Beth to rescind her surrender of custody.

Public policy considerations surrounding this case focus on the interests of the child and of the parents. Custody of Baby M was determined by the contractual provisions and not by the child's best interests. Furthermore, policy demands that the child be kept with its natural parents to the extent possible. No such intentions are found in the actions of the Whiteheads or the Sterns. Equal rights for custody and the lack of counseling received by the natural mother were also policies ignored in the surrogacy arrangement.

With the surrogacy contract considered null and void, the remaining issue was the actual custody of Baby M. Ultimately, the court based its award of custody on the stability of the two families. Testimony indicated the Whitehead family was in financial trouble; Mr. Whitehead was an alcoholic, and Ms. Whitehead had not been recently employed. Additionally, several witnesses testified to Ms. Whitehead's disdain for professional help and her controlling nature, factors that could interfere in her doing what would be in the best interests of the child.

Conversely, the Sterns were a portrait of stability. Their finances, social class, and happy marriage all suggested an environment in which Baby M would flourish. On this contrast alone, the court awarded custody to the Sterns. Because it was determined that Mary Beth's maternal rights were not terminated, visitation orders had to be determined. This matter was remanded to the trial court.

IMPLICATIONS: At the very least, surrogacy motherhood challenges the legal parameters of adoption, parental rights, and child custody. It usually uproots the emotional well-being of entire families (Blyth, 1993; Schwartz, 1990) and undermines the best interests of the child. "Surrogacy raises profound questions regarding the rights of women as mothers, the definition of parenthood, the social value we place on children, and how we relate to each other in a society that becomes more and more commercialized" (*Matter of Baby M*, p. 537).

The risks to children are of alarming concern. Among the psychological dangers are "deliberate separation from her/his birth mother, the loss of half her/his genetic history, deceptions about her/his origins, social stigma, and psychological damage . . ." (Blyth, 1993).

Adoption statutes seek to minimize these emotional ramifications by banning the selling of babies. Yet, in the case of surrogacy motherhood, the prohibition of money does not ultimately protect the child's welfare. "Whilst these risks [of emotional problems associated with adoption] are presumed acceptable for a child who already exists and for whom adoption may represent the best possible alternative care, the *deliberate* exposure of a child to such hazards is not" (Blyth, 1993). Granting surrogate transactions places the needs of the infertile couple over the best interests of the child. As the New

Jersey court wrote: " . . . a person's right of privacy and self-determination are qualified by the effect on innocent third persons of the exercise of those rights" [*In re Baby M,* 537 A.2d, 1254]. Much attention has been given to surrogacy as "using" a woman's body without any regard to the bond between natural mother and child (Arditti, 1987). Schwartz (1990) identifies the issue of loss as a central one for the surrogate mother and the effects of bearing someone else's child as a grave threat to the emotional stability of the surrogate family.

Surrogacy is not merely a contract. It is a microcosm of society's beliefs regarding its most deeply held values. Because surrogacy has such strong implications for the lives of all those involved, particularly the child, mandated counseling must be a part of this complicated process. More importantly, legislature should be cautious before enacting specific laws that enable this form of child bearing.

The law in this area is far from settled. Infertility technology now includes in vitro fertilization, gamete intrafallopian transfer, embryo transfer, embryo transplantation, post-menopausal birthing, embryo and gamete freezing, and preliminary steps toward cloning human embryos. As the court wrote, " . . . [t]he problem is how to enjoy the benefits of technology—especially for infertile couples—while minimizing the risk of abuse" (p. 1264).

REFERENCES

Arditti, R. (Fall 1987). The surrogacy business. *Social Policy,* 42-46.

Blyth, E. (1993). Children's welfare, surrogacy and social work. *British Journal of Social Work, 23,* 259-275.

Schwartz, L. (1990). Surrogate motherhood and family psychology/therapy. *American Journal of Family Therapy, 18*(4), 385-392.

Meracle v. Children's Serv. Society of Wisconsin
437 N.W.2d 532 (Wis. 1989)

FACTS: On October 10, 1979, Quentin and Nancy Meracle met with Children's Service Society (CSS) social worker Josephine Braden to make arrangements for the adoption of Erin, a twenty-three-month-old child. The Meracles claimed they were informed of the following: Erin's paternal grandmother had died of Huntington's Disease and that Huntington's was a fatal degenerative brain condition that is genetically communicated between generations. They maintained that Braden reassured them that since Erin's father had tested negative for Huntington's, Erin was at no risk of developing that disorder. Braden denied having promised to the Meracles a child who had no health problems.

The Meracles applied for adoption with CSS in 1977, at which time they related their preference for adopting a "normal, healthy child"—one, not suffering from a "disabilitating" or "terminal disease." On September 25, 1985, the Meracles filed suit against the Children's Service Society of Wisconsin, an adoption agency, alleging that at the time of adoption, the agency negligently misrepresented the risk of Erin contracting Huntington's Disease.

The Meracles sought compensation for damages on two claims: (1) for emotional pain and suffering regarding their daughter's impending death, and (2) loss of anticipated extraordinary medical expenses.

ISSUE: May adoptive parents successfully sue for emotional distress and extraordinary medical expenses when an adoption agency negligently misrepresents the health of a pre-adoptive child?

DECISION: No, as to the emotional distress; yes, as to the medical expenses. Victims of wrongful adoption actions are not barred by public policy from pursuing relief for perceived damages afflicted by an adoption agency, if no false or misleading claims were determined to have been made by agency representatives during the adoption process.

REASONING: The court cited a previous case [*Brantner v. Jensen*, 121 Wis.2d 658 (1985)] which held that, "to recover for future expenses due to an injury, a plaintiff must demonstrate that the anticipated expenses are reasonably certain to occur" (pp. 663-664). In this case, it was acknowledged that future medical expenses will accrue.

In another previous case [*Garrett v. City of New Berlin,* 122 Wis. 2d 223 (1985)], the court held that to recover for negligent infliction of emotional distress, the "plaintiff's emotional distress must be manifested by physical injury" (p. 231). The court justified its decision by maintaining that emotional pain endured by family members regarding a loss or illness of another family member is not uncommon and therefore not recoverable.

During the time this case was heard, there was no state policy which required adoption agencies to disclose health information regarding pre-adoptive children. The court did decide that if health information was disclosed, responsible care and due diligence must be taken to make the disclosure accurate and complete. Therefore, the court held that the social worker misrepresented the child's possibility of developing Huntington's Disease.

Several points were made. Recovery against an adoption agency will be difficult if (1) the adoptive child's injury is too remote from the alleged negligence of the agency; (2) such recovery would allow for fraudulent claims; or (3) recovery would place social workers in a position of such extreme uncertainty that they could not carry out their professional responsibilities.

IMPLICATIONS: The policy of having adoption agencies refrain from proffering conclusive information about the health of a child has the intended effect of protecting agency workers from liability. But, it does not foster greater confidence in the accuracy and integrity of the adoption process and in the information received.

Numerous states have allowed adoptive parents to recover damages from adoption agencies for improperly representing facts in an adoption proceeding (Amadio, 1989). This case does not mean that adoption agencies are effectively the guarantors of the health of each child available for adoption. All courts agree that while adoption agencies are not guarantors, they must take reasonable precautions to share relevant information with adoptive parents. Often, adoptees themselves are eager to search for their biological parents because they need medical information (Campbell, Silverman, & Patti, 1991; Gross, 1993).

In 1851, Massachusetts passed the first law regulating adoption. Until recently, little or no information pertaining to the natural parents of the child was shared with the adoptive parents. The consequences of these restrictive laws have resulted in lawsuits alleging fraud, misrepresentation, and most recently, a handful of states recognizing a new cause of action called "wrongful adoption" [*e.g., MacMath v. Maine Adoption Placement Servs.,* 635 A.2d 359 (1993); *Gibbs v. Ernst,* 615 A.2d 851 (1992); *M.H. v. Caritas Family Srvs.,* 488 N.W.2d 282 (1992); *Engstrom v. State,* 461 N.W.2d 309 (1990); *Foster v. Bass,* 575 So.2d 967 (1990)]. Today, as a result of legislative activity, many courts no longer dictate whether or not adoptive parents may have access to the pre-adoptive child's medical history. Rather, many states charge state-licensed adoption agencies with the responsibility of investigating and reporting all relevant medical data of the child and natural parents to the prospective adoptive parents.

In previous years adoption was shrouded in secrecy and privacy. With the appearance of childhood illnesses that may only be evident in later life (HIV/AIDS, drug addiction, and Fetal Alcohol Syndrome), there is a compelling tendency to disclose more information, This is preferable to a post-adoptive disruption in which the child, natural parents, and adoptive parents all needlessly suffer. To affect this possibility, a trend has developed to offer an array of open adoptions (Berry, 1991):

(1) Restricted open adoptions: The adoptive family shares pictures and information with the biological parents for a limited period of time following placement, with the agency acting as a liaison between the families

(2) Semiopen adoption: Biological parents meet the adoptive family, but there is no further sharing of information

(3) Fully open adoption: The adoptive family and the biological parents meet and share information for a limited period of time

(4) Continuing open adoption: The biological and adoptive families plan to continue to contact each other over the course of the adopted child's growing up (pp. 638-639).

REFERENCES

Amadio, C. (1989). Wrongful adoption--a new basis for litigation, another challenge for Child Welfare. *Journal of Law and Social Work, 1*(1), 23-30.

Berry, M. (1991). The effects of open adoption on biological and adoptive parents and the children: The arguments and the evidence. *Child Welfare, 70*(6), 637-651.

Campbell, L., Silverman, P., & Patti, P. (1991). Reunions between adoptees and birth parents: The adoptees' experience. *Social Work, 36*(4), 329-335.

Gross, H. (1993). Open adoption: A research-based literature review and new data. *Child Welfare, 72*(3), 269-284.

In re Roger B.
418 N.E.2d 751 (Ill. App. 1981)

FACTS: Plaintiff, born in 1949, had limited knowledge of his birth. Given up for adoption as a newborn, he grew up with adoptive parents. In 1978, as an emotionally stable and financially secure man, he began his search for his biological parents. Under the present laws of Illinois, this information is inaccessible to a plaintiff and because of this, he brought a lawsuit.

ISSUE: By restricting the access to birth records of adopted children and their biological families, does a state violate a "fundamental" right, a privacy right, or a right to freedom of information?

DECISION: No. The court determined that in so far as a statute is rationally related to a state's legitimate purpose for the creation of the statute, it is not a violation of a fundamental right, privacy right, or freedom of information.

REASONING: The relevant portion of the statute reads: "Upon motion of any party to an adoption proceeding the court shall, or upon the court's own motion the court may, order that the file relating to such proceeding shall be impounded by the clerk of the court and shall be opened for examination only upon specific order of the court, which order shall name the person or persons who are to be permitted to examine such file" (Ill.Rev.Stat.1977, ch.40, par. 1522, p. 752). While the plaintiff argued that this portion of the statute applies to him, the court reasoned that the confidentiality of adoption records is at the heart of this institution. Many women would suffer if forced to abort or live in burdensome conditions if not for the ability to give up a child for adoption.

Referring to the violation of a fundamental right argument, the court, following a lower court's findings, supported the "good cause test." This test was implemented by the court to establish an exception to the confidentiality standard set by statute, where certain circumstances require information be divulged. The court reasoned that since the legislature provided for exceptions to the rule, to be determined by the courts, it necessarily implied that some sort of standard would be needed and that the courts would have the responsibility of determining this standard.

With this standard in mind, the court addressed the "fundamental right" argument postulated by the plaintiff, who stated that the "right to know his own identity [was] a fundamental right" (p. 753) and that this fundamental right is implicit in the right to privacy. The court referred to the Supreme Court, which often finds itself in the position of determining fundamental rights under the Constitution but hesitates to create fundamental rights. The Supreme Court's test of a fundamental right is whether or not the right was implied explicitly or implicitly in the Constitution. The court said this was not the case and that no other courts had found adoption information to be a fundamental right.

The court then went to the next level of evaluation stating that since it was not a fundamental right, the statute had only to be rationally related to legitimate state objectives in order to be upheld. As to the state's objective, the court supports the state's desire to maintain adoption procedures and to facilitate finding homes for unwanted children as well as supporting families involved in this process. In so doing, the state has in fact promised biological parents certain rights and their anonymity is perhaps the only way they are capable of making such a difficult decision—to have a child and give it away. While many might disagree with the court's findings and the state's objectives, most states have confidentiality statutes, and this case typifies the state of the law regarding this area. Finally, the court emphasized the protection of the public welfare and the preservation of a legitimate adoption process. Having balanced all of the interests involved, the court determined that, except in extreme circumstances, records should remain confidential.

IMPLICATIONS: The court made a determination based on the weight of all the interests involved. In so doing, it determined that the biological parents' and their new families' interests are more important than an adopted child's interest in finding his or her history and biological identity. The Constitution does not explicitly set forth fundamental rights, but the courts have historically created them. While some states allow for adoption records to be opened when the adoptee becomes an adult, the majority of states choose to keep them confidential. Controversy concerning open adoptions has been debated extensively (Siegel, 1993; Berry, 1993; Gross, 1993). This case represents another instance where the court is forced to make a judgement call, where the protection of society outweighs an individual's rights.

REFERENCES

Berry, M. (1993). Adoptive parent's perceptions of, and comfort with, option adoption. *Child Welfare, 72*(3), 231-253.

Gross, H. (1993). Open adoption: A research-based literature review and new data. *Child Welfare, 72*(3), 269-284.

Siegel, D. (1993). Open adoption of infants: Adoptive parents' perceptions of advantages and disadvantages. *Social Work, 38*(1), 15-23.

State v. Hosto-Worthy
877 S.W.2d 150 (Mo.App. E.D. 1994)

FACTS: S.H., stepdaughter to Dawn Denise Hosto-Worthy, was brought to a hospital emergency room with a ruptured appendix. Hospital personnel called the Division of Family Services (DFS) informing DFS that the Hosto-Worthys had prior knowledge of S.H.'s condition and had neglected to obtain medical attention for her. In response to the call, Elizabeth Thompson, a child abuse investigator, spoke with S.H.'s father at the hospital regarding the incident. Next, Thompson called the defendant to arrange a home visit to speak with her and the other children. Despite Thompson's explanation to Hosto-Worthy regarding the urgent nature of the visit, the defendant refused to cooperate. Thompson then arranged for a police officer to accompany her to the defendant's home. The defendant was unaware of this arrangement.

Detective Ritter arrived at the home, identified himself as a police officer, and was let into the house. Thompson arrived soon after and was also permitted entry. The defendant and children were questioned about the child abuse allegations, and pictures of certain rooms were taken by Ritter. *Miranda* warnings were not given during their three-hour stay.

Hosto-Worthy requested the suppression of all evidence acquired during the interview in her home because she had not been Mirandized, and there had been no search warrant. The trial court held that the situation warranted *Miranda* warnings and a search warrant. The State asserted that *Miranda* warnings would have been necessary only if there had been a custodial interrogation.

ISSUE: When acting jointly with a social worker, are law enforcement officers required to give *Miranda* warnings in a situation in which child abuse is suspected?

DECISION: Yes. *Miranda* warnings are necessary upon the development of a custodial interrogation.

REASONING: The court cited other cases in which suspects who voluntarily offered information to the police were not read their *Miranda* rights and were then implicated by their self-incriminating statements. These interviews, while initially voluntary, escalated into custodial interrogations when the suspects were no longer able to leave the meeting. *Miranda* warnings were therefore required. Hosto-Worthy testified that she did not feel that she could end the interview nor get Detective Ritter to leave her house at any time throughout the three-hour interview.

IMPLICATIONS: Since social workers are not "peace officers," they are not obligated to "*Mirandize*" suspected perpetrators of child abuse. When accompanying a police officer, however, *Miranda* warnings may be required. The United States Supreme Court has held that, "Coercive police activity is the necessary predicate to finding any statement involuntary and inadmissable" [*Colorado v. Connelly*, 107 S.Ct. 515, 522 (1986)]. If a person is informed of his right to remain silent and thereafter makes incriminating voluntary statements, these may be used as evidence. But, incriminating statements that are extracted by coercion or intimidation are not admissible as evidence into court. A social worker operating at the instruction of the police officer cannot do what the police officer is prohibited from doing.

In Interest of M.A.V.
425 S.E.2d 377 (Ga.App. 1992)

FACTS: M.A.V. is the oldest of two siblings to a mother diagnosed with Munchausen Syndrome by Proxy (MSP). The six-year-old child has been in the care of his grandparent since infancy, his mother having remarried and moved to another state shortly after his birth. B.C.C., the younger child, was taken away from the mother based on a physician's testimony regarding MSP, an illness in which the child's caretaker brings on sickness in the child or harms the child and then solicits medical attention. In fact, the mother had induced respiratory arrest in B.C.C. on two separate occasions. The presence of this illness in the mother led the juvenile court to seek termination of the mother's rights for M.A.V. as well. The mother appealed the court's decision, contending that evidence to support such termination involved B.C.C., not M.A.V.

ISSUE: Is evidence from termination of parental rights for one child usable to support a decision to terminate a parent's rights with regard to another child of the same parent?

DECISION: No. Clear and convincing evidence is necessary to support termination of parental rights in each new case.

REASONING: "Only under compelling circumstance found to exist by clear and convincing proof may a court sever the parent-child custodial relationship" [*Carvalho v. Lewis*, 247 Ga. 94, 95 (1981)]. M.A.V. was found to be deprived on the sole evidence provided for *another* child. Relying on the testimony of a psychiatrist at the deprivation hearing of B.C.C., the juvenile court decided that M.A.V. could possibly be the next victim of appellant's MSP. The doctor never examined M.A.V., reviewed his records, or interacted with the mother. No evidence indicated that M.A.V. ever suffered from the appellant's MSP. Furthermore, M.A.V. is cared for by his grandparent, a living arrangement which will continue into the future. The burden of proof of "clear and convincing" evidence was not met.

IMPLICATIONS: Munchausen Syndrome by Proxy is a disorder first identified in the late 1970s. It usually involves mothers who either imagine or cause health problems in their children. Much of the literature has focused on the medical aspects, with mental health professionals only recently addressing this problem (Shreier & Libow, 1993). In their study, Shreier and Libow (1993) found that diagnosing MSP may be difficult and slow. This may be due to the complexity and relative infrequency of the syndrome and also a lack of familiarity by social workers. According to Mercer and Perdue (1993), Moore (1995), and Jones et al. (1986), some signs that may indicate MSP are (1) a child who is ill without being able to identify a cause; (2) medical evaluations which yield no diagnosis; (3) a parent's eagerness to have their child undergo medical procedures. Experts recommend that a social worker

> needs to assist in obtaining consent from the parents for the child's previous medical records and perhaps for their own records. There often is a pattern of many medical visits and hospitalizations for both the child and the suspected perpetrator, and combing through these records can be informative. Social workers have the ability to obtain and assess family information and to successfully sift through the data until the puzzle pieces are found. The symptoms are complex, and the perpetrator is often sophisticated and skilled in deception. (Mercer & Perdue, 1993, p. 80)

Suspicions or confirmation of MSP should be shared with legal authorities immediately.

REFERENCES

Jones, J., Butler, H., Hamilton, B., Perdue, J., Stern, P., & Woody, R. (1986). Munchausen syndrome by proxy. *Child Abuse and Neglect, 10*, 33-40.

Mercer, S., & Perdue, J. (1993). Munchausen syndrome by proxy: Social worker's role. *Social Work, 38*(1), 74-81.

Moore, K. (1995). Social workers' role with patients with Munchausen syndrome. *Social Work, 40*(6), 823-825.

Schreier, H., & Libow, J. (1993). Munchausen syndrome by proxy: Diagnosis and prevalence. *American Journal of Orthopsychiatry, 63*(2), 318-321.

A.Y. v. Department of Public Welfare
583 A.2d 515 (Pa.Cmwlth. 1990)

FACTS: L.K., a three-year-old girl, was being taken care of by a babysitter, A.Y., on October 28, 1988. According to testimony from L.K.'s mother, a conversation with her daughter revealed that A.Y. had licked L.K.'s vagina and buttocks, in addition to other body parts. L.K. similarly described the evening's events to her father. Upon report of the child's story to the Child Protective Services Department, a caseworker and social worker interviewed the child. Once again, L.K. repeated the story using anatomically correct dolls. Despite A.Y.'s denial of all allegations, her name was subsequently listed on the state's child abuse registry.

A.Y., a twenty-three-year-old college graduate in psychology with plans to work with families in crisis, requested expungement of that record. In defense of her innocence, she offered testimony of her former supervisor who had witnessed A.Y. working with children, testimony of a person who had conducted a polygraph test on A.Y. regarding this matter, testimony of her parents, and reports from her therapist. In turn, the child protective agency presented testimony of both the caseworker investigating the incident and the social worker who had interviewed L.K. as well as the testimony of L.K.'s mother.

It was determined that the report of child abuse in the registry was in fact warranted. A.Y. appealed this decision, claiming that the evidence supported expungement of her name from the child abuse registry.

ISSUES: Can the report of a small child regarding alleged sexual abuse be presented through hearsay testimony by her mother? Can the testimony of a social worker be admitted into evidence when no videotape was made of the interview and no psychologist evaluated the child's credibility?

DECISION: Yes. Both these forms of evidence may be admissible.

REASONING: The guidelines for permitting hearsay testimony from a child in a situation of sexual abuse require that "the time, context and circumstances of this statement provide sufficient indicia of reliability" [*L.W.B. v. Sosnowski*, 543 A.2d 1241 (1988)]. A.Y. contends that testimony from L.K.'s mother is not reliable because of the parent's position as an interested party. Nonetheless, because the incident was brought through the child's initiative and the mother's response was of a non-probing nature, criteria of reliability were sufficiently met.

A social worker's interview with an alleged child abuse victim may always be open to suspicion. While A.Y. believed the social worker's questions to be leading, the court found L.K.'s actions with the anatomically correct dolls to be clear evidence of what had occurred. The lack of ambiguity in the child's response to the social worker was a reasonable indication of the child's clarity regarding the allegations of sexual abuse. Preliminary questions, together with L.K.'s detailed description of her interactions with A.Y. formed the basis of the child's credibility. Though the benefits of both a videotape of the sessions and evaluation of the child by a psychologist would have been helpful, the law does not require that either be used. The testimonies themselves were viewed as substantial evidence for the allegations of sexual abuse. A.Y.'s name was not expunged from the registry.

IMPLICATIONS: Mandatory reporting laws now exist in every state. While controversial (Hutchinson, 1993; Besharov, 1990; Rycraft, 1990) it is agreed that the background, experience, and training of the social worker who does a child abuse investigation is critical. In this case, the court noted that the social worker had an associate degree in early childhood education, a bachelor's degree in home economics, a master's degree in social work, and was working on a master's degree in public health (p. 519).

In a case of expungement, the court will not review all of the evidence *de novo*. Rather, it will ascertain only if "substantial evidence existed to support the conclusion actually reached by the [hearing] officer, not whether substantial evidence did exist or might have existed to support a contrary conclusion" (p. 521).

Numerous states have amended their rules of evidence regarding the testimony of children who have allegedly been abused. These statutes now routinely permit a child to testify without being directly confronted by the accused. In a landmark U.S. Supreme Court case, *White v. Illinois* [112 S.Ct. 736 (1992)], the Court acknowledged that the emotional trauma of being in a courtroom, confronted by the alleged perpetrator, would not necessarily provide for a fair hearing. Generally, the Confrontation Clause of the Sixth Amendment requires that a declarant appear at trial or be physically unavailable in order for that person to be able to make an out-of-court statement that will be admitted into evidence. But the Supreme Court acknowledged that an exception to this rule needed to be made. Child hearsay evidence may be used if it bears "particularized guarantees of trustworthiness" [*Ohio v. Roberts*, 100 S.Ct. 2531, 2539 (1980)], or if the child's statements "might be considered the functional equivalent of in-court testimony because the statements arguably were made in contemplation of legal proceedings" [*White v. Illinois,* 112 S.Ct. 736, 747 (1992)].

The Sixth Amendment states, in pertinent part: "In all criminal prosecutions, the accused shall enjoy the right to be confronted with the witnesses against him . . ." (U.S. Const. Amend. VI). In *Maryland v. Craig* [110 S.Ct. 3157 (1990)], the United States Supreme Court decided that the Confrontation Clause is not compromised by legislation which permits the use of one-way closed circuit television hook-ups to allow child witnesses to testify in their own abuse cases. The Maryland statute was upheld. It specified numerous precautions and stipulations that are still in effect today:

* The testimony should be taken during the court proceeding.
* The judge must determine that testimony by the child victim in the courtroom would result in serious emotional distress such that the child could not reasonably communicate.
* Only the prosecutor, defense attorney and judge may question the child.
* The television operator must be unobtrusive.

Thus, while live confrontation may enhance the overall fact-finding potential, the ability to cross-examine is adequately preserved by use of closed circuit television (see Aravzo, Watson, & Hughes, 1994).

REFERENCES

Aravzo, A., Watson, M., & Hughes, J. (1994). The clinical uses of video therapy in the treatment of childhood sexual trauma survivors. *Journal of Child Sexual Abuse, 3*(4), 37-57.

Besharov, D. (1990). *Recognizing child abuse.* New York: Free Press.

Hutchinson, E. (1993). Mandatory reporting laws: Child protective case finding gone awry? *Social Work, 38*(1), 56-63.

Rycraft, J. (1990). Redefining abuse and neglect: A narrower focus could affect children at risk. *Public Welfare, 48,* 14-21.

The People v. Cabral
15 Cal.Rptr.2d 866 (Cal.App. 5 Dist. 1993)

FACTS: On January 22, 1993, the Court of Appeals convicted defendant Gregory Cabral on charges of ongoing sexual abuse of his daughter, J., from the age of eight, until she reported the abuse in 1991, at age fourteen. J. was born April 26, 1976. Gregory Cabral and J.'s mother, R. Cabral, were divorced in 1984 or 1985 but continued living together after the divorce. J. testified that she was forced to engage in sexual activity with her father out of fear of being hurt by him, having on numerous occasions witnessed her father's physical abuse of her mother.

The Cabrals first came to the attention of Child Protective Services (CPS) following an incident in which Mr. Cabral hit T., J.'s older brother. J. did not report the sexual abuse at the time. CPS maintained contact with the family for over two years after that point, until J. finally reported her father's actions to the police in May 1991. A physical examination confirmed J.'s report of long-term sexual abuse.

Once in custody, and possibly facing a 140-year prison sentence, Gregory Cabral was informed by two other prisoners of a program called Parents United, an adult sex offender treatment program, which might be able to secure for him a shorter sentence. In order to accomplish this, Gregory Cabral was told he would be required to complete a sex offender program and admit to the allegations of sexual molestation. The treating psychotherapist testified that in a letter written to her by Gregory Cabral, Cabral acknowledged sexually molesting his daughter and asked to be admitted into her program. The psychotherapist did not reply to the correspondence. The court admitted this letter into evidence.

Gregory Cabral appealed the court's decision asserting that the court was prejudicial in allowing into evidence a letter written to a psychotherapist.

ISSUE: May a letter written to a psychotherapist, other than for the purpose of securing a diagnosis or treatment, be protected under the psychotherapist-patient privileged communication statute?

DECISION: No. In order for a confidential communication to be protected under the psychotherapist-patient privilege statute, a psychotherapist-patient relationship must be definitively established. In this case, there was no conclusive psychotherapist-patient relationship.

REASONING: The court's decision was based on the assessment that Gregory Cabral was not consulting with the psychotherapist with the intention of securing a diagnosis or treatment of his mental or emotional disorder which would have affirmed his status of patient. Rather, there was every indication that the correspondence was driven by an ulterior motive—securing probation rather than incarceration. Gregory's contention that the purpose of obtaining treatment was "implicit" in his letter was deemed insufficient.

The court cited a comparable case [*Montebello Rose Co. v. Agricultural Labor Relations Board*, 173 Cal.Rptr. 856 (1981)] in which it addressed the issue of attorney-client privilege. It wrote that, "To make the communication privilege the dominant purpose it must be for transmittal to an attorney in the course of professional employment" [*Holm v. Superior Court*, 42 Cal.2d 500, 507, 267 P.2d 1025 (1954)]. The legal and clinical nature of a communication must be affirmatively established as the dominant purpose in order for the privilege to adhere.

IMPLICATIONS: The principle of confidentiality between mental health professionals and clients who contract to work together is well established. Ethical and functional guidelines dictating the application of confidentiality and privileged communication are critical for the relationship to be successful.

Section II(H) of the National Association of Social Workers' *Code of Ethics* (1990) states, "Confidentiality and Privacy—The social worker should respect the privacy of clients and hold in confidence all information obtained in the course of professional service" (p. 1). However, one exception states, "the social worker should share with others confidences revealed by clients without their consent only for compelling professional reasons"(p. 6).

Does breach of such confidences and their admissions for examination by the judicial system constitute prejudicial action? What constitutes "compelling professional reasons?" The service provider, having agreed to enter into a contract of safeguarding her clients' confidential information, may at times be faced with a conflict in loyalties—to the client or to society. Many social workers are critical of such external demands being made on them by outside agents such as government entities and the courts. The profession's reaction has been to increase pressure for legislation offering greater protection for social workers under "privileged communication" (Kirkland & Irey,

1981). To date, the legal system has assumed the exclusive responsibility of judging what is and is not a "compelling" enough reason.

REFERENCES

Kirkland, J.M., & Irey, K.V. (July 1981). A reappraisal of confidentiality. *Social Work, 26*(4), 319-322.

National Association of Social Workers. (1990). *Code of Ethics.* Silver Spring: NASW.

M.R.F. v. Depart. of Public Welfare
595 A.2d 644 (Pa.Cmwlth. 1991)

FACTS: L.F. suspected her estranged husband, M.R.F., of sexually abusing their daughter, M. Upon reporting her suspicions to a child protective agency, an investigation of her husband's activities was conducted, and a report of child abuse was filed. As a result, M.R.F. was listed on the child abuse registry.

M.R.F. appealed the decision that denied expungement of this report. The Pennsylvania child protective services law states:

> At any time, a subject of a report may request the secretary to amend, seal or expunge information contained in the Statewide central registry on the grounds that it is inaccurate or it is being maintained in a manner inconsistent with this act . . . [Section 15(d), 11 P.S. § 22159 (d)].

M.R.F. believed that the evidence was insufficient to warrant the listing of his name on the central registry.

ISSUE: In cases of expungement of a name from a child abuse registry will "substantial evidence" be sufficient to keep a perpetrator's name on the registry?

DECISION: Yes. Only with substantial evidence provided by the child protective agency is an individual's name allowed to be listed in the statewide central registry for child abusers.

REASONING: Contrary to M.R.F.'s claim that his daughter was not molested, three interviews between the social worker and the child proved otherwise. M.'s clear and consistent verbalization of the acts of sexual abuse committed against her were indicators of the sexual molestation she had suffered. Her unusual knowledge of sexual matters confirmed the allegations of abuse. Psychological evaluations of the child supported this conclusion as did medical reports referring to constant vaginal infections and abrasions.

M.R.F. asserted there was insufficient evidence to identify him as the perpetrator. Yet, in investigating the activities of other males who had unsupervised contact with the child, the child protective agency found no evidence of sexual abuse. M. consistently and spontaneously named M.R.F., her father, as the sex offender.

Finally, M.R.F. sought to discount his daughter's testimony because of its status as hearsay. The court specifically addressed the difficulty in obtaining testimony from small children in sexual abuse cases:

> Where a caseworker has recorded or carefully noted a child's lucid words, the hearing officer could find the declaration to be reliable. Moreover, the hearing officer could regard the caseworker witness, as a professional person, to be disinterested and therefore reliable, in contrast to the possibly biased testimony of warring parents and others. [*L.W.B. v. Sasnowski*, 543 A.2d 1231, 1247 (1988)].

The social worker's testimony was therefore accepted as credible and the information she provided was viewed as substantial evidence of M.R.F.'s sexual abuse of his daughter. Consequently, M.R.F.'s name was not expunged from the record of child abuse.

IMPLICATIONS: The state child protective services agency bears the burden of proving that an alleged perpetrator is in fact the perpetrator in the case being investigated (Fryer, 1990). The standard of proof is only "substantial evidence." As one court has written, "Evidence is substantial where it so preponderates in favor of a conclusion that it outweighs in the mind of the fact finder any inconsistent evidence and reasonable inferences drawn therefrom." [*G.S. v. Department of Public Welfare,* 521 A.2d 87 (1987)].

Three criteria of reliability may be looked at when deciding whether to admit hearsay evidence: time, content, and circumstances. If all three are in close proximity or closely related to the alleged occurrence, a court may allow hearsay evidence in.

REFERENCES

Fryer, G. (1990). Detecting and reporting child abuse: A function of the human service delivery system. *Journal of Sociology and Social Welfare, 17*(2), 143-159.

Hildebrand v. Hildebrand
736 F.Supp. 1512 (S.D.Ind. 1990)

FACTS: In 1989, plaintiff Susan Hildebrand filed a complaint against her father, Dr. William Hildebrand, alleging that he physically and sexually abused her when she was a minor. The allegations were made after Susan had numerous years of counseling and "discovered" that she was suffering from "post-traumatic stress disorder" and had either repressed or not connected memories of abuse with her depressions as an adult. Specifically, Susan alleges that her father struck her, beat her with a belt, and fondled her genitals and breasts. From 1980 to 1987 Susan met with various counselors and psychologists for her depression but never mentioned the alleged abuse. It was not until March 1987 that Susan connected her depression with the abuse and within two years brought a lawsuit alleging assault and battery, emotional distress, and parental negligence.

Dr. Hildebrand denied all the allegations and asserted that, even if they were true, Indiana's two-year statute of limitations for personal injuries is an affirmative defense. Susan contends that her father fraudulently concealed his behavior, and therefore the statute of limitations should not adversely affect her lawsuit.

ISSUE: May a statute of limitations be a bar to a successful civil lawsuit regarding physical and sexual abuse?

DECISION: Yes. A state may properly protect defendants from lawsuits by specifying that claims must be brought within a proscribed reasonable period of time.

REASONING: The court began its opinion by noting that, "When legal issues involve such sensitive, volatile areas, it is particularly important for courts not to let the emotional impact of the alleged facts obscure the applicable legal principles" (p. 1516). While the opinion seems to be sympathetic to Susan's alleged plight, Indiana law holds that a cause of action accrues "when resultant damage is ascertained or ascertainable by due diligence" [*Burkes v. Rushmore,* 534 N.E.2d 1101, 1104 (1989)]. It is the time that Susan could have ascertained she had been damaged, not when she was allegedly harmed, that is crucial. Nonetheless, the court intimated that Susan knew she had been abused but did not associate her depression with the abuse, rather than the traumatic effect of the abuse having suppressed her recollection of the abuse. The court denied her father's request for summary judgement but conceded that Susan's case was not a strong one when it went back before a jury.

IMPLICATIONS: Issues of repressed memory and post-traumatic stress syndrome are still relatively new to courts. This particular court cautions that "statutes of limitations cannot be abrogated every time a patient gets a new diagnosis" (p. 1523). Other courts have been more lenient or more strict in allowing a statute of limitations to be tolled (temporarily suspended). The traditional course has been to acknowledge that

> The defense of the statute of limitations is not a technical defense but substantial and meritorious . . . .
> Such statutes are not only statutes of repose, but they supply the place of evidence lost or impaired by lapse of time, by raising a presumption which renders proof unnecessary . . . . Statutes of limitations are vital to the welfare of society and are favored in the law. They are found and approved in all systems of enlightened jurisprudence. They promote repose by giving security and stability to human affairs. [*United States v. Oregon Lumber Co.*, 43 S.Ct. 100, 103 (1992)]

The more recent view is to delay the deadline for filing a lawsuit until the plaintiff is cognizant of the events that might be judiciable. Physical and psychological injuries may arise only after an extended period of time, and a plaintiff should not be penalized for not knowing that wrongful conduct would later result in an injury.

The concerns regarding post-traumatic stress syndrome and repressed memory cases revolve around the issue of long-term damage that may have been caused by events long ago. The ability to scientifically measure, document, and authenticate such events is troublesome. When is a memory inadvertently "suggested" by a therapist? When is it truly a repressed memory that has been rekindled? Silberg (1993) notes that:

> The consequences of false allegations are devastating not only to the accused, but to the entire family . . . .
> Once a therapist believes sexual abuse may be involved, she might encourage a patient to break off all relations with family members (p. 1599).

REFERENCES

Silberg, J. (1993). Memory repression: Should it toll the statutory limitations period in child sexual abuse cases? *Wayne Law Review, 39,* 1589-1613.

CHAPTER 2
Social Worker Liability & Immunity

Tobias v. County of Racine
507 N.W.2d 340 (Wis.App. 1993)

FACTS: Diana Jo White ran away from her own home and from foster homes numerous times during the period 1988 to 1990. When Diana Jo reached the age of adulthood she agreed to continue to receive counseling services from the Racine County Human Services Department (RCHSD). A short time later, Diana Jo ran away again. Social workers finally located her in a dangerous neighborhood in Racine. Because no "pick up" order had been issued, the social workers could not have her arrested. On May 27, Diana Jo was killed by an unknown assailant in a drive-by shooting. Her mother, Sheree, brought a lawsuit against RCHSD for negligence that resulted in the wrongful death of her daughter.

ISSUE: May a department of social services be liable for damages caused by a superseding cause?

DECISION: No. The injury to Diana Jo was too remote from the negligence the department may or may not have effected.

REASONING: The court cited the Restatement (Second) of Torts §448 (1964) which states:

> The act of a third person in committing an intentional tort or crime is superseding cause of harm to another resulting therefrom, although the actor's negligent conduct created a situation which afforded an opportunity to the third person to commit such a tort or crime, unless the actor at the time of his negligent conduct realized or should have realized the likelihood that such a situation might be created, and that a third person might avail himself [or herself] of the opportunity to commit such a tort or crime.

The court conceded that arguably, the county's negligent failure to issue a "pick up" order created "a situation which afforded an opportunity to a third person to commit . . . a crime." This argument was rejected:

> . . . the county could not have anticipated that an unknown assailant would take advantage of Diana Jo's runaway status

and shoot her. Diana Jo was in no more or less danger of being shot than was any other child on the street at that time. The likelihood of being killed in a random shooting is so remote that we will not impose liability upon the county for failure to anticipate it. We conclude that Diana Jo's death was too remote from the county's negligence to impose liability.

IMPLICATIONS: Determining who is a "runaway" in need of interventive services is a complicated problem. There is in fact no consensus (Finkelhor et al., 1990). There is disagreement regarding which government agencies have primary responsibility for this problem.

In some samples of youth in a residential program for runaways, 29% reported being thrown out of their homes, while a street survey found that 33% reported being pushed out (Kufeldt et al., 1992). In a study of runaways in New York City shelters, 9.3% indicated being thrown out of their homes, and most reported that problems at home were their primary reason for leaving (Rotheram-Borus & Kooperman, 1991). Hier, Korboot, & Schweitzer (1990) found significantly lower levels of hostility and antisocial behavior for those who left on their own volition (runaways) compared to those who were forced to leave (throwaways), suggesting that throwaway children may not have been functioning "ideally," and thus were forced to leave by their parents. Among their sample of runaway youth with a history of maltreatment, over one-third were "pushed-out" (Powers, Eckenrode, & Jacklitsch, 1990). The distinction between runaways/throwaways may not always be clear. Such individuals may be living in abusive relationships or are not having their needs met by their familial living arrangements (which may include foster care). Assessment might show that the running behavior in such circumstances is both appropriate and functional. Evidence exists that gay male youth may be at high risk for being forced out of their homes because of their sexual orientation (Kruks, 1991).

Public Law 102-586 (1990), as amended, outlines the Federal government's role and responsibility in addressing runaways and homeless youth. Congress made ten critical findings in assessing these issues:

1. Juvenile runaways are at risk of incurring serious health problems.

2. The exact nature of the problem is unknown because no reliable national statistics exist.

3. Runaways are in need of temporary shelter and counseling services.

4. Local police departments and juvenile justice agencies should not be saddled with this problem.

5. Therefore, there is a need for the federal government to intervene.

6. Runaways have inadequate access to health care and intensive aftercare services.

7. There is a need for runaways to further their high school education and obtain employment.

8. The federal government is responsible for creating a national reporting system.

9. Early intervention services are needed to avert runaways.

10. Street-based services are needed to reach out to runaways where they are presently found (42 U.S.C. §5701).

There are large numbers of runaways. Many are at high risk for suicide, drug use, prostitution, illegal activities, and disease infection. Social workers need to be developing prevention, outreach, and rehabilitation services to address this population.

REFERENCES

Finkelhor, D., Hotaling, G., & Sedlak, A. (1990). *Missing, abducted, runaways and throwaway children in America*, First Report. Washington, D.C: U.S. Department of Justice, Office of Juvenile Justice and Delinquency Prevention.

Hier, S. J., Korboot, P.J., & Schweitzer, R.D. (1990). Social adjustment and symptomatology in two types of homeless adolescents: Runaways and throwaways. *Adolescence, 25*(100), 761-771.

Kruks, G. (1991). Gay and lesbian homeless/street youth: Special issues and concerns. *Journal of Adolescent Health, 12*(7), 515-518.

Kufeldt, K., Durieux, M., Nimmo, M., & McDonald, M. (1992). Providing shelter for street youth: Are we reaching those in need? *Child Abuse and Neglect, 16*(2), 187-199.

Powers, J.L., Eckenrode, J., & Jacklitsch, B. (1990). Maltreatment among runaway and homeless youth. *Child Abuse and Neglect, 14*(1), 87-98.

Rotheram-Borus, M.J., & Kooperman, C. (1991). Sexual risk behaviors, AIDS knowledge, and beliefs about AIDS among runaways. *American Journal of Public Health, 81*(2), 208-210.

Gloria G. v. State DSRS
833 P.2d 797 (Kan. 1992)

FACTS: Brothers A. and D. were born to biracial parents. Their biological mother was Caucasian, and their father was African-American. As a result of abuse and neglect, A. was placed into the custody of the Kansas Department of Social and Rehabilitation Services (DSRS). At various times, he was placed with the Goza family, who were both Caucasian and with Gloria G., a single African-American woman. After his name was placed on several adoption registries, D. was placed with Ms. Ford, a single African-American woman. He was eventually adopted by her. A. had been in the process of being adopted by the Gozas when a home study team determined that the Gozas' daughter sexually abused A. A. was removed abruptly from the Goza home and was eventually adopted by Gloria G.

Gloria G. (and A.) brought a lawsuit against DSRS, alleging that the abrupt removal from the Goza home caused emotional and psychological damage to A. She alleges that race was one of the motivating factors for the removal.

ISSUE: May a state social services agency be liable for acts its employees commit which are "discretionary" under a Tort Claims Act?

DECISION: No. The court concurred that A. was removed from the Goza home not because of race but because of the confirmation of sexual abuse. The removal was a discretionary act entitling DSRS to immunity.

REASONING: Gloria G., and A. asserted that DSRS was at fault for (1) denying his adoption by the Gozas based on race, and (2) negligently removing him from the Goza home without regard to the emotional harm which would follow. The court relied on a Kansas law which reads:

> A governmental entity or an employee acting within the scope of the employee's employment should not be liable for damages resulting from: . . . any claim based upon the exercise or performance or the failure to exercise or perform a discretionary function or duty . . . whether or not the discretion is abused and regardless of the level of discretion involved (K.S.A. 75-6104).

The Kansas Supreme Court held previously that the discretionary function exception is applicable "only when no clearly defined mandatory duty or guideline exists which the government agency is required to follow " [*Collins v. Board of Douglas County Comm'rs*, 249 Kan. 712, 721 (1991)]. The court determined that no specific guidelines existed to determine the proper course of action of finding A. has been abused by the Gozas' daughter. Therefore, the court held in favor of DSRS.

IMPLICATIONS: Transracial adoption has been occurring in the United States for decades. The adoption of black children by non-black parents has, since 1972, been the subject of considerate debate. The National Association of Black Social Workers considered it genocide. This condemnation was heeded by many adoption professionals. Consequently, the number of black children waiting for adoption and in foster care rose dramatically. Nationally, 40% of children waiting to be adopted are black (Jones, 1993).

Some argue that a black child adopted by non-black parents will suffer from low self-esteem and be racially unidentified. Others have argued that transracial adoption has undeniable political and ideological overtures that are not ultimately in the best interest of the children needing to be adopted (Hayes, 1993). Further, "just as the assumption of a homogeneous community exaggerates the extent of social conformity, so the assumption that racism is ubiquitous exaggerates its prevalence at an individual level" (Hayes, 1993, p. 307).

If the number of unadopted black children continues to escalate, the pressure to embrace the pragmatism of transracial adoption will increase proportionally. Adoption agencies should attempt to place a child with the family in which the child will be embraced as a full family member. Race may be a factor but should not be the only factor.

REFERENCES

Hayes, P. (1993). Transracial adoption: Politics and ideologies. *Child Welfare, 72*(3), 301-310.

Jones, C. (October 24, 1993). Debate on race and adoptions is being reborn. *The New York Times*, A1.

Caldwell v. LeFaver
928 F.2d 331 (9th Cir. 1991)

FACTS: The plaintiff, a father with joint custody of his two children, appealed from a lower court decision upholding the legal actions of two social workers who removed the children from the plaintiff's home and sent them out of state to their mother.

On April 21, 1987, social workers Gwen Farnsworth and Russell Francetich, believed that the plaintiff's two daughters were in imminent danger. On an "emergency basis" they removed the children and placed them in temporary custody. Soon after, and without notice to the father, Farnsworth and Francetich sent the children by bus to their mother in Washington.

Plaintiff claims his legal rights were denied when he was denied a hearing before a judicial officer or even notice prior to the removal of his children. Farnsworth and Francetich maintain that they were acting lawfully within the realm of their duties and were therefore protected by absolute immunity.

ISSUE: Does a theory of absolute immunity or qualified immunity apply where a social worker removes children from one guardian to the care of another legal guardian in an emergency situation and the original guardian brings a civil suit?

DECISION: Defendants are entitled to absolute immunity "when performing quasi-prosecutorial functions connected with the initiation and pursuit of child dependency proceedings" (p. 333). Regarding qualified immunity, the court stated that "because the defendants were not acting under the supervision of a court, it is the qualified immunity standard, rather than the absolute immunity standard, which must govern their conduct" (p. 333).

REASONING: The court reasoned that there are circumstances when social workers will be entitled to "absolute immunity." In ascertaining whether the "qualified immunity" standard would apply, the court stated that by default, it is the qualified immunity standard that, if applicable to this set of circumstances, protects social workers. Continuing from this standpoint, the court stated that "under the doctrine of qualified immunity, social workers are shielded from liability where their official conduct does not violate clearly established statutory or constitutional rights of which a reasonable person would have known" (p. 333). Once it was established that the qualified immunity standard was to be implemented, the defendant's actions needed to be examined to ascertain whether or not the plaintiff's rights had been violated.

The court first established that "in an emergency situation, a state agency may remove children from their parents' custody when the children are subject to immediate or apparent danger or harm" (p. 333). While the facts are not clear, the court seemed to concede that this situation constitutes an emergency; thus the removal of the children was justified.

The next hurdle the court addressed was whether the father had a due process right to a post-deprivation hearing. The court distinguished this case from earlier decisions where this right was established because here there was a guardian who enjoyed joint legal custody, and this constituted no violation of due process rights.

Finally, the court pointed to section 41-3-301 of the Montana Code, which provided guidelines for removing children and placing them in emergency protective service: "A petition shall be filed within 48 hours of emergency placement of a child unless arrangements acceptable to the agency for the care of the child have been made by the parents" (p. 884). This signifies that where there is a parent with whom arrangements for the children can be made, no obligation to file a petition exists. Therefore, plaintiff's rights in this case were not violated as a parent was available to care for and take custody of the children.

IMPLICATIONS: This case exemplifies society's willingness to compromise what appears to be constitutional and fundamental rights where children are involved so long as the circumstances for emergency removal are carefully circumscribed. Factors to be considered are the immediacy of the danger, the degree of danger, and the extent of physical evidence indicating danger and the presence of subsequent due process rights available to the parents. Many states require that a police officer be present if a child is going to be removed under an "exigent circumstances" doctrine. A social worker can make the decision to remove, but a police officer must be present when the child is removed. Ideally, if time permits, a court order should be obtained prior to removal.

This decision, however, does not stand for the proposition that if there had been no other legal guardian and the children had been placed in a foster home, for example, a hearing or notice would still not be required. This is a separate issue and one of which social workers must be aware.

The Montana statute section 41-3-301 states "(1) Any child protective social worker of the Department of family services, a peace officer, or the county attorney who has reason to believe any youth is in immediate or apparent danger of harm may immediately remove the youth and place him in a protective facility . . ." (p. 334). Thus, the determination of an emergency situation for a social worker, should be both a consideration of statutory mandate as well as a reasoned determination. Despite the increasing number of lawsuits being filed against social workers (Reamer, 1995), the commitment to use sound, professional judgement in emergency situations remains the best defense against litigation.

REFERENCES

Reamer, F. (1995). Malpractice claims against social workers: First facts. *Social Work, 40*(5), 595-601.

Babcock v. Tyler
884 F.2d 497 (9th Cir. 1989)

FACTS: After being transferred from Louisiana to Washington pursuant to an interstate compact, four girls were sexually abused while placed in the home of their maternal uncle. The uncle had previously been convicted of forcible rape, attempted rape, and sexual assault. Had the social workers looked at the uncle's criminal record, these facts would have been discovered. As a result of the abuse, the guardians and parents of the four girls sued two Washington Department of Social and Health Services social workers. The plaintiffs alleged that the girls were deprived of their Fourteenth Amendment liberty interest to be free from harm while in the state's custody. To these allegations, the social workers sought absolute immunity from liability.

ISSUE: Are social workers who perform investigative and placement services following child dependency proceedings entitled to absolute immunity?

DECISION: Yes. The performance of a social worker's duty "in child dependency proceedings is no less entitled to the protection of absolute immunity than is the performance of a prosecutor's duty in a criminal proceeding. Their immunity must be absolute to permit them to perform their duties without fear of even the threat of litigation" [*Coverdell v. Dept. of Social and Health Services,* 834 F.2d 758, 764 (1987)].

REASONING: In this very "pro" social worker case, a United States Court of Appeals held that the social workers were given absolute immunity because their participation in the investigation and placement process was considered to be a part of a judicial process. As such, it is firmly established that

> judges, advocates and witnesses enjoy absolute immunity from liability for acts performed in judicial proceedings to assure that they can perform their respective functions without harassment or intimidation. [*Butz v. Economou,* 438 U.S. 478, 512 (1978)]

The key determinant in granting absolute immunity is whether the functions for which the immunity is claimed are an integral, not just incidental, part of the judicial process. In this case, the court ruled that dependency proceedings include post-adjudication activities as well as acts by which the proceedings are initiated.

> Throughout this process case workers need to exercise independent judgement in fulfilling their post-adjudication duties. The fear of financially devastating litigation would compromise case workers' judgement . . . and would deprive the court of information it needs to make an informed decision. [*Meyers v. Contra Costa County Dept. of Social Servs.*, 812 F.2d 1154, 1157 cert. denied, 484 U.S. 829 (1987)]

IMPLICATIONS: Because these social workers were seen as performing a quasi-judicial function, they were granted absolute immunity from liability. Had the court determined that the social workers were not engaged in the judicial process, the result could have been different. The more obvious it is that a social worker is doing a ministerial or official function on behalf of a court, the greater the likelihood that absolute immunity will attach.

Some judicial jurisdictions have recognized the absolute immunity of social workers [*Salyer v. Patrick,* 874 F.2d 374 (6th Cir. 1989); *Vosburg v. Dept. of Social Services,* 884 F.2d 133 (4th Cir. 1989); *Fanning v. Montgomery County Children & Youth Services*, 702 F.Supp. 1184 (E.D.Pa. 1988)] engaged in child protection work. Others have granted only qualified immunity, especially when the social workers are engaged in administrative functions [*Snell v. Tunnell*, 698 F.Supp. 1542 (W.D.Okla. 1988)]. Qualified immunity is often afforded if the social worker is involved in any "discretionary function" unless her conduct is clearly a violation of a statute or constitutional principle.

The United States Supreme Court has held in *Harlow v. Fitzgerald* [102 S.Ct. 2727, 2738 (1982)] that

> bare allegations of malice should not suffice to subject government officials either to the costs of trial or to the burdens of broad-reaching discovery. We therefore hold that government officials performing discretionary functions, generally are shielded from liability for civil damages insofar as their conduct does not violate clearly established statutory

or constitutional rights of which a reasonable person would have known.

Rowe v. Bennett
514 A.2d 802 (Me. 1986)

FACTS: Plaintiff Mary Rowe sued her social worker/psychotherapist, Louise Bennett, claiming that Bennett caused her to suffer mental and emotional distress due to Bennett's beginning a romantic relationship with Rowe's lover, Jane W., whom Bennett was also counseling. In fact, Bennett ceased counseling Rowe on an individual basis and had her transferred to group therapy. Bennett falsely told Rowe that her agency's policy was to limit individual counseling to just six months. At the trial court, Bennett was granted summary judgement. The court ruled that the defense of charitable immunity barred Rowe's claim.

ISSUE: May a client successfully sue a social worker for negligent infliction of emotional distress if the client cannot show any physical injuries or if the client cannot show an underlying tort?

DECISION: Yes. The Supreme Judicial Court of Maine decided that a client may maintain an action for negligent infliction of emotional distress against a social worker when the distress allegedly caused by the social worker is serious, even if there was not an underlying tort committed by the social worker.

REASONING: In this very unusual case, the court reviewed Maine's history of circumstances under which negligent infliction of emotional distress will be actionable. Initially, a plaintiff could not maintain a negligent claim based only on mental or emotional distress. A physical injury had to also be shown. In a 1921 case [*Herrick v. Evening Pub. Co.*, 113 A. 16 (1921)], the court noted that, "At common law it was well settled that mere injury to the feelings or affections did not constitute an independent basis for the recovery of damages" (p. 17).

Later, the court ruled that recovery could only be had if the mental distress suffered was "serious," defined as existing

> where a reasonable person normally constituted, would be unable to adequately cope with the mental stress engendered by the circumstances of the event.[*Culbert v. Sampson's Supermarkets Inc.*, 444 A.2d 433, 437 (1982)]

Still later, the court arrived at its present general principle:

Mental distress is insufficient in and of itself to establish the harm necessary to make negligence actionable, without either accompanying physical consequences, or an independent underlying tort. [*Rubin v. Matthews International Corp.*, 503 A.2d 694, 698 (1986)]

To this general principle, however, the court was willing to make an exception: "We held that because of the nature of the psychotherapist-patient relationship, an action may be maintained by a patient for serious mental distress caused by the negligence of his therapist despite the absence of an underlying tort" (p. 806).

IMPLICATIONS: While serious emotional distress may be difficult to prove, the court was unwilling to allow a difficulty of proof to preclude even the right to file an action against the social worker. In order to win this lawsuit, the plaintiff had to establish that the social worker was under a duty to uphold an articulated standard of conduct and that a breach of that duty caused the plaintiff's serious emotional distress. In general, a person who undertakes to provide social work/psychotherapist services implicitly acknowledges that a heightened degree of skill exists. In this particular case, Bennett had an MSW, was working for an agency, and was subject to Maine's social work licensing law. These factors all led to her fall under the "exception" and open to being sued.

A client comes to a therapist assuming that the therapist is ethical, trustworthy, and wants to be helpful (Dean & Rhodes, 1992). For this very reason, the client is less apt to be suspicious of what would otherwise be improper or inappropriate behavior. The National Association of Social Workers, the American Psychiatric Association, and the American Psychological Association have determined that sexual interaction between clients and therapists is unethical. The *NASW Code of Ethics* (1993) specifically states: "The social worker should under no circumstances engage in sexual activities with clients" (p. 5). Nevertheless, various studies have concluded that as many as 10% of therapists may engage in some improper physical contact. Courts have recognized this improper behavior (Kagle & Biebelhausen, 1994; Jorgenson et al., 1991; Conte & Karasu, 1990) by awarding large damage awards [*St. Paul Fire & Marine Ins. Co. v. Love,* 459 N.W.2d 698 (Minn. 1990); *Johnson v. Arkansas Board of Examiners in Psychology*, 808 S.W.2d 766 (1991)]. Whether the sexual contact begins because of "transference," erotic fantasies, patient vulnerability, seductive behavior, or dependence, a healthy therapeutic client-therapist relationship cannot coexist with a sexual relationship.

A client who experiences improper sexual advances may seek various legal remedies. These include contacting the appropriate professional organization, the state attorney general, private legal counsel, or licensing boards. Unfortunately, a person who once experiences unwanted sexual advances in a therapeutic setting may be hesitant to renew therapy with a different therapist.

REFERENCES

Conte, H., & Karasu, T. (1990). Malpractice in psychotherapy: An overview. *American Journal of Psychotherapy, 44*(1): 232-246.

Dean, R., & Rhodes, M. (1992). Ethical-clinical tensions in clinical practice. *Social Work, 37*(2), 128-132.

Jorgenson, L., Randles, R., & Strasburger, L. (1991). The furor over psychotherapist-patient sexual contact: New solutions to an old problem. *William and Mary Law Review, 32*, 643-729.

Kagle, J., & Biebelhausen, P. (1994). Dual relationships and professional boundaries. *Social Work, 39*(2), 213-220.

National Association of Social Workers. (1993). *NASW code of ethics.* Washington, DC: Author.

Franz v. Lytle
997 F.2d 784 (10th Cir. 1993)

FACTS: On October 19, 1988, police officer Richard Lytle was dispatched to investigate a report of a child, Ashley Franz, who was possibly abused. The child's next-door-neighbor had called to report that the two-year-old girl was unsupervised, wet, and unclean. The neighbor told Lytle that Ashley had a severe diaper rash and stank of urine. Lytle asked the neighbor to remove Ashley's diaper, without notifying the child's mother. He touched Ashley's vaginal area and took photographs of what he believed to be a severe rash. Lytle then went to Ashley's home and notified her mother, Katherine Franz, that he had examined Ashley and that Franz would be contacted by Kansas Social and Rehabilitative Services (SRS).

When Lytle returned to the police station, he filled out an investigation form and told his supervisor he was investigating a "possible molestation case." He was concerned about leaving the child in the home because he feared the child would be molested, believing that the child's rash was in fact caused by abuse.

The supervisor advised Lytle to take the child for a medical exam. The next day, Lytle, accompanied by a female officer, returned to see Ashley again. Both wore uniforms and carried firearms. Franz allowed them to enter and allowed them to examine Ashley. Once again, Lytle touched the child's vaginal area, and this time asked if she was in pain when he touched her.

Franz told Lytle that she was trying to toilet train the child. Lytle told her she would have to take the child to a local hospital to have her examined, or else he would take the child into protective custody. Franz then called her husband, who left work to come home. Again, Lytle threatened to take the child into protective custody if they did not take the child voluntarily to the hospital. Escorted by the officers, the Franzes took Ashley to the hospital. The doctor found the child to have a mild rash but found no indication of molestation. The officers apologized, but the Franz family sued Lytle and the female officer accompanying him.

ISSUE: Does a police officer have qualified immunity to conduct a warrantless search of a child's body for child abuse?

DECISION: No. The Court of Appeals affirmed that the child's rash and wet diaper did not justify a warrantless search of home and child's body and also that the more liberal standard of probable cause for social workers did not apply to a police officer investigating criminal sexual abuse.

REASONING: Lytle had argued that when a police officer acts in a social worker's role, the same standard of immunity should apply. The court found that police officers have more knowledge of the standards for searches and seizures, as the Fourth Amendment clearly forbids unreasonable and warrantless searches. Therefore, unless there is an emergency, a police officer knows that he or she must get a warrant in order to conduct a search.

Social workers often find themselves in the homes of clients. When they see an indication of abuse or neglect, they must have some protection against lawsuits if they are to investigate. The role of the police officer is very different. They are trained with regard to the need for warrants in order to conduct searches. The court was disturbed by the police officer touching and photographing the child without her parents' knowledge, and was also taken aback by his threat to take the child into protective custody.

The case was then sent back to the trial court to allow the jury to hear evidence and decide whether the plaintiffs had their Fourth Amendment rights violated.

IMPLICATIONS: This case reminds us that although social workers often must investigate and report abuse, the Constitution protects citizens against unreasonable searches by the police. While in many cases, social workers can gain entry into homes by virtue of their special role and have some immunity from lawsuit, police officers have a very different role. Social workers must understand that while they might want a police officer to do something which might seem quite reasonable, if the officer hesitates and decides a warrant is needed, the social worker must appreciate that there are very good reasons for such hesitation.

Search and seizures is a large subject and cannot be covered in this short space. The right of privacy, never mentioned by name in the Constitution, emanates from the Fourth Amendment, which protects the security of our home and our persons. It is much more than an inconvenience; it is a guarantee against the intrusion of the government into our privacy, and it is only the Constitution which protects it. Warrants can be obtained, and indeed, without them, evidence found during improper searches will be excluded, no matter how damaging. This case illustrates that the police are trained to be aware of the need for such warrants, and that their concern for the welfare of a child can only override the need for a warrant if a true emergency exists.

CHAPTER 3
Mental Health Issues

In re Schouler
723 P.2d 1103 (Wash. 1986)

FACTS: Loretta Schouler was brought to the Yakima Valley Memorial Hospital on August 11, 1983. At that time she was disoriented and had not been eating or sleeping. Nor was she taking medication prescribed at an earlier visit. She was also experiencing difficulty in communicating her birth date and address. During 1983 she was admitted four times to the hospital for mental illness.

Five days later, a hearing was held to determine whether or not to involuntarily commit Schouler for a fourteen-day evaluation and treatment period. During the hearing, Dr. McCarthy, one of Schouler's treating physicians, requested that Schouler be subjected to electroconvulsive therapy (ECT). He had demonstrated earlier that it had been effective in treating mental illness and was often used and recommended. Schouler's attorney objected because she had been unaware that this would be requested at the hearing.

The following day, after Schouler was examined by two psychiatrists, arguments were heard on the issue of giving Schouler ECT. Schouler's attorney consistently objected. ECT treatment had not helped Schouler in the past, and conflicting diagnoses existed, making ECT treatment questionable. Dr. McCarthy insisted that ECT was the recommended treatment in such a case. Without it, Schouler would be in jeopardy of falling into "a vegetative state and [might] be confined to the back wards of a state hospital for the rest of her life" (p.1106).

The court ordered ECT treatment for Schouler. The appellate court heard the case on its merits, though no remedy was available. Since the trial court did not order to stay Schouler's treatment during the proceedings, the ECT was administered. Effective legal relief was no longer available. As this is a controversial issue, the court heard the case to decide the merits for future reference.

ISSUE: Can a court decide for an incompetent individual whether or not ECT treatment is an appropriate medical treatment?

DECISION: Yes. The "trial court can order electroconvulsive therapy for a non-consenting patient [but] only after considering and setting forth findings on the nature of the patient's desires, whether the state has a significant interest in treatment, and whether therapy is necessary and effective" (p. 1103).

REASONING: The court addressed many issues regarding ECT as a controversial and "highly intrusive medical procedure" (p. 1107). One of the issues was the long-term and short-term effects of the treatment. The court's caution was a result of the state's desire and goal not to interfere with an individual's fundamental rights. In this case, the right at issue was the "privacy of the mind and freedom from unwanted ECT" (p. 1108) and ultimately the choice to undergo or forego medical treatment. The court followed earlier decisions, stating that "a person involuntarily committed due to a mental disorder retains a fundamental liberty interest in refusing ECT" (p. 1108).

Once this was established, the court addressed the issue of a nonconsenting patient. First the court looked to the "patient's desires" (p. 1108). In evaluating her desires, the court stated that several things should be taken into consideration. "The court should consider previous and current statements of the patient, religious and moral values of the patient regarding medical treatment and electroconvulsive therapy, and views of individuals that might influence the patient's decision" (p. 1108). The court went on to state that if the patient could not understand the nature of ECT, a "substituted judgement" should be made by the court "that is analogous to the medical treatment decision made for an incompetent person" (p. 1108). On this issue, the court ruled that no reasonable investigation was made to determine the patient's desires, nor was ample time permitted for the patient's attorney to contact her family.

The second and third issues, as set forth by the decision, were the state's interest in compelling patients to undergo ECT therapy and the effectiveness and necessity of ECT in furthering the state's interest. While many cases before this established that a fundamental liberty may be limited, it is only under specific circumstances that this may occur. Specifically, there must be a compelling state interest, and the regulation be narrowly drawn. These work as safeguards to prevent misuse of the system and to ensure presumption of fundamental rights in all but the most extreme cases. Specifically in regard to medical treatment, the court looked to earlier decisions where four state interests had been established and commonly mentioned: "(1) the preservation of life; (2) the protection of interests of innocent third parties; (3) the prevention of suicide; and (4) maintenance of the ethical integrity of the medical profession" (p. 1108). On the issue of necessity and effectiveness, the court stated that medical prognosis with or without ECT and alternative treatments should be considered. The court mentioned these "threshold questions" as compelling state interests and requirements and found that the lower court's decision on this issue showed the beginnings of a constitutional requirement. The court's vague discussion on this issue leaves these interests and the possibility of new state interests in the hands of future courts.

IMPLICATIONS: Only mentioned in a footnote, the opinion notes that "as a practical matter, a court probably can find a compelling state interest to treat an involuntarily committed person with ECT relatively often" (p. 1109). Because of this attitude, there is an acknowledged purpose in regulating ECT. Leong and Eth (1991) note some concerns regarding ECT: "(1) ECT's intrusiveness; (2) potential violations of First Amendment rights to free speech and privacy; (3) ECT as a drastic, last resort treatment that does not conform to the rule of least restrictive treatment (alternative); and (4) its history of abuse" (p. 1008). These concerns are not without foundation. Documented side effects of ECT may include schizophrenia, depression, disorientation, memory loss, drug-resistant mania, and affective disorders (Katz, 1992; American Psychiatric Association, 1990; Coffey & Weiner, 1990).

Electroconvulsive therapy has been a treatment for mental illness since the early 1930s. At various times it has been viewed as a cure-all or the end of inhuman torture. It appears that ECT is now a recognized and legitimate method of treatment so long as the client is fully apprised of the risks, gives informed consent, and the treatment is applied in a responsible manner.

REFERENCES

American Psychiatric Association. (1990). The practice of electroconvulsive therapy: Recommendations for treatment, training, and privileging. *A task force report of the American Psychiatric Association.* Washington, D.C.: Author.

Coffey, E., & Weiner, R. (1990). Electroconvulsive therapy: An update. *Hospital and Community Psychiatry, 41*(5), 515-521.

Katz, G. (1992). Electroconvulsive therapy from a social work perspective. *Social Work in Health Care, 16*(4), 55-68.

Leong, G., & Eth, S. (1991). Legal and ethical issues in electroconvulsive therapy. *Psychiatric Clinics of North America, 4*(4), 1008-1020.

Brookhouser v. State of California
13 Cal.Rptr.2d 658 (Cal.App. 6 Dist. 1992)

FACTS: Sharon Brookhouser, an involuntarily committed mentally ill person on leave from an unlocked mental care facility, was injured by walking onto a highway and being struck by a car. Brookhouser brought suit against the state and social worker Ellen Mary Farr, assigned to care for the plaintiff. Brookhouser's guardian asserted negligence on the part of the social worker for failing to forewarn the care facility operator of Brookhouser's tendency and prior history of walking away from various locked and unlocked mental facilities, thereby, by omission, causing Brookhouser to sustain injury.

On appeal, the court found Farr and the state in violation of California law for failing to provide the mental care facility with information regarding Brookhouser's previous conduct. This omission contributed to Brookhouser being injured. On final appeal, however, the court concluded that there did not exist sufficient evidence indicative of a direct cause-and-effect relationship definitively linking Brookhouser's injuries to Farr's neglect to inform. Additionally, Farr and the state were found to be legally immune from liability.

ISSUE: Can a social worker's and state's breach of duty to care, via a negligent act of omission, be construed as being causative of harm that might otherwise have been avoided?

DECISION: No, unless it can be determined that the injury would not have occurred *but for* the defendant's conduct, or, if the defendant's conduct was a *substantial* factor in causing the injury. Even if the defendant's conduct meets the "but-for" test of causation, he or she may not be liable if there is more than one cause of the injury and the defendant's conduct.

REASONING: The court cited legislation affording public entities' and employees' statutory immunity from liability—providing that "[n]either a public entity nor a public employee is liable for . . . an injury to, or the wrongful death of, an escaping or escaped person who has been confined for mental illness or addiction" (Government Code Section 856.2). Given that Brookhouser had been "confined" at a mental care facility as a matter of law, her leave was deemed a *crime* of escape, defined as the "unlawful departure from the limits of custody" [*People v. Davis,* 166 Cal.App.3d 760 (1985)]. The limits of custody in case involve legitimately imposed limitations and controls, the violation of which constitutes the act of escape.

Regarding Brookhouser's argument of Farr's negligence in making the discretionary decision to admit the plaintiff into an unlocked, rather than a locked facility, the court held that "[n]either a public entity nor a public employee acting within the scope of his or her employment is liable for an injury resulting from *determining* in accordance with any applicable enactment . . . whether to confine a person for mental illness . . . or the terms and conditions of confinement for mental illness . . . " and that "[a] public employee is not liable for *carrying out with due care* [such] a determination . . . ."

Finally, the court concluded that there does not exist sufficient evidence to tie Farr's failure to fully inform the facility of Brookhouser's history to her injuries.

IMPLICATIONS: This case allows facility managers and public officials who are responsible for making decisions bearing on limitations and controls of mentally ill persons to make sound discretionary judgements about confinements, based solely on each patient's medical needs, without being overly tainted by concerns of possible resulting liability. Irrespective of intent or will, a patient exceeding the reasonable limits of confinement may be regarded as an escaped person within the definition of California law, thereby absolving the manager or official of liability.

Involuntarily committed mental health patients may have greater due process rights to safety and security than do voluntarily committed patients. This is because the state has deprived an involuntary patient of this liberty. A voluntary patient has given up their liberty of their own choosing.

O'Connor v. Donaldson
422 U.S. 563 (1975)

FACTS: Kenneth Donaldson's father initiated the commitment of his son because he believed the son was suffering from delusions. A hearing was held before a Pinellas County, Florida, judge, and it was determined that Donaldson was suffering from paranoid schizophrenia. As a result, in January 1957 Kenneth Donaldson was civilly committed to the Florida State Hospital in Chattahoochee for care, maintenance, and treatment.

For the next fifteen years, Donaldson remained confined in the state hospital. During Donaldson's commitment, he made many requests to be released. Donaldson repeatedly claimed that he was dangerous to no one and that he was not mentally ill. Donaldson also stated that the hospital was not providing treatment for his supposed illness. Furthermore, Donaldson's demands for his release were supported by responsible people who were willing to care for him if it was so required after his release. Donaldson claimed that, by continuing to confine him, the hospital's superintendent and staff had deprived him of his constitutional right to liberty.

For most of Donaldson's fifteen-year commitment, the superintendent of the hospital was Dr. J.B. O'Connor. O'Connor claimed that he had acted appropriately since state law allowed for the indefinite commitment of the "sick." It was asserted that limitless confinement was permissible even if treatment was not given and even if the "sick" individual's release would not be harmful under the state law.

ISSUE: Is it a violation of the Constitution's Fourteenth Amendment for a state to confine a non-dangerous individual who is capable of living safely in society?

DECISION: Yes. A unanimous U.S. Supreme Court held that a state that confines a non-dangerous individual against his or her will is violating that individual's Fourteenth Amendment liberty interest.

REASONING: Donaldson's claim that he was never a danger to himself or others was clearly supported. Moreover, Donaldson's frequent requests for release were supported by accessibility to care if he should need it. For instance, in 1963 a letter was written to O'Connor by Helping Hands, Inc., a halfway house for mentally ill individuals, asking for Donaldson's release to its care. In addition, it was clearly demonstrated that during Donaldson's confinement, the hospital was merely providing custodial care and was not providing treatment designed to address his supposed illness. Consequently, the confinement of Donaldson was based solely on his mental illness.

The finding of mental illness does not justify a State's indefinite involuntary commitment of an individual in "simple custodial confinement" (p. 575). The existence of mental illness does not deny a person the opportunity to choose his or her residence. Nor may the state confine an individual simply to improve that person's living standard.

A state may also not confine a mentally ill person to preserve its other citizens from exposure to an individual who is different. The court noted that, "(m)ere public intolerance or animosity cannot constitutionally justify the deprivation of a person's physical liberty" (p. 5750).

IMPLICATIONS: Several court rulings over the past twenty-five years have made it more difficult to involuntarily confine a mentally ill individual. During that period, advocates for those in mental hospitals have worked to ensure that the civil rights of those with mental illness are respected (Zastrow, 1990).

As a result of this recognition of the civil rights of mentally ill individuals, many persons with mental illness no longer reside in hospitals. However, since hospitals have been effectively eliminated as a source of food and shelter for many individuals suffering from severe mental illness, there has developed a preponderance of homeless and incarcerated people with mental illness (Johnson, 1991). Indeed, many of the mentally ill have become homeless or wards of the justice system (Elpers, 1987).

There exists a consensus that a substantial number of the homeless suffer from severe and chronic mental illness. However, much of the homeless population is invisible to researchers and is therefore not well understood (Bachrach et al., 1990). Nor do many of the mentally ill homeless have access to community-based mental health services. Consequently, it is only after there has been contact with the police that there is emergency contact with mental health treatment (Belcher, 1991).

Significant numbers of the mentally ill who are no longer hospitalized now populate prisons and jails. An arrest often occurs after a mentally ill person engages in an activity which is a manifestation of mental illness (i.e., drunkenness or trespassing). In addition, incarcerations also occur due to so-called "mercy bookings" where police officers invent charges to get the mentally ill person a place to sleep and a meal. As a result, it is estimated that 7.2 percent of all inmates in the nation's jails suffer from serious mental illness.

REFERENCES

Bachrach, L., Santiago, J., & Berren, M. (1990). Homeless mentally ill patients in the community: Results of a general hospital emergency room study. *Community Mental Health Journal, 26*(5), 415-423.

Belcher, J. (1991). Moving into homelessness after psychiatric hospitalization. *Journal of Social Service Research, 14*(314), 63-77.

Elpers, J. (1987). Are we legislating reinstitutionalization? *American Journal of Orthopsychiatry, 57*(3), 441-446.

Johnson, A. (1991). *Out of Bedlam.* New York: Basic Books.

Zastrow, C. (1990). Mental health issues in the 1990s. *Journal of Independent Social Work, 5*(1), 9-21.

Ricci v. Okin
781 F.Supp. 826 (D.Mass. 1992)

FACTS: As a result of a number of class action lawsuits filed by residents of two Massachusetts mental health institutions against the State, various consent decrees were agreed to between the parties and ordered by the court concerning the quality of care to be provided by the State. In the Fall of 1991 three subsequent hearings were held before the United States District Court to interpret the prior consent decrees concerning the Paul A. Dever State School (Dever). The first hearing was scheduled because there had been reports from the Office of Quality Assurance (OQA) and the Department of Public Health (DPH) that serious shortcomings existed in the services to students living at Dever in violation of prior consent decrees.

At the first hearing, the court asked the Health Care Finance Administration (HCFA) to thoroughly inspect Dever to ascertain the extent of the school's problems. HCFA reported at the second hearing that the Dever had many serious deficiencies in its organization, utilization, and training of staff. HCFA informed Dever that the problems had to be corrected by February of 1992 or the school would be in jeopardy of losing its Medicaid certification and federal funding.

Compounding problems at Dever was a June 1991 announcement by the Governor that there would be a consolidation of several institutions operated by the Department of Mental Health and DPH. The plan called for the placement of several hundred institutional residents in community programs throughout the state, the movement of residents between and among the institutional settings, a concomitant movement among staff, and the closing of Dever within three years. Although the Governor announced these plans, he did not specifically outline how this consolidation would be realized. As a result of the Governor's announcement, combined with previous Dever layoffs that were initiated in November 1990, staff absenteeism increased and staff morale declined.

ISSUE: If there is a plan for the closing of an institution, does that institution remain responsible during the interim for adhering to previously-agreed-upon rules and guidelines governing the care of the residents of the institution?

DECISION: Yes. The fact that Dever would be closed did not allow the school to ignore requirements governing staffing and living conditions set forth in applicable regulations and previous consent decrees.

REASONING: As a result of prior class actions and subsequent consent decrees involving the improvement of the quality of care provided by Dever, there existed clearly established procedures for the care of Dever residents. Included in Dever's care requirements, as called for by Title XIX of the Social Security Act, was the implementation of Individual Service Plans (ISP) for the residents. The ISPs "address the individual's residential and programmatic needs, vocational work needs and capabilities, medical needs, physical needs, equipment needs, guardianship needs and habitational needs . . ." (p. 827). In keeping with these well-established care requirements, the court held that all services and staffing levels must be maintained as called for in the consent decrees. Furthermore, the court stated that until a detailed plan was in place for the relocation of Dever residents and related resources, the defendants should not assume and act as if the closure of Dever was a certainty.

The court clarified that it is not opposed to the consolidation plan or the eventual closure of Dever. It did emphasize the need to maintain the required level of services to Dever residents while consolidation plans were being worked out. Specifically, the service requirements include "maintenance of adequate personnel levels at [a] state school, the ongoing provision of services in accordance with class members' ISPs, and the utilization of evaluation and monitoring mechanisms" (p. 828).

The court noted that Dever should continue to adhere to procedures developed by the defendants and HCFA to ensure the maintenance of adequate services for Dever inhabitants if there is movement from the school to the community or when any transition occurs that would lead to changes in staffing levels. These procedures call for various quality assurance and reporting procedures to ensure that any adjustments in personnel levels due to staff reassignments do not adversely impact the maintenance of required school services. Thus, the court emphasized Dever's responsibility to maintain and monitor services set forth in residents' ISPs even in the face of institutional transition (i.e., the movement of residents from an institutional environment to a community setting). The court noted in its memorandum that it expected the parties to work together to ensure that the class members' best interests are well served.

IMPLICATIONS: The long history of institutionalizing mentally retarded people came into question in the 1960s. This questioning was the result of several factors including an economic component. Perhaps the most important elements pushing towards deinstitutionalization of the mentally retarded were the compelling reports of and investigations into the brutally inhumane conditions which existed in many institutions. Moreover, the deinstitutionalization movement was further strengthened in 1975 with the passage of the Education for All Handicapped Children Act. It required states to provide a free and appropriate public education for all disabled children (Lakin, 1991).

Thus, the community group home approach to treatment developed. This type of setting was further supported by a both legal and societal acceptance that mentally retarded individuals have the right to be treated in the least restrictive setting possible. Consequently, the treatment of the mentally retarded shifted from a few large establishments to many small facilities. Due to this change, many new and important issues arose. One is the important challenge of seeking a least restrictive setting while maintaining high-quality treatment. As is seen in this case, this is particularly true when a client is in transition from a more to a less restrictive environment. As a result, to successfully realize this goal, the endeavor must be well organized including the design and implementation of specific techniques germane to this effort (Buchard & Harrington, 1985, 1986).

As treatment efforts are deinstitutionalized, numerous questions are being raised. Is a smaller community-based setting, by definition, a better treatment environment? Are not some large institutions less restrictive than some small settings (Zigler, Hodapp & Edison, 1990)? Do the large number of facilities that exist in the community require the dedication of substantial resources to monitor the quality of treatment? This may be particularly true since many group homes are operated by non-professionals. Is the quality of treatment potentially compromised by the often high turnover (as much as 200% in some areas) of the inspectors responsible for the enforcement of treatment standards? Has the anticipated decrease in institutional budgets been realized (Lakin, 1991)? Deinstitutionalization is being scrutinized to determine if it has met societal goals. As part of this ongoing process, social workers play an important role in obtaining and communicating information regarding treatment of the mentally retarded.

REFERENCES

Buchard, J.D., & Harrington, W.A. (1985/86). Deinstitutionalization: Programmed transition from the institution to the community. *Child and Family Behavior Therapy, 7,* 17-34.

Lakin, A. (1991). Deinstitutionalization of the mentally retarded: Big v. little—A national and Florida perspective. *Medical Science and the Law, 31*, 313-321.

Zigler, E., Hodapp, R., & Edison, M. (1990). From theory to practice in the care and education of mentally retarded individuals. *American Journal of Mental Retardation, 95*, 1-12.

Lessard v. Schmidt
349 F. Supp. 1078 (1972)

FACTS: On October 29, 1971, Alberta Lessard was picked up by two police officers in front of her home in West Allis, Wisconsin. She was taken to the Mental Health Center, North Division, in Milwaukee where police officers filled out an "Emergency Detention for Mental Observation" form, and Ms. Lessard was held on an emergency basis. On November 1, 1971, the same police officers appeared before a judge in an *ex parte* hearing and reaffirmed what was contained in the written petition for emergency detention. Based on this hearing the judge issued an order permitting the confinement of Lessard for an additional ten days. On November 4, 1971, a doctor stated in an "Application for Judicial Inquiry," that Lessard was suffering from schizophrenia and recommended permanent commitment. The judge ordered two physicians to examine Lessard. He also signed a second temporary detention document which permitted Lessard to be detained for ten more days. An additional extension was granted on November 12, 1971. Throughout this period, neither Ms. Lessard nor anyone acting on her behalf was informed of the proceedings.

Without notice, the judge interviewed Lessard at the Mental Health Center on November 5, 1971 and informed her that two doctors had been appointed to examine her and a guardian *ad litem* would be named to represent her. The judge asked Lessard if she would like her own doctor to examine her and she replied that she did not have a doctor. After the meeting, a guardian *ad litem* was appointed by the judge.

On her own initiative, Lessard retained counsel through Milwaukee Legal Services. On the afternoon of November 15, 1971, Lessard was informed that a commitment hearing would be held the following morning. The hearing was adjourned and reset for November 24, 1971, in order to enable the appearance of Lessard's attorney. A request at this time by Lessard that she be allowed to go home during this interim time period was denied.

At the November 24, 1971 hearing, the judge committed Lessard for an additional thirty days. The judge's decision was based on the hearing testimony of one police office and three physicians. The judge found Lessard to be "mentally ill." Three days after the November 24, 1971 hearing, Lessard was allowed to return home on an outpatient "parole" basis. Until the time the case was heard nearly a year later, the thirty-day commitment order was extended for one month each month after the November 24th hearing.

Lessard filed a class action suit on behalf of herself and all other persons eighteen years of age and older who were being held against their will after a temporary or permanent commitment provision was invoked, based on the Wisconsin involuntary commitment statute. The lawsuit, which sought changes in Wisconsin's procedures for involuntary commitment and detention of those alleged to be suffering from mental illness, was filed in the U.S. District Court of the Eastern District of Wisconsin. Lessard also asked the court to issue a restraining order preventing Wisconsin officials from further proceeding against or detaining her.

ISSUE: Does an involuntary civil commitment statute violate a person's right to due process by denying a timely fair hearing and by failing to provide an easily understandable standard for detainment and commitment?

DECISION: Yes. The court concluded that the Wisconsin civil commitment procedure was "constitutionally defective" because it violated due process procedures in the areas of notice of charges and rights, permitting detention without hearings, inadequate representation for detainees, lack of protection against self-incrimination and hearsay evidence, insufficient evidence to prove that the patient is both mentally ill and dangerous, and failure to consider less restrictive alternatives to commitment.

REASONING: In the past, due process procedural safeguards have been relaxed for civil commitments based on the state's role as *parens patriae*, "parent of the country." This implies that the state acts in the best interest of the individual. The community may limit individual liberties as part of that role. Consequently, involuntary commitment of those deemed mentally ill has been sanctioned because the guidance and rehabilitation that the state provides to the individual are believed to be in the best interest of the community and the individual. The *parens patriae* role taken by the state in a civil commitment is in stark contrast to the adversarial role taken by the state in a criminal commitment.

Parens patriae has been interpreted to imply that the state has a responsibility to provide treatment to those involuntarily committed. Access to treatment is seen as an integral part of the state's function in rehabilitating and assisting the individual. However, the court pointed out that this approach is fundamentally flawed because the presumed helpfulness of the state in an involuntary commitment fails to take into account committed persons who do not want to be treated, the often-questionable efficacy of treatment, and the likelihood that prolonged hospitalization may increase rather than decrease symptoms of mental illness.

The court explained that a commitment to a mental institution brings with it the loss of several civil rights, including restrictions in making contracts, engaging in certain professions, and holding a driver's license. In addition, former mental patients face stigmatization which often causes increased difficulty in buying or leasing a home and in obtaining a job. Possibly the most serious effect of commitment is the finding that those committed to a mental institution have a much greater chance of dying than those at large. The court found that since the impact of a civil commitment on a mentally ill individual is often negative, adherence to stringent due process procedural requirements is as essential in a civil commitment as it is in a criminal proceeding.

IMPLICATIONS: During the 1960s and 1970s there was a push for the deinstitutionalization of the civilly committed mentally ill. The deinstitutionalization effort came from several areas, including those who saw it as a method to control ever-growing state budgets as well as those who believed that involuntary commitment is an obstruction of the mentally ill person's civil right to liberty. Thus, in the past two decades, it has become increasingly difficult to involuntarily confine someone without a finding that he or she is dangerous to himself or herself or others (Slovenko, 1993).

The concept of the least restrictive alternative to treatment provides that the state, in its *parens patriae* role, may restrict fundamental liberties only to the extent necessary to effectuate the state's interest (Slovenko, 1993). Community mental health agencies now provide needed services to the mentally ill in a non-restrictive environment. However, "mental health dollars did not follow the patient from the inpatient setting to the community" (Wilk, 1988, p. 580). Unfortunately, one consequence of deinstitutionalization without adequate community supports has been the growth of homelessness. It is estimated that a large proportion of the homeless population may be attributed to deinstitutionalization. Furthermore, as a result of the use of the "danger to self and others" standard, mental health advocates have complained that mental illness is being criminalized. State hospitals are being filled with anti-social and sociopathic people and more and more often mentally ill people have wound up in corrections facilities. This imbalance has further pressured the already stressed services in both prisons and hospitals (Ludwig, 1991).

Social workers are left to deal with this societal dilemma. The pendulum has swung from institutionalizing people for idiosyncrasies that made the average American uncomfortable to allowing record numbers of mentally ill to wander the streets. Must a person be allowed to deteriorate to an extreme degree before society can forcibly intervene for that person's own welfare and the benefit of the community? What now is the role of the state's benevolent *parens patriae* power?

REFERENCES

Ludwig, E.V. (1991). The mentally ill homeless: Evolving involuntary commitment issues. *Villanova Law Review, 36*, 1085-1111.

Slovenko, R. (1993). The hospitalization of the mentally ill revisited. *Pacific Law Journal, 24*, 1107-1123.

Wilk, R.J. (1988). Implications of involuntary outpatient commitment for community mental health agencies. *American Journal of Orthopsychiatry, 58*, 580-591.

Addington v. Texas
441 U.S. 418 (1979)

FACTS: Between 1969 and 1975, Frank Addington had been temporarily committed to various Texas state mental hospitals. Following his arrest on a charge of "assault by threat," Addington's mother petitioned for Addington to be indefinitely committed. At the trial, the jury had to determine: (1) whether Addington was mentally ill, and if so, (2) whether he required hospitalization in a mental hospital for his own welfare and protection or the protection of others, and if so, (3) whether he was mentally incompetent. Following a six-day trial, the trial judge gave the jury instructions by which to decide the case. Addington disagreed with the "standard of proof" portion of the jury instructions articulated by the judge and appealed his case to the U.S. Supreme Court.

ISSUE: What standard of proof is required by the Fourteenth Amendment in a civil proceeding brought under state law to commit an individual involuntarily for an indefinite period of time to a state mental hospital?

DECISION: Clear and convincing evidence. There are three major standards of proof: (1) beyond a reasonable doubt, (2) clear and convincing evidence, and (3) a preponderance of the evidence. The purpose of a standard of proof is to "instruct the factfinder concerning the degree of confidence our society thinks he should have in the correctness of factual conclusions for a particular type of adjudication" [*In re Winship,* 397 U.S. 358, 370 (1970) (Harlan, J., concurring)].

REASONING: The Court reviewed the history of the three major standards of proof. At one end of the spectrum is the typical civil case involving a monetary dispute between private parties. Since society has a minimal concern with the outcome of such private suits, plaintiff's burden of proof is a mere preponderance of the evidence. The litigants thus share the risk of error in roughly equal proportion.

In a criminal case, on the other hand, the interests of the defendant are of such magnitude that historically, and without any explicit constitutional requirement, they have been protected by standards of proof designed to exclude as nearly as possible the likelihood of an erroneous judgement. In the administration of criminal justice, society imposes almost the entire risk of error upon itself. This is accomplished by requiring, under the Due Process Clause, that the state prove the guilt of an accused beyond a reasonable doubt.

The intermediate standard was chosen by the court for symbolic as well as for practical reasons. Intermittent, idiosyncratic behavior is something everyone displays. What appears as mental illness to one person may be within the "normal" range to another observer. "The reasonable doubt standard of criminal law functions in its realm because there the standard is addressed to specific, knowable facts" (p. 430). On the other hand, the vagaries of psychological diagnosis and treatment are open to interpretation. To expect an assessment which is consistently conclusive and certain is expecting too much of both mental health professionals and lay jurors. Therefore, the "clear and convincing" standard of proof was chosen.

IMPLICATIONS: This case demonstrates that an adult's liberty interest is compelling enough to require a standard of proof greater than the customary civil case, yet not so demanding as that of a criminal case where the state and the defendant are adversaries. In a civil commitment, the objective is not to deprive an individual of freedom solely because he is dangerous, but rather, to confine the individual so that quality treatment can be offered.

Over the past decade, sincere concern about the number of challenged people residing in communities has resulted in a relaxation of civil commitment laws (Treffert, 1986). This effort has been decried by some and hailed by others (Sullivan, 1992; Wilk, 1994).

For the foreseeable future, the intermediate standard seems to navigate between society's genuine need to intervene and treat a person who can benefit from such treatment and to protect itself from dangerous persons, and the individual's right to be free from society's overreaching into its citizens' private lives.

In law, the involuntary treatment of mental illness is perceived as a deprivation of liberty, not a philosophical discussion focusing on whether treatment is medically indicated or is a form of control of social deviance. In practice, most states require two independent factors to justify an involuntary commitment: first, that the individual be mentally ill, and second, that due to this mental illness the individual may be dangerous to himself or to others. While this standard has been faulted for being ambiguous and highly conclusionary, social workers are nevertheless called upon to use this rather elastic concept to predict the relative "dangerousness" of an individual.

REFERENCES

Sullivan, W. (1992). Reclaiming the community: The strengths perspective and deinstitutionalization. *Social Work, 37*, 204-209.

Treffert, D. (1986). The obviously ill patient in need of treatment: A fourth standard for civil commitment. *Hospital and Community Psychiatry, 36*, 259-267.

Wilk, R. (1994). Are the rights of people with mental illness still important? *Social Work, 39*(2), 167-175.

Grkman v. Dept. of Public Welfare
637 A.2d 761 (Pa.Cmwlth. 1994)

FACTS: Mary Grkman became a resident of the Westmoreland Manor Nursing Home in December of 1989. She was receiving intermediate care at the facility when in November of 1991 a plan of care team determined that Ms. Grkman no longer needed intermediate care. The facility then sent written notice to Ms. Grkman's family informing them of the facility's plan to move Ms. Grkman to their domiciliary care program.

After being informed by the facility that his sister was no longer in need of intermediate care, Ms. Grkman's brother filed an appeal and request for intervention with the Office of Hearings and Appeals, Department of Public Welfare (DPW) in December of 1991. In response to Ms. Grkman's brother's appeal and request for intervention, she remained at the facility.

At the end of March of 1992, Ms. Grkman was reevaluated, and a diagnosis was made of her physical condition. As a result of this examination, "the attending physician certified that Grkman did not meet the criteria for intermediate care and agreed with the transfer to domiciliary care" (p. 762). However, the hearing officer for Ms. Grkman's appeal received a letter written by Miriam Cohen, MSW, of the Forbes Regional Health Center Geriatric Assessment Center. The letter attested that "the transfer of Grkman from the facility's intermediate care unit to [its] domiciliary care program would be detrimental to Grkman's psychological well being" (p. 672). Moreover, Ms. Grkman testified that she did not want to leave the facility because of her well-established friendships.

In May 1992 the hearing officer denied Ms. Grkman's appeal. The rejection was based on the clinical record, indicating that Ms. Grkman's condition had improved and she therefore did not require the more extensive health services of an intermediate care facility. The hearing officer also pointed out that the potential negative impact of the transfer on Ms. Grkman's mental status was not substantiated in any of the medical documentation.

This decision was affirmed by the Director of the Office of Hearings and Appeals and, after reconsideration, upheld by the Secretary of the Department of Public Welfare. Ms. Grkman then filed a petition review with the court.

ISSUE: Must a hearing officer's decision confirming the transfer of a nursing home patient to domiciliary care be supported by substantial evidence?

DECISION: Yes. Since both state and federal regulations only require clinical record evidence to support a provider's decision to transfer or discharge a patient, the attending physician's reports that supported the appropriateness of Ms. Grkman's transfer were considered adequate. Thus, the burden of proof is on the resident to show the incorrectness of the decision.

REASONING: The court noted at the outset that the scope of its review of the hearing officer's decision was limited to a determination of whether constitutional rights were violated, an error of law was committed, or necessary findings were supported by substantial evidence. Ms. Grkman's clinical record included her attending physician's reports, which clearly supported the appropriateness of her transfer. The argument that the physician's report was insufficient because it may have been based on hearsay was considered by the court to be irrelevant. In keeping with state and federal law, it was found that the decision to transfer or discharge must be based on the clinical record regardless of the source of information. Thus, it was determined that the DPW provided sufficient documentation to support its judgement that Ms. Grkman was suitable for transfer to domiciliary care.

In addition, the court rejected the argument that the DPW failed to consider Ms. Grkman's mental and psychological well-being in regard to the appropriateness of her transfer to domiciliary care. The court noted that the hearing officer specifically rejected the social worker's letter indicating that the transfer would be detrimental to Ms. Grkman's psychological well-being and Ms. Grkman's testimony because they were not substantiated by medical documentation in the clinical record.

IMPLICATIONS: We take for granted our ability to make the fundamental choices which determine the course of our daily lives. However, when someone becomes dependent on long-term health care, the freedom to make life choices is often diminished. This is particularly true of the elderly.

Due in part to changes in the structure of society and significantly increased longevity, families frequently turn to outside sources to care for aging and debilitated members. Consequently, it is expected that over the next fifty years the nursing home population will triple (Altman et al., 1992).

The recipients of institutionalized care, such as residents of nursing homes, are often unable to take part in the decisions which greatly impact their lives. There often exist institutional structures that limit the degree to which a client can be part of any decision-making process. However, the degree to which individuals can control decisions about their physical and social environments will influence their health status, utilization of medical care, activity levels, feelings of well being and mortality rates. For instance, participating in decision making is directly related to the degree to which an elderly individual is able to adjust after being moved from one health care setting to another (Abramson, 1990).

Until these structures can be modified, social workers can provide clients with a sense of choice within existing parameters. A seemingly modest intervention, such as working out ways for the client to increase a client's level of comfort, can enhance perceived control and client well-being. Moreover, in keeping with the National Association of Social Worker's Code of Ethics, which calls for client self-determination, social workers must use their advocacy role to more fully bring their clients into the health care decision-making process in the future.

REFERENCES

Abramson, J. (1990). Enhancing patient participation: Clinical strategies in the discharge planning process. *Social Work in Health Care, 14*(4), 53-70.

Altman, W., Parmelee, P., & Smyer, M. (1992). Autonomy, competence, and informed consent in long-term care: Legal and psychological perspectives. *Villanova Law Review, 37*, 1671-1704.

CHAPTER 4
Aging

McKennon v. Nashville Banner Publishing Company
115 S.Ct. 879 (1995)

FACTS: Christine McKennon was an employee of the Nashville Banner Publishing Company for thirty years. She was discharged under the presumption that the company was cutting back its employment force due to "cost considerations." Believing that the company fired her due to her age, 62, McKennon filed suit, seeking legal and equitable remedies under the Age Discrimination in Employment Act (ADEA) of 1967 (81 Stat. 602, as amended, 29 U.S.C. at 621 et seq.). Information during the deposition in preparation of her case revealed that McKennon, during her last year of employment, had photocopied and brought home confidential documents regarding the company's financial condition. McKennon said that she had done so because she feared that the company was going to dismiss her due to her age.

Nashville Banner claimed that this misconduct itself would have been enough for termination had it known of her actions. Therefore, McKennon was "fired" again. For purposes of summary judgement, Nashville Banner conceded it had acted discriminatorily towards McKennon. McKennon sought judicial relief notwithstanding her misconduct, arguing that the ADEA was intended to protect people in these situations, and her misconduct discovered after the fact was not a bar to recovery.

ISSUE: Is employee misconduct discovered after an employee has been unfairly discharged in violation of the Age Discrimination in Employment Act of 1967 a complete bar to recovery?

DECISION: No. "An employee discharged in violation of the ADEA is not barred from all relief when, after her discharge, her employer discovers evidence of wrongdoing that, in any event, would have led to her termination on lawful and legitimate grounds had the employer known of it" (p. 879).

REASONING: The purpose of the 1967 Age Discrimination in Employment Act was to deter employers from discrimination in the workplace and compensate employees who had been discriminated against for injuries suffered. Specifically, the Act makes it illegal for employers "to discharge any individual or otherwise discriminate against any individual with respect to his compensation, terms, conditions, or privileges of employment, because of such individual's age" [29 U.S.C. at 623 (a) (1)]. Therefore, the Act would seem to be ineffective if there were actions which could override the protections afforded by the Act, therefore permitting and condoning age discrimination. However, the courts and the legislature had to show some deference to employers to make decisions in the workplace, and the court was quick to note this.

The Court of Appeals found the misconduct to be supervening grounds, and therefore McKennon could be terminated and no compensation given regardless of the discrimination. The Supreme Court flatly overruled the decision, finding that, while the misconduct may have given Banner Publishing enough reason to terminate McKennon's employment, the initial discrimination could not be ignored. Once the Court determined there had been discrimination, it wrote "the employer could not have been motivated by knowledge it did not have and it cannot now claim that the employee was fired for the nondiscriminatory reason" (p. 885). Therefore, the evidence of discrimination, notwithstanding the misconduct that had occurred, could not be disregarded when the Company said it would have fired McKennon on other grounds.

While an employer's interests are relevant considerations and will not be ignored, the Court found a compromise when ascertaining the actual remedies to be awarded. While the holding supported the notion that a violation of the ADEA merits relief, misconduct in the workplace significant enough to terminate employment merits attention when determining relief.

The Court, in its conclusion regarding compensation, stated that "the beginning point in the trial court's formulation of a remedy should be calculation of backpay from the date of the unlawful discharge to the date the new information was discovered" (p. 886).

IMPLICATIONS: With this case we witness a rare occurrence—a unanimous United States Supreme Court. This precedential decision is important for equal protection concerns and imperative for the growing older population better known as the "baby boom generation." While Fourteenth Amendment cases have in the past endeavored to protect racial discrimination, age discrimination has not been historically a "suspect class" and has largely been ignored. With elderly workers increasing in disproportionate numbers, the Court, in overruling numerous previous cases barring relief in similar situations, has set a standard of review for relief indicating that age discrimination and after-acquired evidence (Mills, 1994; White & Brussack, 1994) will not be tolerated. This decision serves to resolve earlier conflicting decisions which made this area of the law confusing. While recognizing both the employer's and employee's interests regarding the ADEA (Cuellar, 1989) yet standing strongly on the underlying presumption that discrimination will not be tolerated, the Court has set a standard of protection for the elderly as a group.

This decision comes after a long line of anti-discrimination cases and legislation going back the 1960s and the civil rights movement. What is unique about this case is that we are no longer dealing with a societal minority whose voice cannot be heard. While workers' rights have been an issue since the early 1900s with laws protecting minimum wages, hours, and unions, this constitutes another class. Age discrimination will potentially touch a large number of citizens in the near future.

REFERENCES

Cuellar, J. (1989). The Age Discrimination in Employment Act: Handling the element of intent in summary judgement motions. *Emory Law Journal, 38*, 523-562.

Mills, S. (June 1994). Toward an equitable after-acquired evidence rule. *Columbia Law Review, 94*, 1525-1557.

White, R., & Brussack, R. (1994). The proper role of after-acquired evidence in employment discrimination litigation. *Boston College Law Review, 35*, 49-94.

Billingslea v. State of Texas
780 S.W. 2d 271 (Tex.Cr.App. 1989)

FACTS: Ray Edwin Billingslea was charged with and convicted of injuring his ninety-four-year-old live-in mother, Hazel Billingslea. His appeal to the Dallas Court of Appeals granted him an acquittal, based on the absence of a statutory duty to care for an elderly individual.

Hazel Billingslea first came to the attention of Adult Protective Services in 1984 when attempts by her granddaughter to make contact with Ms. Billingslea proved unsuccessful. The Texas Department of Human Resources was notified, and a formal inquiry into Ms. Billingslea's welfare was requested.

Ms. Billingslea had been residing with her son Ray Billingslea, his wife, and their son in her small two-story frame house since 1964 and had become bedridden in March 1984. When Adult Protective Services worker Velma Mosley, accompanied by two Dallas police officers and a police social service employee, visited Ray Billingslea at his home, they found Ms. Billingslea near death.

Ms. Mosley testified that Ms. Billingslea was discovered lying in bed, moaning and asking for help. Ms. Billingslea's heel, hip, and back had been eaten away to the bone by large bedsores. She had suffered massive muscle loss, was disoriented, and was emaciated from having not eaten for some time. She had sustained second-degree burns and blisters on her inner thighs from lying in her own urine, and maggots had settled into her open bedsores. A doctor testified that the bodily injury evidenced by Ms. Billingslea would have taken, at the least, four to six weeks to accrue.

The State asserted that the absence of a statutory duty to act was deficient and that the evidence warranting an indictment was sufficient.

ISSUE: Does failure to care for and secure medical attention for an ailing, live-in parent constitute criminal negligence?

DECISION: No, unless there is an explicit statutory duty to act on behalf of the ailing individual. It is unconstitutional to criminalize an act of omission without specific and clear warning that failure to perform such a duty would result in punishment.

REASONING: The court justified its decision by stating that the law under which Ray Billingslea was charged failed to stipulate a duty to care for an ailing, elderly individual. A legislative amendment to the

Texas Penal Code later added that, "a person who omits to perform an act does not commit an offense unless a statute provides that the omission is an offense or otherwise provides that he has a duty to perform the act" [V.T.C.A., Penal Code § 1.07(a)(23), 6.01, 6.01(c)].

The court cited a similar case [*Ronk v. State*, 544 S.W.2d 123 (Tex.Cr.App. 1976)] in which it ruled that the defendant was not negligent in failing to secure medical treatment for a child due to the absence of a special relationship between the defendant and the child which would have provided that the defendant comply with a statutory duty to act on behalf of the child. Rather, this duty to act was found in V.T.C.A. Family Code, § 12.04(3), which dictated that parents had a duty to "support the child, including providing the child with clothing, food, shelter, medical care, and education."

Although the new legislative amendment includes a clear statutory duty to act that did not exist previously, applying the amended provisions retroactively would be impermissible.

IMPLICATIONS: Although elder abuse and neglect is not a new phenomenon, society has only recently begun to recognize its pervasiveness. Whether the increase in awareness of elder maltreatment is due to greater publicity and research, improved reporting procedures, or an actual rise in the number of maltreated elderly, is yet unclear. The response by many states to this heightened awareness has been to develop protective programs to intervene in cases of elder abuse and initiate case management protocols (Soares & Rose, 1994) as well as to institute mandatory reporting laws.

Many experts suggest that the issues of dependency, financial abuse, physical and/or emotional abuse are strong factors in this society's steady increase in cases of elder maltreatment. However, rather than examine the circumstances that contribute to such cases— the stress of elderly persons' dependency on their children (Steinmetz, 1983) or the sense of powerlessness experienced by the children who are dependent on their aging parents (Pillemer, 1985)—this case looks at the legal implications of such relationships.

Its decision is based on the important distinction between the moral versus the legal duty to care for dependent elderly and recognizes that in order for liability to be established, a legal obligation must exist. Wolf, Strugnell and Godkin (1982) assert that active neglect is the refusal or failure to fulfill a caretaking obligation. This definition limits neglect to dependent elders and assumes a legal obligation of care. Absent such a statutory duty, there can be no obligation and therefore no liability.

REFERENCES

Pillemer, K. (1985). The dangers of dependency: Domestic violence. *Social Problems, 3,* 146-158.

Soares, H., & Rose, M. (1994). Clinical aspects of case management with the elderly. *Journal of Gerontological Social Work, 22*(3/4), 143-156.

Steinmetz, S.K. (1983). "Family violence toward elders." In Susan Saunders, Ann Anderson, and Cynthia Hart (eds)., *Violent individuals and families: A practitioners handbook.* Springfield, IL: Charles C. Thomas.

Wolf, R., Strugnell, C.P., & Godkin, M. (1982). *Preliminary findings from three model projects on elderly abuse.* Worcester, MA: University of Massachusetts Center on Aging.

In re Byrne
402 So.2d 383 (Fla. 1981)

FACTS: A social worker employed by the Florida Department of Health and Rehabilitative Services took into custody an elderly man, Herbert Byrne, after visiting him in his home and finding Byrne naked and surrounded by debris and excrement. The social worker had him involuntarily transported to a medical facility pursuant to a Florida statute which provided that:

> (1) Upon probable cause to believe that an individual suffering from the infirmities of aging is being abused, maltreated, or neglected, a representative of the department, accompanied by a law enforcement officer, may enter a premises, after obtaining a court order and announcing their authority and purpose. Forcible entry shall be attained only after a court order has been obtained, unless there is probable cause to believe that the delay incident to obtaining such an order would cause an individual suffering from the infirmities of aging to incur a substantial risk of life-threatening physical harm.

> (2) When, from the personal observation of a representative of the department and a law enforcement officer, it appears probable that an individual suffering from the infirmities of aging is likely to incur a substantial risk of life-threatening physical harm or deterioration if not immediately removed from the premises, the department's representative may, when authorized by court order, take into custody and transport, or make arrangements for the transportation of, the individual to an appropriate medical or protective services facility.

> (3) When action is taken under this section, a preliminary hearing shall be held within 48 hours, excluding Saturdays, Sundays, and legal holidays, to establish probable cause for grounds for protective placement.

> (4) Upon a finding of probable cause, the court may order temporary placement for up to 4 days, pending the hearing for a need for continuing services.

(5) When emergency services are rendered, a report of the exact circumstances, including the time, place, date, factual basis for the need for such services, and the exact services rendered, shall be made.

Byrne sought to dismiss the petition of involuntary custody on the ground that the above statute was unconstitutional because it did not afford him due process of law.

ISSUE: Is an adult protective service statute constitutional that allows a department of social services to take emergency involuntary custody of an elderly person if sufficient probable cause and safeguards are evident?

DECISION: Yes. If sufficient procedural safeguards are in place, emergency involuntary custody may be initiated by a department of social services.

REASONING: The specific safeguards evident in the Florida statute were (1) the requirement that a member of the department and a law enforcement agency must personally observe the emergency situation; (2) the relocation order must be authorized by a court; and (3) within 48 hours there must be a preliminary court hearing to determine whether there is probable cause for protective placement.

IMPLICATIONS: The Florida Supreme Court articulated the purpose of this adult protective act: "to free persons suffering from infirmities of aging from dangerous or oppressive conditions. The stated purpose of the statute—to protect the elderly—is genuine and not a euphemism for punishment" (p. 385).

It has been estimated that the incidence of domestic elder abuse in the United States ranges from 1 to 10 percent (Tatara, 1993; Pillemer and Finkelhor, 1988; Gioglio and Blakemore, 1983; Steinmetz, 1981). Overall criminal victimization against the elderly has also been well documented (Bachman, 1993; Bachman, 1992; Bachman and Pillemer, 1992; Fattah and Succo, 1989). A recent Congressional report (1981) estimated that 1.5 million elderly persons are abused each year. Although the number of elder abuse and neglect cases that actually go to trial is not known, no adult protective services statute has yet been held to be unconstitutional. As adult protective services become more legalized (Pollack, 1992) the professional tension between social workers and lawyers becomes more acute. Behavior that a social worker defines as placing an elderly client at risk may not be sufficient for legal action to be taken. Alternatively, social services, rather than court intervention, may often be the more appropriate and pragmatic action.

REFERENCES

Bachman, R. (1992). *Elderly victims.* (NCJ Pub. No. 138330) Washington, D.C.: Bureau of Justice Statistics, U.S. Department of Justice.

Bachman, R. (1993). The double edged sword of violent victimization against the elderly: Patterns of family and stranger perpetration. *Journal of Elder Abuse and Neglect, 5*(4), 59-76.

Bachman, R., and Pillemer, K.A. (1992). Epidemiology and family violence involving adults. In R.T. Ammerman and M. Hersen (Eds.), *Assessment of family violence: A clinical and legal sourcebook* (pp. 108-120), New York: John Wiley and Sons, Inc.

Fattah, E.A., and Succo, V.F. (1989). *Crime and victimization of the elderly.* New York: Springer-Verlag.

Gioglio, G.R., and Blakemore, P. (1983). *Elder abuse in New Jersey: The knowledge and experience of abuse among other New Jerseyans.* Trenton, New Jersey: New Jersey Department of Human Resources. House Select Comm. on Aging, 97th Cong., 1st Sess., *Elder abuse: An examination of a hidden problem.* (Comm. Print. 1981).

Pillemer, K., and Finkelhor, D. (1988). The prevalence of elder abuse: A random sample survey. *The Gerontologist, 28,* 51-57.

Pollack, D. (1992). Record retention management: A key element in minimizing agency and worker liability. *Journal of Law and Social Work, 2,* 89-94.

Steinmetz, S.K. (1981, January/February). Elder abuse. *Aging,* 6-10.

Tatara, T. (1993). Understanding the nature and scope of domestic elder abuse with the use of state aggregate data: Summaries of the key findings of a national survey of states APS and aging services. *Journal of Elder Abuse and Neglect, 5*(4), 35-57.

Goldman v. Krane
86 P.2d 437 (Colo.App. 1989)

FACTS: In this Colorado case, a social worker employed by the Denver Department of Social Services was found by the trial court to have unilaterally and improperly assumed guardianship of a ninety-year-old widow living alone in senior citizens' housing. Upon receiving guardianship, social worker Mary Krane had Anna Barshop transferred to a hospital and then to a nursing home. While at the hospital, Barshop was subjected to an extensive examination and was not permitted to call anyone. To accomplish the transfer, Krane had used a guardianship petition pre-signed by her agency director. At the trial court, Barshop received a damage award of $135,000 from the Denver Department of Social Services for deprivation of her constitutionally protected liberty interest.

ISSUE: May a department of social services be liable for damages when a social worker uses a pre-signed petition for guardianship to take custody of and transport a person?

DECISION: Yes. A jury could reasonably conclude that a department of social services may be liable for permitting social workers to use pre-signed guardianship petitions.

REASONING: The department asserted that Krane's actions were an isolated instance of a single employee. While this action might have led to Barshop's deprivation of a constitutionally protected right, it did not implicate the department. The trial court and the appellate court disagreed. The appellate court acknowledged that "a jury could reasonably infer that the act of the social worker in this instance was the direct consequence of the director's policies" (p. 439).

The department also urged that the jury should have been required to find that the department "acted with deliberate indifference toward Barshop's constitutional rights in petitioning for temporary guardianship" (p. 440). Once again, the court disagreed. It referred to a landmark U.S. Supreme Court case [*Monell v. Department of Social Services*, 98 S.Ct. 2018 (1978)] which held that constitutional deprivations resulting from this kind of policy were clearly foreseeable. "Thus, the existence of the policy or custom itself presumed a tolerance or deliberate indifference on the part of the department as to the consequences of such policy or custom" (p. 440).

IMPLICATIONS: A department of social services may be held liable for actions of its employees or agents when the employee is carrying out agency policies or customs sanctioned by department officials who have policy making authority. Once it is established that a social worker is working under the authority and control of the department, the department may be liable for the social worker's actions. Factors that may indicate authority and control are the ability of the department to specify the details of the social worker's job, the right of the department to set the social worker's hours of work and to specify tasks to be done, and the right of the department to require that the social worker maintain certain professional skills. As long as the social worker does not substantially deviate from the usual and customary work assignments, the department will be vicariously liable for actions of its employees.

This case highlights some of the difficulties and challenges faced by social workers who are placed in supervisory positions. How does the social service provider who is besieged by a large caseload make important decisions on behalf of clients? And how can a provider successfully cope with demands from government agencies which may not serve the interest of vulnerable clients?

Pressures like these add to the difficulties already present during the assessment phase of a guardianship petition. Additionally, guardianship procedures are in themselves complicated and ambiguous. Although guardianship of an elder is in many cases a necessity to preserve the safety of an incompetent person, in other cases it is a serious infringement of an older person's autonomy and civil liberties. Because it is so difficult to make accurate assessments for clients, the potential for improper decisionmaking is high.

These difficulties are compounded by ambiguities present in the judicial system. In most cases, the petition for guardianship is not made by the alleged incompetent person. Instead, reports made by nurses, physicians, and family caretakers form the basis for guardian proceedings. However, statements made by physicians are often vague and dated, and fail to consider the possibility of rehabilitation and treatment (Bulcroft, Kielkopf & Tripp, 1991; Iris, 1988). This may be due to the fact that there is a lack of reliable instruments to make accurate medical assessments of competency. Legal reports appear to be sketchy as well, because the guardian *ad litem*, who is often an attorney, views relevant facts from a legalistic, rather than a medical perspective (Iris, 1988). Although some reforms have begun to be enacted, petitions generally neglect to outline the specific circumstances or reasons necessitating guardianship (Keith & Wacker, 1993).

Other reforms call for more adequate legal representation of the ward. Although there is some controversy over whether a guardianship hearing should be adversarial, it is clear that without legal representation that is in the interest of the ward, as opposed to the guardian *ad litem* who acts "in the ward's best interest as determined by the attorney" (Keith & Wacker, 1993, p. 83), it is unlikely that the petition will be challenged.

Older people are generally discouraged from appearing in court due to the fact that psychiatrists and other mental health personnel often feel that the strain of judicial proceedings would be too disturbing for a proposed ward to endure. However, in many cases, the patient, as well as legal and medical staff, could benefit from the presence of the proposed ward in the courtroom. Witnessing firsthand the effects of legal processes as they relate to an older person's personal and property rights might facilitate a therapeutic outcome (Butler, Lewis & Sunderland, 1991). In many other cases, the petitioning process itself is so demoralizing that "the challenge to one's competency, of itself, reduces the ability to challenge it" (Bulcroft, Kielkopf & Tripp, 1991, p. 162).

Guardianship of the elderly is a subject that is and will continue to be challenging for those who work with the frail elderly. The elderly, particularly the very old, are currently the fastest growing demographic group in the United States. Current projections indicate that due to increased longevity, life expectancy is expected to increase from 74.9 years to 77.6 years by the year 2005, and by the year 2080, the projected life expectancy will increase to 81.2 years. For this reason it is important that the process associated with guardianship be fair and appropriate to the needs of this vulnerable population. While advocacy for legal reform is an essential component in guardianship research, social workers should approach questions regarding guardianship with great care and at the same time develop stronger relationships within their agencies.

REFERENCES

Bulcroft, K., Kielkopf, M., & Tripp, K. (1991). Elderly wards and their legal guardians: Analysis of country probate records in Ohio and Washington. *The Gerontologist, 31*(2), 156-164.

Butler, R., Lewis, M. & Sunderland, T. (1991). *Aging and mental health*. New York, Merrill Publishing, Inc.

Iris, M. (1988). Guardianship and the elderly: A multi-perspective view of the decisionmaking process. *The Gerontologist, 28*, suppl., 39-45.

Keith, P., & Wacker, R. (1993). Implementation of recommended guardianship practices and outcomes of hearings for older persons. *The Gerontologist, 33*(1), 81-87.

CHAPTER 5
Women

The People v. Hudson
6 Cal.Rptr.2d 690 (Cal.App. 2 Dist. 1992)

FACTS: In early 1985, defendant Warren Hudson, employed as a telephone solicitor for a company in California, began to write letters and send flowers and gifts to Kelly Lange, a television journalist for the National Broadcasting Company (NBC) in Los Angeles. She ignored these overtures and had no contact whatsoever with Hudson. Later in 1985 Hudson wrote Lange a note that read, "You are going to walk out of the studio some night and you will never know what hit you." Lange informed the police.

On August 9, 1989, Hudson told a co-worker that he had some bullets with him and was going to shoot Lange. The co-worker saw the bullets and believed Hudson was serious about the threat. The co-worker notified the police who, in turn, notified Lange. Two days later Hudson was arrested under California's stalking law. He had in his possession a .38 caliber revolver and a half dozen .38 caliber bullets.

Hudson asserted that the law was overbroad and therefore was unconstitutional and in violation of the First Amendment.

ISSUE: May a state enact a stalking law which is sufficiently narrow to be constitutional?

DECISION: Yes. California and several other states have passed stalking laws that are constitutional.

REASONING: California's Penal Code section 422 reads in part:

> Any person who willfully threatens to commit a crime which will result in death or great bodily injury to another person, with the specific intent that the statement is to be taken as a threat, even if there is no intent of actually carrying it out, which, on its face and under the circumstances in which it is made, is so unequivocal, unconditional, immediate, and specific as to convey to the person threatened a gravity of purpose and an immediate prospect of execution, shall be punished . . . by imprisonment in the state prison if he or she cause another person unreasonably to be in sustained fear for his or her or their immediate family's safety.

Whether or not the maker of the threat intends to carry it out is irrelevant. So long as the statement is a threat to commit murder or great bodily injury, the statement may be considered a "true threat." Hudson contended that he did not intend his co-worker to convey his threat to Lange, and also, that the threat caused Lange to be "in sustained fear."

The court determined that the "person threatened need not be the intended victim" (p. 694), even though the legislature did not specify whether or not this was its intention. As to an insufficient showing that Lange was in "sustained fear," there was evidence that private armed security guards were hired immediately and retained until Hudson was arrested. "There is no particular period of time during which the fear must be sustained. The time will vary depending on the individual and the circumstances" (p. 697).

IMPLICATIONS: A majority of states now have stalking laws. Many were enacted to work in concert with domestic violence laws, though their passage was due to celebrities being stalked. While there are no firm numbers regarding the incidence of stalking, it is generally agreed that the stalker and the victim usually had a relationship prior to the commencement of the stalking. Often this relationship was an abusive one.

The difficulties in enforcing stalking laws are many. They (1) demand a great deal of time and personnel, (2) are difficult to document, (3) may not be enforced at the request of the victim, out of fear of retaliation, (4) may not favor complaints brought by private citizens as opposed to those brought by a prosecuting attorney, and (5) are inapplicable when the victim does not "overly communicate a threat" (Bernstein, 1993, p. 559). As with other offenses which impinge on the First Amendment right to freedom of speech, stalking laws are often open to interpretation.

REFERENCES

Bernstein, S. (1993). Living under siege. *Cardozo Law Review, 15*(1-2), 525-567.

Syndex Corp. v. Dean
820 S.W.2d 869 (Tex.App.- Austin 1991)

FACTS: A female former employee sued her supervisor and employer for, among other things, sexual harassment in violation of the state's Human Rights Act. The District Court entered judgement for the employee, and this appeal was made. The Court partially reversed, but the Supreme Court reversed and remanded. On remand, the Court of Appeals held that the employer was liable to the employee for the supervisor's conduct because the supervisor acted within his delegation of authority as employer's branch manager and that the testimony of a certified social worker and psychotherapist fell within the medical-treatment exception to hearsay rule.

Syndex Corporation owned Smith Produce, which hired Mary Dean in 1978. She was eventually promoted and became an office manager. Bill Bushell was branch manager of Smith Produce and was Dean's immediate supervisor when she was an office manager.

Though they initially had a good working relationship, by December 1983 Bushell became flirtatious and sexually aggressive with Dean, buying her meals and soft drinks, discussing with her his fantasies and problems with his wife's sexual performance. He grabbed Dean in front of other employees and tried to kiss her. One day in 1984, Bushell ordered Dean to have an affair with him. After she refused, he later looked at her in front of other employees and observed that "everything has a price and can be bought."

Later, Bushell became very cold with Dean and increased her workload. She eventually quit her job.

ISSUE: If an employer does not ratify or authorize a supervisor's sexually harassing conduct, can the employer still be liable under the state's Human Rights Act?

DECISION: Yes.

REASONING: The Texas Human Rights Act makes it unlawful for an employer to "discriminate against an individual with respect to compensation or the terms, conditions, or privileges of employment because of . . . sex." Sexual harassment, like racial harassment, is universally recognized as employment discrimination. Courts have recognized two distinct categories of claims, including a hostile work environment.

This case involves a hostile work environment, which "has the purpose or effect of unreasonably interfering with an individual's work or creating an intimidating, hostile, or offensive working environment" *(Meritor Sav. Bank v. Vinson,* 477 U.S. at 65-66). The jury found that Dean was subjected to unlawful sexual harassment by Bushell.

There were no Texas cases establishing a test for employer liability under the Act. However, it is modeled on federal law. Its purpose is to carry out the policies embodied in Title VII of the federal Civil Rights Act of 1964. Therefore, defendant Syndex relied on federal case law in arguing its position. The Court found that even though Syndex did not know of its employee's harassment of Dean, because he was acting in the scope of his duties as a supervisor when he harassed her, the Court found Syndex liable through the concept of "agency." In other words, even if Syndex did not know of Bushell's harassment, the acts took place in the scope of Bushell acting as a supervisor doing his job for the Syndex Corporation, and so the Corporation was responsible for injuries resulting from these acts.

Deena Mersky was a certified social worker and psychotherapist. Dean's family doctor referred Dean to Mersky for treatment for depression. During the course of treatment, Mersky saw Dean approximately thirty times and took a detailed history. Mersky testified at the trial and said that obtaining the history was a part of the diagnosis and treatment of Dean's depression. Her testimony was within the medical-treatment exception to the hearsay rule, which generally prohibits such evidence from being admitted in court. According to Texas rules of evidence, a medical exception need not be a statement made to a physician so long as it is made for the purpose of medical treatment.

IMPLICATIONS: Sexual harassment in the workplace does not need to be directed or even be observed by the owner of the company in order for the company to be liable for the acts of its workers. This is because the workplace is under the authority or control of the company, and the company is responsible for the acts of those it hires as managers while those individuals are acting as managers.

With sexual harassment, the issue is not whether the company knew about the acts of the manager but whether those acts took place within the "scope" of his work for the company. This is the "agency" aspect discussed in the case. "Agency," used in this case, means that when a person works for another person or company, he or she is acting under the authority of the "principal," or the owner. The acts of the "agent," if done in the course of working for the "principal," or in the "scope" of his employment, will be imputed to the principal, even if the principal did not know the agent was doing those acts. This concept is not unique to sexual harassment cases but is rather a concept used throughout business litigation. Illegal, overt sexual harassment is the exception.

Subtle behavior that tests the boundaries of freedom of speech and expression is more frequent yet more difficult to categorize as sexual harassment. Title VII of the Civil Rights Act of 1964 outlaws sexual conduct, submission to which is either an explicit or implicit condition of employment. Also outlawed is conduct that has the purpose or effect of interfering with an employee's work or creating an intimidating, hostile, or offensive work environment. Defining this latter category of circumstances can be done from the "reasonable person's" perspective, or it can be done from the "reasonable woman's" perspective. Courts are divided as to which standard to use [see, e.g., *Trotta v. Mobil Oil Corp.,* 788 F.Supp. 1336 (S.D.N.Y. 1992); *Campbell v. Kansas State University,* 780 F.Supp. 755 (D. Kan. 1991); *Austen v. State of Hawaii,* 759 F.Supp. 612 (D.Hi. 1991); *Robinson v. Jacksonville Shipyards,* 760 F.Supp. 1486 (M.D. Fla. 1991)]. Whichever standard prevails, there are objective and subjective criteria to consider. Has the aggrieved notified the alleged perpetrator of her discomfort? Was this done in writing? Were there witnesses to the behavior? Were there multiple incidents or only one? Was the behavior "sufficiently severe or pervasive [so as] to alter the condition of [the victim's] employment and create an abusive working environment" *Meritor Savings Bank v. Vinson* [477 U.S. 57 (1986)]?

Men and women have sincerely different perceptions as to what constitutes sexual harassment. Men and women disagree even among themselves. This may be due to child-rearing patterns, disregard or denial of sexual harassment as offensive, or a lack of awareness (correctable by education and training). Whatever the explanation, there is a perception gap that is difficult to define. For now, employers and employees individually and collectively share the burden of being role models, providing training, and affording opportunities to discuss and write meaningful sexual harassment policies. These remedial steps will go a long way to avoiding workplace rancor and costly lawsuits.

Thurman v. City of Torrington
595 F.Supp. 1521 (1984)

FACTS: A woman and her son brought a civil rights action against the City of Torrington and police officers of the city, alleging that their constitutional rights were violated by the nonperformance of official duties by police in regard to threats and assaults by the wife's estranged husband. Specifically, they alleged that a violation of the plaintiff's Fourteenth Amendment rights were violated because it was alleged that the city and the police officers used an administrative classification of assault complaints that was discriminatory and violative of the Equal Protection clause of the Fourteenth Amendment. They alleged that police protection was fully provided to persons abused by someone with whom the victim had no domestic relationship, but the police consistently afforded lesser protection when the victim was a woman abused or assaulted by a spouse or boyfriend or when a child was abused by a father or stepfather.

In October 1982, Charles Thurman attacked his wife, plaintiff Tracey Thurman, at the home of friends in Torrington, Connecticut. The friends made a formal complaint of the attack to police and requested their help in keeping Charles Thurman off their property.

In November of the same year, Charles returned to his home and, using physical force, took his child from the home. Tracey and one of her friends went to Torrington police headquarters to make a formal complaint. The police officer refused to accept the complaint.

Several days later, Charles screamed threats at Tracey while she sat in her car. A police officer stood in the street watching Charles scream threats at Tracey until he broke the windshield of his wife's car while she sat in the car. Charles was arrested for breaking the windshield and was convicted the next day of breach of peace. He received a suspended sentence of six months and a two-year conditional discharge, during which he was ordered to stay away from Tracey and the home of her friends and commit no further crimes.

In December, while Tracey was at her friend's home, Charles again returned and threatened her. She called the police. Although informed of the violation of the conditional discharge, the police made no attempt to find Charles Thurman or to arrest him.

Between January and May of 1983, Tracey and her friend, by telephone, reported to the police that Charles threatened to shoot both of the plaintiffs. On May 4 and 5, Tracey and her friend took a written complaint to the police. The complaint stated that Tracey was seeking an arrest warrant for her husband because of his death threat and his violation of the conditional discharge. The police refused to take the written complaint. Tracey was told to return three weeks later when another police officer could seek a warrant for the arrest of her husband. On May 6, she filed an application for a restraining order against Charles, and the court issued a restraining order forbidding him from assaulting, threatening and harassing Tracey. The City was informed of the order.

On May 27, Tracey requested police protection to get the police department to issue a warrant for her husband's arrest. She was told she would have to wait until after the Memorial Day weekend.

On May 31, she appeared again at the police department to request a warrant. She was told that no one was there to help her and that she would have to wait until an officer returned from his vacation. Her brother-in-law also called to protest the lack of action, and was told that Charles would be arrested on June 8, 1983. No such arrest was made.

On June 10, Charles appeared at the home of Tracey's friends and demanded to speak with her. She remained indoors and called the police department, demanding Charles be arrested for this violation of his probation. After 15 minutes, she went outside to keep him from taking or hurting their son. Soon after, Charles began to stab Tracey in the chest, neck, and throat. Ten minutes later, a police officer arrived. Charles was holding a bloody knife. In front of the officer, Charles kicked Tracey in the head and went into the home and came out with his child. He then dropped the child on his bleeding mother and kicked Tracey in the head again. Soon, three more policemen arrived but allowed Charles to wander in the crowd and to threaten Tracey. When Tracey was on the ambulance stretcher, he approached her again. Finally, the police arrested him.

ISSUE: May a city police department be sued for failure to adequately enforce an order of protection?

DECISION: Yes.

REASONING: The standard to be used is that a complaint should not be dismissed unless it appears that the plaintiff could prove no set of facts in support of her claim which would entitle her to relief. Since the plaintiff here did state such a set of facts, the court ordered that the case would not be dismissed for this reason and ordered the case to go forward.

The city claimed that the complaint of the plaintiff should be dismissed for failing to allege a deprivation of a constitutional right. The complaint stated that the police failed to guarantee her Equal Protection under the Fourteenth Amendment. The city argued that the Equal Protection clause only prohibits intentional discrimination that is racially motivated. The court held that this is a misstatement of the law and that application of the Equal Protection Clause of the Fourteenth Amendment will invalidate state laws that classify on the basis of gender unless they are substantially related to an important governmental objective.

The plaintiffs alleged that the defendant used a classification that created discriminatory treatment in violation of the Fourteenth Amendment. The classification allowed less police protection of women in domestic relationships with an assailant. The court held that "if the City wishes to discriminate against women who are the victims of domestic violence, it must articulate an important governmental interest for doing so."

IMPLICATIONS: This case graphically illustrates how lack of police response in a domestic violence situation can create more violence. In this instance, the police classified women who are victims of violence at the hands of people with whom they had "domestic relationships," differently from other victims of violence. These "classifications" needed to be examined by the court. Classifications according to gender are given a close look, and the government must show an important interest for doing so and show that this classification is rationally related to achieving an important governmental interest.

It is hard to think what governmental interest would be "important" given that domestic violence is so detrimental to society's interests. Does the supposed reduction in police budgetary expenditures meet the test? What about the interests of "privacy" of families which look for the police to intervene in these cases? Does one family member's asking for help mean the family's privacy interests are waived? Does the high incidence of domestic violence make it something the police can ignore or treat differently?

Attitudes about domestic violence are hard to change and are probably somewhat ingrained in many police officers, prosecutors, judges, and members of the public. This case makes it clear that the battered woman can seek government help, including the arrest of her batterer, and have the system fail her at every turn in spite of courageous efforts and family support.

What are some of the ways the police and the judicial system could have protected the safety of Tracey Thurman? Are they overly expensive or intrusive? What about the larger social cost of families and individuals who want to escape violent relationships, finding themselves unable to free themselves? What effect is seen on the children of such families?

Simmons v. State
504 N.E.2d 575 (Ind. 1987)

FACTS: On October 14, 1983, J.Y. was approached by her track coach, Wendell Simmons, outside of the high school she attended. Simmons threatened her at knifepoint and forced her to a secluded area. He then ordered her to undress and lie down on his jacket. While holding the knife to her throat, Simmons raped J.Y. Afterward, Simmons repeatedly told J.Y. that unless she would agree to go along with a fabricated story about how the rape occurred, he would kill her. She went home and reported the fabricated story to her father and to the police. Later, she testified as to her true recollection of the evening's events. During her testimony she did not recall some crucial items. These lapses, testified social workers Linda Kepner and Brenda Turnbloom, were due to J.Y. having "rape trauma syndrome."

After a hung jury at the first trial, Simmons was convicted of multiple charges. He appealed, asserting that, among other things, the "rape trauma syndrome" testimony should not have been admitted.

ISSUE: Is "rape trauma syndrome" admissible as evidence in a criminal proceeding?

DECISION: Yes, but only in some states.

REASONING: The court noted that Kepner and Turnbloom were both employees of Women's Alternatives, Inc., an organization that aids rape and sexual assault victims and had a number of years experience in this area. The court wrote:

> The witnesses here were properly qualified psychiatric social workers, specifically trained in treatment of rape victims. Their testimony tended to show the victim's behavior was consistent with the clinically observed behavior pattern known as "rape trauma syndrome" . . . The decision to allow the opinion of an expert is left to the discretion of the trial judge and will be reviewed . . . only if the trial court exceeds his discretion (p. 579).

IMPLICATIONS: Rape trauma syndrome is a post-traumatic stress disorder which was first admitted into evidence by expert testimony in the early 1980s. State appeals courts have had a mixed reaction to its reliability [see *Henson v. State,* 535 N.E.2d 1189 (1989); *State v.*

Saldana, 324 N.W.2d 227 (1982)]. Objections include (1) that the rape may not have occurred at all. Therefore, it is prejudicial to allow testimony regarding rape trauma syndrome that presumes the rape did occur; (2) that rape trauma syndrome has not been generally adopted by the scientific community; and (3) that the particular evidentiary use of this kind of expert testimony is unclear. If it speaks to the credibility of the defendant rather than the state of mind of the victim, this may be unfair to the defendant.

Some advocates have suggested that, just as "battered child syndrome" and "battered spouse syndrome" have received a positive reception in some judicial circles, so too should "rape trauma syndrome." And, they argue, the jury is always free to decide for itself whether or not the expert testimony offered is credible or not. Further, the court is free to decide on a case-by-case basis whether the expert testimony will be more probative than inflammatory and, therefore, whether to admit the testimony.

Social services for battered women and rape victims have been available for several decades (Davis et al., 1992, 1994; Edleson, 1992). As more states admit rape trauma syndrome as evidence, social workers who counsel rape victims will increasingly be called upon to be expert witnesses (Beebe et al., 1994; Brookings et al., 1994; Dallager & Rosen, 1993).

REFERENCES

Beebe, D., Gulledge, K., Lee, C., & Replogle, W. (1994). Prevalence of sexual assault among women patients seen in family practice clinics. *Family Practice Research Journal, 14*(3), 223-228.

Brookings, J. McEvoy, A., & Reed, M. (1994). Sexual assault recovery and significant others. *Family in Society, 75*(5), 295-299.

Dallager, C., & Rosen, A. (1993). Effects of a human sexuality course on attitudes toward rape and violence. *Journal of Sex Education and Therapy, 19*(3), 193-199.

Davis, L., & Hagen, J. (1992). The problem of wife abuse: The interrelationships of social policy and social work practice. *Social Work, 37*, 15-20.

Davis, L., Hagen, J., & Early, T. (1994). Social services for battered women: Are they adequate, accessible, and appropriate? *Social Work, 39*(6), 695-704.

Edleson. J. (1992). Social workers' intervention in women abuse: 1910-
1945. *Social Service Review, 2,* 304-313.

Webster v. Reproductive Health Services
109 S.Ct. 3040 (1989)

FACTS: This case questions the validity of a Missouri state statute containing approximately 20 provisions. The plaintiffs are concerned primarily with two: (1) the statute calls for a ban on the use of public facilities and public employees in abortion proceedings unless the proceeding is for the purpose of saving the mother's life, and (2) a requirement that a physician do a series of tests in cases when the fetus is twenty weeks or more in order to determine viability.

Plaintiffs brought this class action in July 1986, claiming that the statute violates various constitutional amendments, including the First, Fourth, Ninth, and Fourteenth. They bring this suit on behalf of public facilities performing abortions, women seeking abortions, and health care professionals offering counseling and abortion-related services.

ISSUE: Does a state statute regulating abortions in public facilities by public employees violate the Constitution?

DECISION: No. The Supreme Court ruled that these provisions did not violate any constitutional rights as the state is not required by the Constitution to give assistance to a woman desiring an abortion even though the right to an abortion is a constitutional right. Therefore, a state may prohibit all use of public facilities for abortions.

REASONING: The 5-4 decision narrowly passed. With a number of concurrences and dissents, the Court had difficulty in setting a consistent precedent for future reference. The majority's primary reasoning for validating the statute was the idea that a woman still has a constitutional right to an abortion by going to a private institution. Nowhere in the Constitution, reasoned the court, was "health services" a constitutional or fundamental right that must be offered by the government.

IMPLICATIONS: This case puts into question the series of abortion cases preceding it. The trimester analysis established by *Roe v. Wade* established a woman's fundamental right to an abortion. With this decision, the future of abortion law will likely mean varying state laws and regulations.

While the court reasoned that a woman in Missouri still has a fundamental right to an abortion, it could also be argued that, pragmatically, poor women will have a more difficult time securing this right.

Abortion regulation in the United States first appeared in 1821. While the regulations continued to increase, the active numbers of indictments and convictions were small (Whitney, 1991). The supersensitivity regarding this issue cannot be fully discussed here. It is perhaps enough to note that issues of privacy, public policy, religion, and science intersect to such an extent that it is not surprising that none of the major Supreme Court decisions has been unanimously endorsed (Ross, 1992; Lieberman & Davis, 1992; Hartman, 1991).

REFERENCES

Hartman, A. (1991). Toward a redefinition and contextualization of the abortion issue. *Social Work, 36*(6), 467-468.

Lieberman, A., & Davis, L. (1992). The role of social work in the defense of reproductive rights. *Social Work, 37*(4), 365-371.

Ross, L. (1992). African-American women and abortion. *Journal of Health Care for the Poor and Underserved, 3*(2), 274-284.

Whitney, C. (1991). *Whose life? A balanced, comprehensive view of abortion from its historical context to the current debate.* New York: William Morrow.

CHAPTER 6
Income Support

Loper v. New York City Police Dept.
802 F.Supp. 1029 (S.D.N.Y. 1992)

FACTS: A class action lawsuit was brought by homeless people who were begging in public. A New York law provides that, "A person is guilty of loitering when he . . . loiters, remains or wanders about in a public place for the purpose of begging." The constitutionality of this law was questioned by the plaintiffs on the basis of the First Amendment guarantee of freedom of expression and association.

ISSUE: Is a statute that criminalizes all forms of begging in public constitutional?

DECISION: No. Regulations regarding free speech must be "neutral, support substantial governmental interests, and not completely ban the speech at issue" (p. 1039).

REASONING: Two standards are used by the courts in analyzing statutes and regulations pertaining to the freedom of expression. The U.S. Supreme Court, in *United States v. O'Brien* [88 S.Ct. 1673 (1968)], decided that

> a government regulation is sufficiently justified when: (1) it is within the constitutional power of the Government; (2) it furthers an important or substantial governmental interest; (3) the governmental interest is unrelated to the suppression of free expression; and (4) the incidental restriction on alleged First Amendment freedoms is no greater than is essential to the furtherance of that interest (p. 1679).

Merging with this standard is a standard used to assess time, place, and restrictions on "pure speech." Such restrictions are valid

> provided that they are justified without reference to the content of the regulated speech, that they are narrowly tailored to serve a significant governmental interest, and that they leave open ample alternative channels for communication of the information. [*International Society for Krishna Consciousness*, 112 S.Ct. 2711, 2720 (1992)]

Applying these standards, the court determined that because the ban on begging was all-encompassing, no matter how aggressive or unobtrusive, the statute was unconstitutional.

IMPLICATIONS: This case allows homeless and poor people to bring attention to their impoverished state. It is "a critical message that the beggar has a genuine and legitimate interest in presenting to the public at large" (p. 1042). Balanced against this interest is the public's desire for personal privacy, safety, and the avoidance of what may be perceived to be offensive behavior (see Johnson & Cnaan, 1995).

The criminalization of begging is hardly a recent phenomenon (Trattner, 1994; Guest, 1989). English Poor Laws were enacted to curb groups of homeless people from roaming from one community to another and menacing the general population [see *Papachristou v. City of Jacksonville*, 405 U.S. 156, n.4 (1972)]. It is the range of begging approaches that is difficult to categorize. These include verbal or non-verbal; unobtrusive or aggressive; polite or intimidating; non-physical to quasi-assaultive. A beggar has a right to communicate in any manner in which he or she chooses, so long as it is not unduly intrusive. Many lawsuits regarding the finer points of this issue have been filed [e.g. *Young v. New York City Transit Authority*, 903 F.2d 146, cert. denied, 498 U.S. 984 (1990)], but the Supreme Court has yet to hear a case which specifically delineates the impact of the First Amendment on the right to beg as distinguished from the right to solicit for other charitable purposes.

REFERENCES

Guest, G. (March 1989). The boarding of the dependent poor in Colonial America. *Social Service Review, 63*, 92-112.

Johnson, A., & Cnaan, R. (1995). Social work practice with homeless persons: State of the art. *Research on Social Work Practices, 5*(3), 340-382.

Trattner, W. (1994). *From poor law to welfare state*. New York: Free Press.

State of Louisiana, Dept. of Social Srvs. v. Jones
638 So.2d 699 (La.App. 3 Cir. 1994)

FACTS: The Louisiana Social Services Support Enforcement Service brought suit against Victorian Jones, Jr., claiming that he is the father of K.B. Green. K.B. Green was born on March 26, 1987. Wyezeta Green, K.B.'s mother, claimed that she was exclusively seeing Victorian Jones in the fall of 1986 when K.B. was conceived.

In 1986, Mr. Jones and Ms. Green were co-workers at the City of Natchitoches police department. She was a dispatcher and he was a patrolman. She claimed that she had three sexual relations with Jones. Ms. Green said that she had no other sexual relations at that time. Jones claimed to have never even dated Ms. Green.

Ms. Johnson, also a dispatcher at the police department, testified that Ms. Green told her that Mr. Jones was K.B.'s father. However, inconsistent with Green's testimony, Ms. Johnson testified that Ms. Green told her that K.B. was conceived in Chicago. Ms. Johnson also testified that Ms. Green had dated a man named Bill McDaniel. Another police employee stated that she thought Mr. McDaniel was K.B.'s father. Likewise, Ms. Kathy Berryman, also a police department employee, testified that Ms. Green had confided in her that Mr. McDaniel was K.B.'s father. None of the witnesses could recall ever seeing Ms. Green and Mr. Jones together socially.

Blood tests of Jones were taken to make a DNA comparison with K.B. The results indicated that the Probability of Exclusion (P.E.) was 99.49% (exclusion of all other males except the defendant) and the Combined Paternity Index (P.I.) was 341.12 to 1 (the odds that the defendant is the father of the child). Despite the fact that the DNA evidence pointed to Jones as K.B.'s father, Delores Mercer, a state representative, testified that Mr. Jones continually and consistently denied that he was K.B.'s father. The trial court held that the state failed to carry the burden of proof that Mr. Jones was the father. The state appealed.

ISSUE: Is DNA testing alone sufficient proof of paternity?

DECISION: No.

REASONING: The purpose of DNA testing is to exclude falsely accused men from a finding of paternity. Even if an alleged father is not excluded, scientific testing is not 100% conclusive and is alone insufficient to prove paternity. However, it is persuasive. Other supportive testimony can help prove paternity by a preponderance of evidence.

In this case, the non-scientific evidence did not sufficiently establish the putative father's paternity. There were numerous discrepancies in Ms. Green's testimony. For example, her original testimony about her sexual contact with Mr. Jones differed from what she said when cross-examined. Likewise, there was testimony from other witnesses that failed to support Ms. Green's claim that Mr. Jones was K.B.'s father or that they even had a social relationship.

In light of these inconsistencies, the appellate court found that the trial court's decision was a reasonable one. It noted that the issue of the sufficiency of proof of paternity is a question of fact that should not be disturbed on appeal in the absence of manifest error. In this case, even though the scientific evidence implicated Mr. Jones, the court held that the trial court's decision was not clearly wrong since there was enough other evidence to support that decision.

IMPLICATIONS: In the late 1980s, nearly two-thirds of births among women under the age of twenty were to non-married women, compared to only 30% in 1970. This represents a ten-fold increase, with one in five births now being non-marital (Wattenberg, 1990, p. 26). In 1990, fewer than 34 paternities were established for every 100 non-marital births (Nichols-Casebolt, 1994, p. 5). The emphasis on paternity is important since "[w]ithout the establishment of paternity, nonmarital children are denied certain filial rights afforded them by law . . . including the right to receive child support . . ." (Nichols-Casebolt, 1994, p. 5). The economic well-being of a non-marital child is further affected by paternity establishment because it affords such children the right to Social Security, worker's compensation, insured health care, and armed service benefits (Wattenberg, 1990). In addition to the economic implications, identification of the father provides the child with a sense of identity and knowledge of his or her biological heritage (Nichols-Casebolt, 1994).

While the non-economic reasons to establish paternity are compelling (Seltzer & Brandreth, 1994; Sonenstein et al., 1993), child support issues have been at the center of paternity-establishment controversies. In 1975, Congress passed Title IV-D of the Social Security Act. This law created the Child Support Enforcement program, which reimbursed states for a large portion of the costs associated with establishing paternity, locating noncustodial parents, and collecting child support. The push for paternity establishment is fueled by findings that indicate that non-marital children are more likely to be poor and welfare dependent and are a growing proportion of all poor children (Danziger & Nichols-Casebolt, 1990).

For seventy years, 1923 to 1993, the test for admitting scientific evidence was stated in the care of *Frye v. United States* [293 F.1013 (D.C. Cir. 1923)]:

> Just when a scientific discovery crosses the line between the experimental and demonstrable stages is difficult to define. Somewhere in this twilight zone the evidential forces of the principle must be recognized, and while courts will go a long way in admitting expert testimony deduced from a well-recognized scientific principle or discovery, the thing from which the deduction is made must be sufficiently established to have gained general acceptance in the field in which it belongs (p. 1014).

The U.S. Supreme Court recently endorsed a different standard that courts should use when ruling an admission of novel scientific evidence. Focus should be upon:

> (1) the soundness and reliability of the process or technique used in generating the evidence
> (2) the possibility that admitting the evidence would overwhelm, confuse, or mislead the jury, and
> (3) the proffered connection between the scientific research or test result to be presented, and particular factual issues in the case [*United States v. Downing* 753 F.2d 1224, 1237 (1985)].

Although the reasons for establishing paternity may seem compelling, it must be acknowledged that there are many legal barriers to paternity establishment. Scientific evidence, no matter how compelling, does not conclusively resolve parentage. There is no consensus that every child has a right to a relationship with his or her father. For example, should paternity be established despite a mother's objection? There are also questions about the due process rights of the father and whether it is always in the best interest of the child to promote the father-child relationship. Consequently, public policy makers are looking beyond paternity establishment to address the issues that are growing out of the increasing numbers of non-marital children.

REFERENCES

Danziger, S., & Nichols-Casebolt, A. (1990). Child support in paternity cases.   *Social Service Review, 64*, 458-474.

Nichols-Casebolt, A. (1994). Establishing paternity: An analysis of cases from two Arizona counties. *Social Work Research, 18*, 5-15.

Seltzer, J. & Brandreth, Y. (1994). What fathers say about involvement with children after separation. *Journal of Family Issues, 15*(1), 49-77.

Sonenstein, F., Holcomb, P., & Seefeldt, K. (1993). What works best in improving paternity rates? *Public Welfare, 51*(4), 26-33.

Wattenberg, E. (1990). Unmarried fathers: Perplexing questions. *Children Today, 19*, 25-30.

Dexter v. Kirschner
984 F.2d 979 (9th Cir. 1992)

FACTS: Sheri Dexter was diagnosed with chronic myelogenous leukemia, a form of cancer that is treatable only with an allogeneic bone marrow transplant as part of its cure. It is undisputed that this transplant is the standard of care for this disease and that the death rate is 100% without treatment. While she did qualify for health care benefits under Arizona's Medicaid program, the state's Medicaid statute does not cover allogeneic bone marrow transplants, a procedure in which a matched donor's marrow is infused into the patient. Conversely, autologous Bone marrow transplants, whereby the patient's own bone marrow is transfused back into the patient, are covered by Arizona's Medicaid plan. However, it is accepted medical fact that autologous bone marrow transplants are ineffective for individuals with Dexter's type of leukemia.

Dexter filed an action seeking declaratory and injunctive relief. Her contentions included Arizona's violation of federal guidelines for the Medicaid program and disregard for Equal Protection by differentiating between varying types of bone marrow transplants. In turn, appellants argued that Arizona's Medicaid law is not unconstitutional and that federal law was upheld in this case.

ISSUE: Do limitations of Medicaid statutes in state law signify a lack of constitutional-based rights for program participants?

DECISION: No. Medicaid statutes in Arizona were found to be constitutional despite their discrimination of critical medical procedures.

REASONING: Federal guidelines regulate the implementation of Medicaid programs in the individual states. Medicaid, established by Title XIX of the Social Security Act, 42 U.S.C. § 1396a-1396e, is a federal-state cooperative program that provides medical assistance to indigent people. The State pays the cost of medical service, which is reimbursed to the extent of 55% by the federal government. Each state writes its own plan, which must cover five categories: (1) inpatient hospital services; (2) outpatient hospital services; (3) laboratory and X-ray services; (4) skilled nursing services; and (5) physicians services [42 U.S.C. § 1396d(a)(1)-(5) (1992)].

Despite the inclusive nature of this federal law, subsequent legislation offers discretion to states with regard to organ transplants

[42 U.S.C. § 1396b(i) [1992)]. Arizona was therefore in compliance with federal requirements in its discretionary funding of transplant procedures.

The constitutionality of the Arizona legislation raises separate issues. States electing to fund transplant procedures are bound by federal regulation: "similarly situated individuals [must be] treated alike . . ." [42 U.S.C. § 1396b(i) (1992)]. The court has defined "similarly situated" as "all patients who can be effectively treated by the same organ transplant procedure" (p. 986). If the appellate court had chosen to interpret the phrase as an indication of anyone suffering from a similar disease, grave implications for the Medicaid system would result. Medicaid would be obliged to fund almost all transplant procedures. Given this distinction, Dexter's right to Equal Protection was not breached. As the court wrote:

> Nonetheless, the inequality is acknowledged but not classified as an infringement on the Equal Protection Clause for an additional reason. In the area of economics and social welfare, a State does not violate the Equal Protection Clause merely because the classifications made by its laws are imperfect. If the classification has some 'reasonable basis', it does not offend the Constitution simply because the classification is not made with mathematical nicety or because in practice it results in some inequality. [*Danridge v. Williams*, 397 U.S. 471 (1970)]

The "reasonableness" in this case was the lack of any allogeneic bone marrow program in the state of Arizona at the time the law was enacted. Furthermore, the decision to fund one transplant over the other was not deemed arbitrary because the two separate treatments deal with two distinct diseases.

IMPLICATIONS: Medical technological advances are proceeding at an unparalleled pace. Access to this technology implicates an ethical and legal dilemma: Are the poor equally entitled to accessing this technology as the non-poor? These are not merely theoretical, philosophical issues. Difficult public policy choices have thus far acknowledged that the small supply of suitable transplant donor matches may in some cases be out of reach to the poor (Dhooper, 1990; House & Thompson, 1988). Their survival rate is thereby compromised. This adverse and disparate impact on the poor has not yet been held to be constitutionally impermissible. Intensified efforts to prolong life through improved medical technology will continue to highlight the competing social values of equity and wealth.

REFERENCES

Dhooper, S. (1990). Organ transplantation: Who decides? *Social Work, 35*(4), 322-327.

House, R., & Thompson, T. (1988). Psychiatric aspects of organ transplantation. *Journal of the American Medical Association, 260*(4), 535-539.

King v. Smith
88 S.Ct. 2128 (1968)

FACTS: In this landmark U.S. Supreme Court case, Alabama had in place a regulation under the Aid to Families with Dependent Children (AFDC) program that effectively denied payments to a family unit if the mother cohabited "in or outside her home with any single or married able-bodied man." The purpose of the AFDC program was (and still is) to assist a dependent child, defined as an age-qualified "needy child . . . who has been deprived of parental support or care by reason of the death, continued absence from the home or physical or mental incapacity to a parent."

Alabama allowed a man to qualify as a "non absent substitute father" under its AFDC regulations if he was frequently visiting the home for the purpose of cohabiting with the child's mother, or even if he cohabited with the mother at another location. As a result of this regulation, the number of children who would otherwise have been able to receive AFDC benefits in Alabama decreased by 16,000 (22%) between 1964 and 1967. This regulation affected plaintiff Smith who "cohabited" with a Mr. Williams at his home on weekends. Williams was not the father of any of Smith's children, and he had no legal obligation to support any of her children.

ISSUE: Can a state disqualify an otherwise eligible needy child solely because the state wishes to discourage what it perceives to be parental immorality?

DECISION: No. The court clearly stated that immorality, illegitimate children, and discouraging illicit sexual behavior are not at issue. Such issues are unrelated and irrelevant to the eligibility of a needy child.

REASONING: The court briefly reviewed the history of public welfare since the mid-1800s.

> A significant characteristic of public welfare programs during the last half of the 19th century in this country was their preference for the "worthy" poor. Some poor persons were thought worthy of public assistance, and others were thought unworthy because of their supposed incapacity for "moral regeneration." This worthy-person concept characterized the mothers' pension welfare programs, which were precursors of

AFDC. Benefits under the mothers' pension programs, accordingly, were customarily restricted to widows who were considered morally fit.

In this social context it is not surprising that both the House and Senate Committee Reports on the Social Security Act of 1935 indicate that States participating in AFDC were free to impose eligibility requirements relating to the "moral character" of applicants. During the following years, many state AFDC plans included provisions making ineligible for assistance dependent children not living in "suitable homes."

In the 1940s, suitable home provisions came under increasing attack. Critics argued, for example, that such disqualification provisions undermined a mother's confidence and authority, thereby promoting continued dependency; that they forced destitute mothers into increased immorality as a means of earning money; that they were habitually used to disguise systematic racial discrimination; and that they senselessly punished impoverished children on the basis of their mothers' behavior, while inconsistently permitting them to remain in the allegedly unsuitable home. Although fifteen states abolished their provisions during the following decade, numerous other States retained them.

In the 1950s, matters became further complicated by pressures in numerous states to disqualify illegitimate children from AFDC assistance. In 1960 the federal agency strongly disapproved of illegitimacy disqualifications. In disapproving this legislation, then Secretary of Health, Education, and Welfare Flemming issued what is now known as the Flemming Ruling:

A State plan may not impose an eligibility condition that would deny assistance with respect to a needy child on the basis that the home conditions in which the child lives are unsuitable, while the child continued to reside in the home (p. 2130).

The Court went on to rule that,

Every effort is to be made to locate and secure support payments from persons legally obligated to support a . . . child. Such parental support can be secured only where the parent is under a state-imposed duty to support the child. Children with alleged substitute parents who owe them no duty or support are entirely unsupported by these provisions (p. 2132).

IMPLICATIONS: Despite a court's propensity to defer statutory interpretation to the implementing state or agency, the Supreme Court in this case reasoned that Alabama's interpretation simply disguised its true intent—to serve fewer illegitimate children. Simply to save money, a state may not curtail AFDC funds by adopting eligibility requirements that conflict with the mandates of federal legislation. A person not fitting the legal definition of "parent" within the meaning of the Social Security Act cannot be charged with a legal duty to support children in a family receiving AFDC benefits. Nor can that person's income be attributed as available for use by those receiving AFDC. Were it otherwise, there would be a disincentive for men to cohabit with families receiving AFDC or to make any monetary contribution to that family. This would undermine the freedom of association between poor men and women and might actually lengthen the time an AFDC household would need to receive benefits.

As the number of single-parent families continues to escalate (U.S. House of Representatives, 1992), poverty rates among children have also risen, and the extent of that poverty has also grown worse (Danziger & Danziger, 1993). The Family Support Act, touted as a measure to assist more people off welfare and into the workforce, has not yet shown appreciable success (Edkin & Jencks, 1992). It appears that tinkering with the eligibility criteria of welfare is no longer the political option it once was. While some social policy experts have advocated reworking the Internal Revenue Code to address institutionalized poverty (Belcher & Fandetti, 1995), a more popular idea has been to limit the length of time recipients may stay on welfare (Halter, 1994). It remains to be seen whether this will increase or decrease the overall poverty rate, especially among children.

REFERENCES

Belcher, J., & Fandetti, D. (1995). Welfare entitlements: Addressing the new realities. *Social Work, 40*(4), 515-521.

Danziger, S., & Danziger, S. (1993). Child poverty and public policy: Toward a comprehensive anti-poverty agenda. *Daedalus, 122*(1), 57-85.

Edkin, K., & Jencks, C. (1992). Reforming welfare, In C. Jencks (Ed.), *Rethinking social policy* (pp. 204-235). Cambridge, MA: Harvard University Press.

Halter, A. (1994). Chipping away at General Assistance: A matter of economics or an attack on poor people? *Social Work, 39*(6), 705-709.

U.S. House of Representatives, Committee on Ways and Means. (1992). *Background materials and data on programs within the jurisdiction of the Committee on Ways and Means* (102nd Congress, 2nd session). Washington, D.C.: U.S. Government Printing Office.

Goldberg v. Kelly
90 S.Ct. 1011 (1970)

FACTS: The U.S. Supreme Court was asked to decide whether New York City had the right to discontinue welfare benefits to a recipient prior to giving that recipient an administrative hearing. In the 1960s, with welfare rolls rising rapidly, New York City sought to save money by giving an administrative hearing only after benefits were cut off. The city argued that it had a legitimate and overriding interest in conserving fiscal and administrative resources.

ISSUE: Does the Due Process Clause of the Fourteenth Amendment require that a recipient of Aid to Families with Dependent Children (AFDC) be afforded an evidentiary hearing before the termination of benefits?

DECISION: Yes. Termination of assistance pending resolution of a client's eligibility may deprive an eligible person of benefits. Pretermination evidentiary hearings are indispensable to ensuring that eligible recipients are not unfairly deprived of benefits due them.

REASONING: The U.S. Supreme Court endorsed the lower court's rationale when it wrote: "Against the justified desire to protect public funds must be weighed the individual's overpowering need . . . not to be wrongfully deprived of assistance." The Supreme Court went on to cite its own precedent [*Joint Anti-Fascist Refugee Committee v. McGrath,* 341 U.S. 123, 168 (1951)]: "The extent to which procedural due process must be afforded the recipient is influenced by the extent to which he may be condemned to suffer grievous loss." The Court noted that the country has acknowledged that often forces not within the control of the poor contribute to their poverty.

IMPLICATIONS: This case did not decide whether welfare benefits were a right or a privilege. It decided only that an administrative hearing, not a trial, must be available to recipients before their benefits can be terminated. Notice of a fair hearing must be in writing and must be sent to the recipient within a statutory time frame. Failure to follow these procedural guidelines will likely result in full restoration of all benefits that were denied. Today, most departments of human resources have a separate office that monitors the fair hearing process. These offices identify and track alleged ineligible recipients so that they are given a fair hearing prior to termination of their benefits.

What is particularly striking about this case is the detailed extent to which the Supreme Court identified a decision-making process that satisfies hearing requirements owed to welfare recipients. It shows an awareness of the Supreme Court that due process demands minimum compliance with procedures that will ensure a measure of fairness. In effect, the Court balanced the consequences of improperly terminating a client's welfare benefits against the state's need to summarily protect scarce fiscal resources (Bowen & Neenan, 1993; Ewalt, 1994).

REFERENCES

Bowen, G., & Neenan, P. (1993). Does subsidized child-care availability promote welfare independence of mothers on AFDC: An experimental analysis. *Research on Social Work Practice, 3*(4), 363-384.

Ewalt, P. (1994). Welfare—How much reform? *Social Work, 39*(5), 485-486.

Wyman v. James
400 U.S. 309 (1971)

FACTS: In 1967, Barbara James applied for Aid to Families with Dependent Children (AFDC) benefits shortly before her son's birth. As part of the application process, a home visit was made by a caseworker. Shortly after the home visit, AFDC benefits were authorized. Two years later, James was informed by mail that a caseworker would visit her home in six days. Ms. James responded to the letter by informing the worker that while she was willing to supply any information needed by the worker, she would not permit the exchange of information to take place in her home. Ms. James was informed that the worker was required by law to visit the home and that refusal to permit the visit would result in the termination of benefits. Nevertheless, James continued her refusal, and termination procedures were implemented.

As part of this process, James was granted the right to a hearing before a review officer. James appeared at the hearing. She continued to refuse permission for a worker to enter her home and offered to give any needed information in a different location. The review officer ruled that the refusal was a proper ground for the termination of assistance. In response, James instituted a law suit.

A Federal District Court held that a mother receiving AFDC relief may refuse to comply with the New York State required periodic home visit regulation without forfeiting her right to AFDC. Ms. James' contention, affirmed by the Court, was that home visitation is a search, which, when not consented to or when not supported by a warrant issued due to probable cause, violates the beneficiary's Fourth and Fourteenth Amendment rights. The state appealed the District Court's decision, and the U.S. Supreme Court agreed to hear the case.

ISSUE: May a beneficiary of AFDC refuse a mandated home visit by a caseworker without risking the termination of benefits because of the beneficiary's rights protected by the Fourth and Fourteenth amendments?

DECISION: No. The home visit which was provided for by New York State's law governing AFDC benefits was reasonable and did not violate any right guaranteed by the Fourth and Fourteenth Amendments.

REASONING: The Supreme Court held that although the Fourth Amendment affords "(t)he right of the people to be secure in their persons, houses, papers and effects against unreasonable searches and seizures . . ." the court was not concerned with a search by the New York social service agency. The majority noted that although the caseworkers' visit might have rehabilitative and investigative components, the visit does not violate the Constitution since it is not compelled or forced and is not a search in the traditional criminal law context of the Fourth Amendment. Thus, if visitation consent is refused, the only consequence will be the denial of the benefit as opposed to a criminal prosecution.

Even assuming the home visitation constituted a search, the Court held that it was not unreasonable. It is the public's interest to protect and assist the dependent child who is the recipient of the aid. It is also in the public's interest for the agency to assure that its tax benefits reach the intended recipients. The Court illustrated this point by stating that one who gives assistance through private charity has an interest in and an expectation of knowing how those funds are applied. The public should expect the same.

The Court noted that New York State's focus on close contact with the beneficiary through home visits is in the interest of restoring the recipient to "a condition of self support." Although a home visit is not required by federal statute or regulation, it is in keeping with the federal legislation's focus on "assistance and rehabilitation" and was an established standard in states besides New York (p. 320). In addition, New York's home visit procedures were in keeping with guidelines designed to minimize the burden upon the homeowner's right against unreasonable intrusion. These included advance notice of the intended home visit and visitation during working hours.

The court disagreed with James' contention that all the needed information for eligibility determination could be obtained without a home visit. The court stated that a home visit was necessary to "assure verification of actual residence or of actual physical presence in the home, which are requisites for AFDC benefits, or of impending medical needs" (p. 322).

The court stressed the responsibility of the caseworker for the welfare of the benefit recipient because AFDC concerns dependent children and the needy families of those children. Consequently, the objective of the home visit is not a criminal investigation. As such, "if the home visit should, by chance, lead to the discovery of fraud and a criminal prosecution should follow . . . that is a routine and expected fact of life and a consequence no greater than that which necessarily ensues upon any other discovery by a citizen of criminal conduct" (p. 323).

IMPLICATIONS: The AFDC program was created in 1935 as part of the Social Security Act. Because AFDC is a federal program that provides matching funds to states choosing to participate, those states must follow existing federal program regulations. Since its inception, federal regulations have dealt primarily with demonstrating neediness and dependency. AFDC has focused on procedural eligibility, not on getting people off welfare (see Cheng, 1995). Congress has left states with most of the authority to create the rules and procedures for operating and regulating the program (Anders, 1990).

The original rationale for the creation of AFDC was that widows and their children became poor through no fault of their own and were therefore "deserving" of assistance (Anders, 1990). Although AFDC eligibility requirements now focus on parental absence rather than parental death, need and dependency remain an integral part of determining eligibility. At a time when calls for AFDC reform abound in large part due to the costs associated with the program, it is imperative that social workers are able to ensure that the public funds allocated to AFDC are used as intended. For example, it is critical that the social worker is able to assure that children, the primary target of AFDC, experience gain as a result of the benefit. In this role, the dual nature of social work as rehabilitator and investigator, while uncomfortable, is a reality.

REFERENCES

Anders, C. (1990). State intervention into the lives of single mothers and their children: Toward a resolution of maternal autonomy and children's needs. *Law and Inequality, 8*, 567-610.

Cheng, T. (1995). The chances of recipients leaving AFDC: A longitudinal study. *Social Work Research, 19*(2), 67-76.

Pickett v. Brown
462 U.S. 1 (1983)

FACTS: In 1978, the mother of a ten-year-old illegitimate child brought a paternity and support action against the putative father. A Tennessee law provided that a paternity and support action must be brought within two years of the child's birth unless the father provided support or acknowledged his paternity in writing, or unless the child either was or would likely become a public charge, in which case either the state or anyone else could bring a lawsuit prior to the child's eighteenth birthday. The putative father, Braxton Brown, sought to dismiss the lawsuit on the ground that it was barred by the two-year statute of limitation for filing. The mother, Frances Pickett, challenged the constitutionality of this statute and asserted that it violated the Equal Protection Clause of the Fourteenth Amendment. The case was eventually decided by the United States Supreme Court.

ISSUE: Does a statute which imposes a two-year limitation on paternity and child support actions violate the Equal Protection Clause of the Fourteenth Amendment?

DECISION: Yes. The statute unfairly restricts the rights of legitimate children. For the illegitimate child whose claim is not covered by one of the exceptions in the statute, the two-year limitation period severely restricts the rights to paternal support.

REASONING: The Supreme Court supported its decision by citing one of its own precedents [*Weber v. Aetna Casualty and Surety Co.,* 406 U.S. 164, 175 (1972)]:

> [I]mposing disabilities on the illegitimate child is contrary to the basic concept . . . that legal burdens should bear some relationship to individual responsibility or wrongdoing. Obviously, no child is responsible for his birth and penalizing the illegitimate child is an ineffectual—as well as an unjust— way of deterring the parent.

It went on to question whether the two-year limitation period was long enough to provide a reasonable opportunity for plaintiffs to bring a lawsuit on their own behalf. The court inquired whether the time limitation was really substantially related to the state's assertion that it was trying to avoid the litigation of stale or fraudulent claims.

There is no apparent reason why claims filed on behalf of illegitimate children who are receiving public assistance when they are more than two years old would be just as stale, or as vulnerable to fraud, as claims filed on behalf of illegitimate children who are not public charges at the same age (p. 15).

As Justice O'Connor pointed out in an earlier case [*Mills v. Habluetzel,* 456 U.S. 91 (1982)], the relationship between a statute of limitations and the state's interest in preventing stale or fraudulent paternity lawsuits has become difficult to endorse in light of scientific advances in blood and DNA testing.

IMPLICATIONS: In 1576, England first recognized the idea of paternity action at law. Ever since, the search for an accurate method to establish paternity has been underway. The number of illegitimate children has been growing rapidly over the past two decades (Liebmann, 1993). Simultaneously, children "born outside of marriage" have the longest spells of poverty and welfare dependency and are a rising proportion of all poor children (Danziger & Nichols-Casebolt, 1990, p. 458). Garbarino & Associates (1992) report that a majority of American children will spend a significant portion of their childhood in a living arrangement without their fathers in the home. Garfinkel et al. (1992) note that, "Nearly one of every four children is now living apart from at least one parent and therefore is potentially eligible for child support" (p. 505). It is therefore not surprising for one researcher to conclude that "[l]ow child support awards can perpetuate the impoverishment of many single-parent households with whom family practitioners work on a daily basis" (Pirog-Good, 1993, p. 453).

There are still some legally sanctioned differences in the treatment of illegitimate children. The social worker's role in assisting illegitimate children may involve such areas as inheritance, workers compensation, Social Security, and paternity and child support. Generally, if a father acknowledges in writing that the child is his, this is sufficient to establish paternity. Some states require that this be done in a judicial proceeding, while others allow this to be handled administratively.

DNA testing is not yet admissible in every state for purposes of establishing paternity. While companies doing these tests are claiming a 96% to 99.98% certainty rate, the Supreme Court has not yet ruled on its acceptability for purposes of paternity verification. Many states, however, have ruled such testing as admissible evidence and have passed regulations based upon the Uniform Paternity Determination Act ("UPDA"). These statutes acknowledge a presumption of paternity if the testing procedure meets acceptable laboratory standards. State courts or administrative agencies oversee the suitability of testing procedures to protect the putative father's civil rights and to expedite paternity identification. The federal government has also endorsed genetic testing and has required states to set up DNA testing programs if they wish to take full advantage of federal money through AFDC [42 U.S.C.A. 666(a)(5)(A)(West 1991)].

Interestingly, paternity actions are more often brought by government entities than by individuals (Deparle, 1993). The incentive is to locate the putative father (Klawitter, 1994) so that public welfare benefits may be discontinued.

REFERENCES

Danziger, S., & Nichols-Casebolt, A. (September 1990). Child support in paternity cases. *Social Service Review,* 458-474.

Deparle, J. (July 14, 1993). Big rise in births outside wedlock. *New York Times*, A1, A14.

Garbarino, J., & Associates. (1992). *Children and families: The social environment* (2nd ed.). New York: Aldine.

Garfinkel, I., Meyer, D., & Sandefur, G. (1992). The effects of alternative child support systems on Blacks, Hispanics, and non-Hispanic Whites. *Social Service Review, 66*(4), 505-523.

Klawitter, M. (1994). Child support awards and the earnings of divorced noncustodial fathers. *Social Service Review, 68*(3), 351-368.

Liebmann, G. (1993). The AFDC conundrum: A new look at an old institution. *Social Work, 38*, 36-43.

Pirog-Good, M. (1993). Child support guidelines and the economic well-being of children in the United States. *Family Relations, 42*, 453-461.

Siegal v. Kizer
15 Cal.Rptr.2d 607 (Cal.App. 2 Dist. 1993)

FACTS: Judith Siegal, executrix for the estate of her mother (Rose), appealed a decision of the California Department of Health Services denying her mother Medi-Cal (Medicaid) benefits, resulting in a $40,000 loss to the estate.

In 1973, Rose Siegal's three daughters funded a living trust for her benefit. The trust provided that Rose was to receive the income from the trust's assets, and upon her death the trust would be divided between the three daughters. The trust also provided that in the event of an emergency, such as an accident, the trustees were required to pay for Rose's care with a portion of the trust principal as deemed necessary or appropriate by the trustees to meet such emergency. The trustees were given discretion to determine whether there was an emergency that warranted invading the principal. If so, the amount of trust funds needed to deal with the situation would be decided by the trustees. The exercise of discretion by the trustees was final and not subject to question by any person.

In August 1988, Rose, who suffered from Alzheimer's disease, moved into a long-term care facility. In March 1989, Judith Siegal applied for Medi-Cal on her mother's behalf. The Department of Public Services denied the application, arguing that the principal of the trust, approximately $184,938, was available to Rose.

ISSUE: Are discretionary trust funds in which the beneficiary's access to the principal is restricted considered to be available property in determining Medicaid eligibility?

DECISION: No. "[S]ince Rose was the income beneficiary of the trust with no ownership in the corpus and had only restricted access to the principal, the corpus of the trust was, therefore, not an available resource in determining Medi-Cal eligibility" (p. 610). However, the court did note that the income Rose received from the trust was an available eligibility resource.

REASONING: The California State Welfare and Institutions Code 14006 subdivision (c) stated that for determining Medi-Cal eligibility "resources shall be determined, defined, counted, and valued in accordance with the federal law governing resources under Title XIX of the federal Social Security Act." Therefore, resources considered exempt under the Social Security Act would be excluded from consideration when determining Medi-Cal eligibility.

Section 50489 of the California Code of Regulations, which governs eligibility for Medi-Cal benefits, provided in part that "real or personal property held in trust for the applicant or beneficiary shall be exempt if the applicant or beneficiary cannot obtain access to the principal of the trust." This law also stated that "provisions of this section shall not apply if the trust agreement clearly specifies that the applicant or beneficiary is the income-beneficiary only and has no ownership interest in the corpus of the trust" (p. 610).

The court concluded that since Rose Siegal was only the income beneficiary of the trust with no ownership in the corpus of the trust and only had highly restricted access to the principal of the trust, the resources were not to be considered "available" when considering Medi-Cal eligibility. This court's decision is consistent with decisions made in other states which have held that discretionary trust funds in which the beneficiary's access to the principal is restricted are not available property in determining Medicaid eligibility.

IMPLICATIONS: This case illustrates societal competition for limited resources. Social services are provided to those members of society who would otherwise be unable to gain access to these benefits. Since these services are scarce and often of significant real dollar value, fair and efficient disbursement is sought through instituting eligibility requirements. In the case of Medicaid, a determination of ineligibility can result in significant personal financial loss to the applicant. Thus, for potential beneficiaries, there may exist a financial motivation to manipulate personal resources to ensure access to Medicaid.

The elderly may find themselves in this situation because Medicaid may cover only a percentage of "reasonable charges" for medical services (Gilfix & Gilfix, 1993). Due to this lapse in coverage, the acutely ill elderly often experience the need to "spend down." Spend-down occurs when chronically ill individuals spend their assets down to the threshold of Medicaid eligibility. Although Medicaid was designed to protect older Americans against impoverishment, lapses in coverage and the costs associated with care for a chronic illness have caused many elderly to experience spend-down requirements (Branch et al., 1988).

To avoid this impoverishment, a trust is often used as a means to secure assets and ensure Medicaid eligibility. When assets are transferred out of an estate and into a trust, Medicaid ineligibility may still exist for up to thirty months. The same thirty-month ineligibility applies when real property (i.e., a house) is transferred to anyone other than a spouse or a disabled or minor child (Gilfix & Gilfix, 1993). The trust exemplified in this case was one which was created for the parent by the child. As shown in this example, this type of trust can coexist harmoniously with Medicaid requirements.

Unfortunately, the effect of this manipulation of resources to ensure Medicaid eligibility may compromise the overall efficiency of the system, causing fewer resources to be available for those most needy. It must be ensured that the rules governing resource allocation have their intended effect and lead to the greatest service accessibility to those most in need of those resources. Furthermore, the issues of acute illness, spend-down, and Medicaid eligibility bring into sharp focus the need to further discuss policy to address the medical care requirements of the chronically ill.

REFERENCES

Branch, L., Friedman, D., Cohen, M., Smith, N., & Socholitzky, E. (1988). Impoverishing the elderly: A case study of the financial risk of spend-down among Massachusetts elderly people. *The Gerontologist, 28*, 648-652.

Gilfix, M., & Gilfix, M.G. (June 1993). Elders and nursing home expenses: Preserving client assets. *Trial*, 37-40.

Anderson v. Edwards
115 S.Ct. 1291 (1995)

FACTS: This case is concerned with the "family filing unit" rule, 42 U.S.C. sec. 602(a)(38), which is a federal statute created to determine the status and eligibility for benefits to families with dependent children. The law requires that "all cohabiting nuclear family members be grouped into a single 'assistance unit' (AU)" for the above purposes (p.1293). Simultaneously, California has a law, the 'non-sibling filing unit rule,' which groups all children living in the same household under the care of one adult, regardless of their status to each other, in the same classification as the federal statute.

Plaintiffs in this case are a grandmother and her dependent granddaughter, and two dependent grandnieces who are sisters. Upon application of the California statute, this family, and many others, had a decrease in benefits because the children were considered as a "unit" under federal law even though they did not comprise a "nuclear" family in the usual sense of the term. Thus, under the state statute they were eligible for less assistance. Verna Edwards and her dependents brought this suit against the California Department of Social Services, which is in charge of administering the Aid to Families with Dependent Children program (AFDC).

ISSUE: Does the federal family filing unit law prohibit California from removing the distinction between a "nuclear" family unit and a family consisting of an adult and various dependents not directly related, thereby decreasing benefits under the AFDC?

DECISION: No. The Supreme Court stated "this statute [the California statute] is reasonably construed to allow States, in determining a child's need (and therefore how much assistance she will receive), to take into consideration the income and resources of all cohabiting children and relatives also claiming AFDC assistance" (p.1293).

REASONING: The Supreme Court, taking into account the national implications of potential inconsistencies in the application of the federal statute, granted *certiorari* to resolve this issue. In its discussion, it explained that AFDC was "designed to provide financial assistance to needy dependent children and the parents or relatives who live with and care for them" [*Shea v. Vialpando*, 94 S.Ct. 1746, 1750 (1974)]. The Court argued that the purpose of the federal assistance program was to provide for children and families' needs regardless of their actual familial relations. The court reasoned that the primary purpose of the legislation is to provide as much assistance to the largest number of eligible persons possible. By creating a state law further narrowing eligibility, individual children might be eligible for less funds, but more families could benefit from the state's resources. The court further stipulated that when a state is legislating with regard to a federal statute, it has great latitude. The Supreme Court, like the lower federal courts, often chooses to defer to state legislatures. Here, the ultimate issue is one of state funds and the way in which they will be dispensed.

While the court found the California law valid, it argued, citing section 233.20(a)(2)(viii), that a state cannot create a situation in which AFDC eligibility is invalidated or decreased "solely because of the presence in the household of a non-legally responsible individual" (p.1299). The Court further explained that it is not for this reason that plaintiffs had a reduction in assistance but rather because of the very definition of the AU that was implemented as a measure of an "income unit" within this level.

In conclusion, the Court referred to the inequities that would be present without the California law as the numbers of dependents got larger. It found that "the California Rule sensibly and equitably eliminates these disparities by providing that equally sized and equally needy households will receive equal AFDC assistance" (p. 1299).

IMPLICATIONS: This decision exemplifies the public assistance dilemma which exists in this country and persists at the core of many debates both on the state and federal level (Hagen & Davis, 1994; Halter, 1994; Meyer, 1994). The opinion shows a trend toward no longer "rewarding" those with more dependents, regardless of whether they are the caretaker's children or other relations. It also sets a standard whereby needs will be met as equitably as possible and also encourages those involved in the AFDC program to seek employment and leave welfare rolls (Hamilton et al., 1994; Coulton et al., 1993; Caputo, 1993).

REFERENCES

Caputo, R. (1993). Family poverty, unemployment rates, and AFDC payments: Trends among blacks and whites. *The Journal of Contemporary Human Services, 74*(9), 515-526.

Coulton, C., Crowell, L., & Verma, N. (1993). How time-limited eligibility affects general assistance clients: An Ohio study shows that few former recipients are finding work. *Public Welfare, 51*(3), 29-36.

Hagen, J., & Davis, L. (1994). Women on welfare talk about reform. *Public Welfare, 52*(3), 30-40.

Halter, A. (1994). The Family Support Act: Reinventing the wheel? *Social Work, 39*(5), 526-532.

Hamilton, W., Burstein, N., Moss, D., & Hargreaves, M. (1994). New York State's experiment with economic incentives. *Public Welfare, 52*(1), 6-17.

Meyer, C. (1994). The latent issues of welfare reform. *AFFILIA: The Journal of Women amd Social Work, 9*(3), 229-231.

CHAPTER 7
Social Workers in Court

State v. Bush
442 S.E. 2d 437 (W.Va. 1994)

FACTS: The defendant, Denzil Bush, was convicted on two counts of second degree murder for the shooting deaths of his former girlfriend and her boyfriend. At trial, he acknowledged that he killed the victims. This appeal is based on his claim that the state violated his Fifth Amendment right against self-incrimination by introducing testimony as to his mental competency from a licensed clinical social worker, Robin Straight, and a licensed clinical psychologist, William Fremouw. Both individuals had performed pre-trial psychological tests of the defendant.

At the request of the sheriff's department, Straight examined the defendant within several hours after the crime. Fremouw examined the defendant prior to trial pursuant to an order of the court after the defendant indicated that he "may rely upon the defense of insanity . . . but if he does so, [he] does not intend to introduce any expert testimony" (p. 438).

During the trial the defendant testified that he was not capable of committing first-degree murder because he was under the influence of drugs and alcohol. In response, the state presented Straight, who testified that the defendant was " . . . fully oriented to person, place and time. There was no evidence of hallucinatory [or] . . . delusional thinking. His recent and remote memory were fully intact. He showed no peculiarities in his mood or affect. His general fund of information was not impoverished" (p. 438). Straight also testified that she believed the defendant was able to formulate intent at the time of the murders. Similarly, Fremouw attested that the defendant was "not suffering from a psychotic condition, he [was] not mentally retarded and the effects of drugs and alcohol did not diminish his ability to premeditate" (p. 439). The trial record established that neither expert witness revealed any self-incriminating statements that the defendant may have made during the course of their respective examinations.

ISSUE: Does expert testimony concerning a defendant's mental capacity from witnesses who had performed psychological evaluations on a defendant at the request of the state violate that defendant's right against self-incrimination?

DECISION: No. The testimony did not violate the defendant's Fifth Amendment rights since the defendant raised the issue of diminished capacity, and the expert testimony did not include incriminating statements that may have been made by the defendant. The court noted that the defendant's testimony on drug and alcohol usage put his competency at issue even though he did not assert an insanity defense.

REASONING: The Fifth Amendment provides that "[n]o person . . . shall be compelled in any criminal case to be a witness against himself." The court noted that prior case law has interpreted this right to apply to court-ordered psychiatric examinations. If the state orders a defendant to undergo a forced examination, any incriminating statements made are protected and inadmissible in court. In addition, although Straight did not perform a court-ordered evaluation of the defendant, she conducted a psychological evaluation as an agent of the state since it was performed at the request of the sheriff's department. Consequently, the appellate court applied the same analysis as to whether her testimony violated the defendant privilege against self-incrimination as it applied to Fremouw's testimony, which was based on a court-ordered evaluation.

The court held that neither expert witnesses' testimony violated the defendant's right against self-incrimination since it did not contain statements about what led to the murders, the murders themselves, or any of the defendant's statements about the murders. The testimony only contained statements as to the defendant's self-reported drug use and mental status.

Although the defendant did not use an insanity defense, he put his competency at issue. The defendant sought to reduce the murders from first to second degree by suggesting that his alcohol and drug use diminished his ability to formulate a specific intent to kill. Under such circumstances, expert testimony about the defendant's mental status is admissible and not a violation of the defendant's Fifth Amendment right against self-incrimination.

IMPLICATIONS: Since the 1980s, social workers have been recognized as expert witnesses (Gothard, 1989). While this represents an elevation in the state of the profession, it raises important questions. Who is the social worker's client? Is the social worker acting as an advocate for the client or as a court-appointed neutral expert?

The Code of Ethics for the National Association of Social Workers' states in section II(H) that "[t]he social worker should respect the privacy of clients and hold in confidence all information obtained in the course of professional service." An exception to this rule is found in Section II(H)(1) which states that "[t]he social worker should share with others confidences revealed by clients, without their consent, only for compelling professional reasons." Compelling professional reasons include those imposed by state reporting requirements.

The level of confidentiality of the professional relationship is determined by the social worker's role in the relationship (Schultz, 1991). It is therefore important that social workers be clear as to what their professional role is and be able to communicate that role to those with whom they are working. Their role must be disclosed at the start of the professional relationship to ensure that the level of confidentiality in the relationship is understood.

For much of the work in which a social worker engages, the maintenance of confidentiality is essential for the work to progress. However, it is generally accepted that no privilege exists when the client is evaluated as part of a state- or court-ordered evaluation (Seelig, 1990).

REFERENCES

Gothard, S. (1989). Power in the court: The social worker as an expert witness. *Social Work, 34*, 65-67.

Schultz, L. (1991). Social workers as expert witnesses in child abuse cases: A format. *Journal of Independent Social Work, 5*(1), 69-87.

Seelig, J. (1990). Privileged communication. *Journal of Independent Social Work, 4*, 75-80.

Polotzola v. Missouri Pacific R. Co.
610 So.2d 903 (La.App. 1 Cir. 1992)

FACTS: The plaintiff in this case, Dommie Polotzola, was employed as a bridge tender by Missouri Pacific Railroad since 1975. In October of 1986, Polotzola claimed he tripped on uneven boards near the bridge tender's shack and injured his right shoulder as he reached out to break his fall. During the course of treatment for injuries sustained in his fall, Polotzola suffered an allergic reaction to the iodine used in diagnostic tests. The drug Xanac was proscribed to alleviate the symptoms associated with this allergic reaction. Polotzola became addicted to the Xanac and was hospitalized for treatment of this addiction.

Two years after his accident, Polotzola filed suit against the railroad, alleging that the railroad was negligent in maintaining and inspecting the wooden walkway where he fell. He claimed that despite two shoulder surgeries, he was still unable to lift anything with his right arm. He also complained that he continued to experience dizziness, headaches, ringing in his ears, disorientation, and short-term memory loss brought on by his allergic reaction to radiopaque iodine.

At trial, the court allowed the defense to introduce medical records generated during the course of Polotzola's hospitalization for his addiction to Xanac. These records included the report of a social worker. The social worker's records included references made by Mrs. Polotzola regarding her husband's alcoholism, wife beating, and arrest and guilty plea on a marijuana charge.

During the trial, the defense presented evidence that would tend to show that Polotzola drank excessively and that many of the types of psychological problems Polotzola experienced could be caused or aggravated by alcohol use. Testimony of Polotzola's co-workers tended to support the conclusion that no tripping hazards existed at the work site on the day of Polotzola's accident. The jury returned a verdict in favor of the railroad, and judgement was entered dismissing the suit.

Polotzola appealed the judgement, asserting that the admission into evidence of the social worker's notes violated a Louisiana statute which provides that the communications of a client to a board-certified social worker are privileged.

ISSUE: Can client communications to a board-certified social worker lose their privileged status under a state statute?

DECISION: Yes. A plaintiff waives the right to keep confidential communications made to a social worker confidential by bringing an action to recover damages for personal injuries and raising the issue of whether mental and emotional difficulties suffered were due to the complained of injury.

REASONING: Polotzola claimed that his mental and emotional difficulties were solely the result of reaction to the radiopaque iodine used to diagnose his shoulder injury. He thus placed at issue his mental and emotional state both before and after the accident.

The Louisiana statute at issue provided an exception for certain communications that would ordinarily be privileged. La.R.S. 13:3734C(3) provided that, "if any person brings an action to recover damages, in tort or for worker's compensation . . . for personal injuries, such action shall be deemed to constitute a consent by the person who brings such action that any health care provider who has attended such person may disclose any communication which was necessary to enable him to diagnose, treat, prescribe or act for said patient." The psychiatrist responsible for treating Polotzola during his hospitalization for treatment of his Xanac addiction testified that he used the social worker's notes in treating Polotzola. Given that testimony, communications made to the social worker during group therapy could not be claimed as privileged under the statute.

IMPLICATIONS: Many states provide a privilege for communications made to health care providers, including social workers, for treatment of a condition affecting the patient's physical or mental health. It is clear, however, that this privilege may be waived when a patient brings a suit for personal injuries in which the patient alleges that the acts of a third party caused some particular physical or mental injury. If the injuries of which the plaintiff complains bear some relationship to health problems for which treatment was sought in the past, the privilege is waived.

What is interesting about this case is that in deciding to whom the privilege applied, the court looked not at who made the communication, but rather at the purpose behind the communication. Since the person making the communication testified that her sole purpose for making the communication was to help her husband get well, the court viewed the privilege as attaching to the person for whose benefit the communication was made. Had Mrs. Polotzola testified that she made the communication with the intent of receiving counseling for her own emotional difficulties, the outcome might have been different. Under those circumstances, the privilege would have applied to Mrs. Polotzola and communications made to the social worker during group therapy may have been deemed privileged, thus preserving the sanctity of the relationship between the social worker and client.

State v. Decker
842 P.2d 500 (Wash.App.Div. 1 1992)

FACTS: In this Washington State case, juvenile Joseph Decker was convicted on an assault charge and ordered by the trial court to have a predisposition psychological evaluation. Without the presence of his attorney, the court agreed to stipulate that "any discussion with the evaluator in reference to matters that have not been adjudicated, will be granted use immunity" (p. 501). Decker appealed this decision, claiming that it violated his Fifth Amendment right against self-incrimination and Sixth Amendment right to counsel.

ISSUE: Absent a showing of special circumstances, do juvenile defendants in non-capital cases have a right to have an attorney present during a psychological examination for pre-sentencing purposes?

DECISION: No. While the United States Supreme Court has generally held that criminal defendants may not be compelled to testify against themselves, the Court has not applied this principle to juveniles in a postadjudicatory proceeding [*In re Gault,* 87 S.Ct. 1428, 1455 n.48 (1967)].

REASONING: The court cited a Washington State precedent [*State v. Escoto,* 108 Wash.2d 1, 735 P.2d 1310 (1987)]:

> It is essential to consider the applicability of the privilege against self-incrimination to the circumstances of this case in light of the unique rehabilitative purpose of the disposition of juveniles. Because it is crucial for the court to have access to information obtained from the psychological evaluation . . . , I believe that less stringent application of the privilege against self-incrimination is warranted under these circumstances than in an adult setting (pp. 10-11).

Neither the *Escoto* court nor the U.S. Supreme Court in *Estelle v. Smith* [101 S.Ct. 1866 (1981)] directly addressed the issue of the constitutional right to have an attorney present during the pre-sentence evaluation. The Supreme Court, in a footnote, ventured that "an attorney present during the psychiatric interview could contribute little and might seriously disrupt the examination" (p. 1866, n. 14).

This court recognized that the trial court and the psychologist agreed that the presence of an attorney might compromise the evaluation. The trial court was sensitive to the need to not undermine other constitutional procedural protections. The psychologist was instructed to avoid discussing unadjudicated matters.

IMPLICATIONS: The Fifth Amendment to the United States Constitution provides that: "No person . . . shall be compelled in any criminal case to be witness against himself." This Amendment protects against coercion to confess to a crime. The Sixth Amendment ensures the right to legal assistance in all criminal proceedings. However, constitutional protections afforded adults charged with crimes are not necessarily applicable to juveniles. Juvenile law and procedures reflect civil law more than criminal law. Rules of evidence are less rigid and procedural safeguards not as stringent.

Is a court-ordered psycho-social, psychological, or a psychiatric interview part of a "criminal" proceeding? The U.S. Supreme Court has not definitely decided. Consequently, states have come up with a multiplicity of approaches. Social workers and other mental health professionals evaluating juvenile offenders must be aware of the legal status of their role. Can they be called upon to testify regarding everything the juvenile related, including incriminating remarks, or may their testimony be limited to their professional judgement of the juvenile's state of mind? This remains a very unsettled area of law and social work.

Gentry v. State
443 S.E.2d 667 (Ga.App. 1994)

FACTS: Appellant Gentry was convicted of two counts of molesting his two stepchildren. The stepchildren's mother, the investigating police officer, and a social worker all testified that the stepchildren had indicated that they had been molested by Gentry. This testimony was admitted into evidence at Gentry's trial. Also admitted were results of a penile plethysmograph test. This procedure involves placing a gauge around a subject's penis, showing the subject various aural and visual stimulation, and then measuring the change in the circumference of the subject's penis. If the subject is aroused by non-normative stimuli or is not aroused by normative stimuli, the results may be evidence of a subject's state of mind. Gentry objected to the results of the penile plethysmograph being admitted into evidence.

ISSUE: Are results of a penile plethysmograph test admissible as scientific evidence?

DECISION: No. The standard for admitting novel scientific evidence is "whether the procedure or technique in question has reached a scientific stage of verifiable certainty . . ." [*Harper v. State*, 249 Ga. 519, 525-526, 292 S.E.2d 389 (1982)].

REASONING: A number of states have addressed the question of admissibility of penile plethysmograph evidence. All have rejected it based on a lack of scientific certainty and unreliability [see *In the Interest of A.V.*, 849 S.W.2d 393 (Tex.App. 1993); *Nelson v. Jones*, 78 P.2d 964 (Alaska 1989); *Dutchess County Dept of Social Services v. Mr. G.*, 141 Misc.2d 641 (1988); *People v. John W.*, 229 Cal.Rptr. 783 (Cal.App. 1 Dist. 1986)]. The court noted that no national guidelines have yet been recognized by the scientific community.

The court noted that there might be sufficient evidence to convict Gentry without the plethysmograph test results. In fact, the stepchildren's testimony was admissible. In making this determination the court stated that child victims' statements could be admissible by taking into account the following:

(1) the atmosphere and circumstances under which the statement *was made* (including the time, the place, and the people present thereat); (2) the spontaneity of the child's

statement to the persons present; (3) the child's age; (4) the child's general demeanor; (5) the child's condition (physical or emotional); (6) the presence or absence of threats or promise of benefits; (7) the presence or absence of drugs or alcohol; (8) the child's general credibility; (9) the presence or absence of any coaching by parents or other third parties before or at the time of the child's statement, and the type of coaching and circumstances surrounding the same; and, the nature of the child's statement and type of language used therein; and (10) the consistency between repeated out-of-court statements by the child. These factors are to be applied neither in mechanical nor mathematical fashion, but in that manner best calculated to facilitate determination of the existence or absence of the requisite degree of trustworthiness [*Gregg v. State,* 411 S.E.2d 65 (1991)].

IMPLICATIONS: As the number of reported sex-offender crimes continues to rise, social workers involved in the human services and criminal justice system are being called as expert witnesses. Social workers may be involved in ascertaining the nature and impetus of deviant sexual behavior, in treating forensic and sex offenders, in caring for the victims of these offenders, and frequently testifying as to the biopsychological factors which may be based on the offenders' fantasies, desires, or psychopathology (Solomon & Draine, 1995; Teplin, 1990). Rehabilitative efforts have been largely ineffective, and therefore extended incarceration has been the recourse of choice. This has been decried by some and applauded by others (Prins, 1990; Prison Reform Trust, 1990; Roman and Gerbring, 1989; The Suzy Lamplugh Trust, 1990). Whether incarceration or rehabilitation is the dominant response, social workers will be increasingly called upon to interact with high-risk sex offenders (Laflen & Sturm, 1994).

REFERENCES

Laflen, B., & Sturm, W., Jr. (1994). Understanding and working with denial in sexual offenders. *Journal of Child Sexual Abuse, 3*(4), 19-36.

Prins, H. (1990). Mental abnormality and criminality: An uncertain relationship. *Medicine, Science, and the Law, 30,* 247-258.

Prison Reform Trust. (1990). *Sex offenders in prison*. Rochdale, RAP Ltd: Author.

Roman, D., & Gerbring, D. (1989). The mentally disordered criminal offender: A description based on demographic, clinical, & MMPI data. *Journal of Clinical Psychiatry, 45,* 983-990.

Solomon, P., & Draine, J. (1995). Issues in serving the forensic client. *Social Work, 40*(1), 25-33.

The Suzy Lamplugh Trust. (1990). *Working with the sex offender: Report of the inter-disciplinary conference.* London: Author.

Teplin, L. (1990). The prevalence of severe mental disorder among male urban jail detainees: Comparison with the Epidemiologic Catchment Area program. *American Journal of Public Health, 80,* 663-669.

CHAPTER 8
Social Workers as Employees

Birthisel v. Tri-Cities Health Services
424 S.E.2d 606 (W.Va.1992)

FACTS: Deborah Birthisel was a social worker employed by Tri-Cities Health Services. As a result of an upcoming accreditation visit from the National Association of Private Psychiatric Hospitals, the staff at River Park Hospital were told by the director to ensure that the master treatment plan of each file contained the relevant treatment strategies that coincided with the weekly planning notes. Staff were asked to add or change information where necessary to comply with the memo. Ms. Birthisel believed this request was unethical. After further clarification from the director, she refused to comply. She "felt that she could not ethically make any changes to the charts she had been asked to review because they were closed charts of patients with whom she had no contact. She feared that to do so would be to falsify the records and would constitute a violation of the West Virginia Social Work Code of Ethics" (p. 609), and would put her in jeopardy of losing her social work license. Ms. Birthisel tendered her resignation and sued the hospital for wrongful discharge.

ISSUE: Is a social worker protected against discharge by claiming that her employer's requests would constitute a violation of a state's public policy?

DECISION: No. A social worker is not protected from discharge unless the state's public policy provides sufficient specific guidance.

REASONING: In general, an employer may terminate an at-will employee. But this right "must be tempered by the principle that where the employer's motivation for the discharge is to contravene some substantial public policy, then the employer may be liable to the employee for damages occasioned by this discharge" [*Harless v. First National Bank in Fairmont,* 162 W.Va. 116, 246 S.E.2d 270 (1978)]. In this case, the statutory language Birthisel relied on was not sufficiently specific, and she could not identify any clear legal violation she was being asked to undertake. Her employer was not asking her to falsify records but to simply determine if the records were complete and up to date.

IMPLICATIONS: While a social worker may read the NASW code of ethics broadly, a court is more apt to hold that only specific statutory or regulatory language will prohibit specific employer behavior. It is unwise for a social worker to rely on extremely general language as an expression of a state's public policy.

"Public policy" is a general term which is difficult to define. Sources of a state's public policy include legislation, administrative rules, regulations, or decisions, and judicial decisions. As the New Jersey Supreme Court wrote in a similar case: "[A]n employee should not have the right to prevent his or her employer from pursuing its business because the employee perceives that a particular business decision violates the employee's personal morals . . ." [*Pierce v. OrthoPharmaceutical Corp.,* 84 N.J. 58, 72 (1980)].

Doe v. City of Chicago
883 F. Supp. 1126 (N.D.Ill. 1994)

FACTS: Plaintiffs, in the process of applying for positions in the Chicago police force, were required to undergo various tests. These included written examinations, psychological examinations, and physical examinations. While both plaintiffs passed the first two and had reason to believe that they would be candidates for the police force, they had yet to pass their physical examinations. One of the plaintiffs, in fact, had been extended a conditional offer which would be final, contingent upon a background check, a fitness test, and the physical examination. The other plaintiff did not have a conditional offer.

The plaintiffs brought this suit against the doctor who performed the physical examinations and the city for conducting HIV tests without their consent and for denying them positions or consideration in the police force solely because they tested positive for the virus. Specifically, the plaintiffs claim that defendants maintain a custom, practice, or policy of: (1) testing candidates for HIV as a condition of employment without medical justification; (2) requiring a physical examination prior to providing candidates with a valid conditional offer of employment; (3) failing to obtain consent or provide counseling with regard to HIV tests; and (4) refusing to hire candidates solely because of their HIV-positive status. The defendants made a motion to dismiss, and the court in this proceeding heard the claims by both parties to decide if plaintiffs have a justiciable claim.

ISSUE: May a public employer test employment applicants for HIV?

DECISION: Yes.

REASONING: Section 504 of the Rehabilitation Act of 1973 establishes that where an organization receives federal funds, medical tests may be done at will by those receiving the funds. The city's argument, therefore, was that they could implement physical examinations to determine a potential candidate's ability to perform the functions required by the potential position (partially federally funded). Although section 504 permits pre-employment testing, it did not permit discrimination based on an HIV-positive blood test. Therefore, the plaintiffs have a valid allegation of discrimination. Therefore, the case will be heard.

IMPLICATIONS: Disability discrimination is a subset of both employment law and civil rights. The purpose of this case was to ascertain the ability of justifiable HIV testing in the public sector as a requirement for employment and to further ascertain if the courts will hear this type of claim. This decision indicates that plaintiffs can maintain a case against a municipality.

Discrimination against people with HIV/AIDS has taken many forms: housing, public accommodations, education, and of course attitudinal. With more than 170,000 deaths reported from AIDS, and one million cases of HIV (Centers for Disease Control, 1993), the spread of negative attitudes will spread as rapidly as the disease itself. Legal remedies are one way to slow the unjustifiable stereotyping and misconceptions. In the area of employment, people with AIDS/HIV are seeking an equality of opportunity, a reasonable accommodation.

REFERENCES

Centers for Disease Control. (1993). *Facts about the scope of HIV/AIDS epidemic in the United States*. Atlanta: Author.

Cunico v. Pueblo School District No. 60
917 F.2d 431 (10th Cir. 1990)

FACTS: Plaintiff, a white social worker, earned a Master's degree which certified her as a social worker under Colorado law. This enabled her to seek employment in the Colorado public schools and after a three-year probation period, earn "tenure status." While the plaintiff was under the impression that this status meant security in her position, Colorado state law does not support this.

During the 1981-1982 school year, the year the plaintiff would achieve tenure status, her school district was forced to examine its budget as it was experiencing financial difficulties. Social workers in the district were scheduled to be dismissed because they were not seen as essential as classroom educators. When the district learned that state law required a minimum of two social workers, it modified its plan and retained the two social workers in the district with the most seniority.

In justification of its employment reductions, the school board explained how it came to its conclusions. It stated that the cancellation of contracts was to be according to seniority. Furthermore, the board supported the policy that "in the event of a reduction in force, the District shall make reasonable effort to maintain, as a minimum, the percentage of minority teachers employed within the District" (p. 435). Implemented along with this policy was a hearing process whereby dismissed employees could make a request to have their dismissal reviewed. A hearing would determine if the cancellation of their contract was "arbitrary or capricious with respect to the individual or otherwise unjustified" (p. 435).

All of the dismissed social workers requested hearings. One of the complaints, by the only black social worker in the district, Wayne Hunter, was reviewed. While officials examining his complaint felt that his dismissal would be a temporary setback in the affirmative action program, his dismissal was neither capricious nor done discriminatorily. The hearing officer found that in Hunter's case there was a special duty to retain a minority employee and special consideration was called for. Hunter was reinstated while the other social workers were permanently dismissed. Sometime later, a fourth social worker, an Hispanic, was rehired for his "ability to speak Spanish" even though speaking Spanish was not a requirement and his seniority was not greater than that of the plaintiff's.

The plaintiff brought suit under 42 U.S.C. Sections 1981, 1983, and under Section 706 of Title VII of the Civil Rights Act of 1964, as amended (42 U.S.C. Section 2000e-5).

ISSUE: May a board of education rehire a black and an Hispanic social worker in keeping with its affirmative action plan, while its seniority policy, if followed, would have retained a white social worker with more seniority?

DECISION: No. "The District may defend its averred interest in assuring at least one position for a black administrator, however, only as a necessary measure to remedy past discrimination. Because there [was] no direct evidence of past or present discrimination against blacks by the District . . ." (p. 439), the District was not justified in overlooking the plaintiff's seniority.

REASONING: The court reasoned that "the purpose of race-conscious affirmative action must be to remedy the effects of past discrimination against a disadvantaged group that itself has been the victim of discrimination" (p. 437). The court had to determine whether this case was a violation of the Equal Protection Clause or Title VII because this would be the determining factor in deciding what level of proof would be necessary in order to justify the hiring or firing practices. The court said this was not a violation of equal protection because the only reason fewer blacks had roles as social workers was due to the lack of blacks in this work force, indicating that no past discrimination needed to be remedied. To avoid a Title VII violation, "the affirmative action plan must be justified by the existence of a manifest imbalance in a traditionally segregated job category" (p. 437). In the case of avoiding an Equal Protection violation, a "strict scrutiny" test would be implemented whereby the court would examine whether or not there exists a compelling state interest and whether the means to attain this interest were narrowly tailored. The court found that the social worker position was to go to the most qualified candidate and that the present system was set up to maintain rather than create a racial balance.

IMPLICATIONS: This case represents the conflict between affirmative action, equal employment policies, and employment rights. When do an individual's rights get trampled upon to further the rights of a community so long discriminated against? Affirmative action was instituted to remedy centuries of discrimination. Today there is a fine line when programs, instituted to create a diverse environment, become discriminatory against others. With more minorities in more elevated positions today, courts are hesitant to uphold affirmative action plans, regarding them as outdated and no longer appropriate. As this court stated,

> to accept defendant's argument would obtain the curious result of allowing employers to escape liability for discrimination by arguing that they would have hired no one if not allowed to discriminate. An employer who might be inclined to hire someone solely for racial reasons is not precluded from making the decision to hire no one, for the command of equal protection is observed either when the state terminates its preferential treatment of the person who benefits from the discrimination or when it extends such treatment to the person aggrieved (p. 442).

The problem remains, however, that in every choice for a candidate, whether it be for a job, a student in a school, or financial aid, there is one person who receives a benefit and one who does not. Choice, however, is not necessarily discrimination. The trend seems to be in the direction of reestablishing the principle that seniority, merit, and fitness will take precedence over traditional affirmative action policies. Statistical disparities, by themselves, will rarely be sufficient proof of discrimination and justify departing from an established policy of seniority and merit employment practices.

Murdock v. Higgins
527 N.W. 2d 1 (Mich.App. 1994)

FACTS: Plaintiff was an eighteen-year-old volunteer at the Kalamazoo Department of Social Services when he was sexually assaulted by his supervisor, Mark Kelley. Defendant Higgins, Kelley's supervisor, had previously received information indicating that Kelley had been seen in a park with young men. Higgins and Kelley had several discussions regarding Kelley's conduct, and Kelley promised to be more discreet. Higgins approached the local sheriff regarding Kelley's conduct, and the sheriff assured Higgins that there had been no reports or noted acts by Kelley regarding his "questionable conduct." Higgins suggested to Kelley, with regard to his sexual orientation, that another community might be more tolerant of him. Later in 1986 Kelley transferred.

In Kelley's new position he had contact with children and was the supervisor for the plaintiff he befriended. One evening they went to dinner and spent time at Kelley's residence. At some point in the evening Kelley "stroked plaintiff's leg, licked his ear, called him 'baby' and repeatedly attempted to push him onto the bed" (p. 3). Murdock tried to avoid this contact and suggested they leave and go to the hot tubs as had been discussed earlier in the evening. On their way there, Kelley told plaintiff "he had everything they needed in his little black bag, including soap, condoms, and vaseline" (p. 3). Once at the hot tubs, Murdock ran to call the police from a friend's home.

Murdock brought suit against the defendants, stating that they had breached a duty owed him by not hiring a competent employee and by not preventing Kelley's acts of misconduct. Furthermore, he alleged that the Kalamazoo Department of Social Services owed him a special duty to transmit "adverse employment information" and to protect him from harm. The defendants appealed.

ISSUE: Does a supervisor have a duty to divulge an employee's sexual activities and suspected homosexuality?

DECISION: No. The court concluded that while Higgins may have had a moral or social obligation to divulge his suspicions, there exists no legal duty to do so.

REASONING: While the court conceded that a duty may exist to use reasonable care in special relationships, it determined that no such relationship existed here. In determining this relationship, the court must ask "whether the plaintiff entrusted himself to the control and protection of the defendant, with a consequent loss of control to protect himself" (p. 3). The court held that when determining this special relationship, it was necessary to

> balance the societal interest involved, the severity of the risk, the burden upon the defendant, the likelihood of occurrence, and the relationship between the parties . . . and other factors which may give rise to a duty include the foreseeability of the [harm], the defendant's ability to comply with the proposed duty, the victim's inability to protect himself from the [harm], the costs of providing protection, and whether the plaintiff had bestowed some economic benefit on the defendant (p. 3).

Since no relationship was found between Higgins and Kelley, Higgins owed no duty to plaintiff to convey any information he may have had or sought out. Furthermore, even though Higgins had suspicions of Kelley's homosexuality, he had no reason to believe that he would be a threat to anyone at the department.

The court further stated that while an employer has a qualified privilege to give information about a former employee to a future employer, there is no legal obligation. Rather, "an imperfect obligation of a moral or social character" (p. 4) exists. Courts usually defer to the legislature's will. Making it a requirement to divulge information of this sort is not appropriate for the judiciary.

IMPLICATIONS: This case exemplifies the classic tension between an individual's right to privacy and the public's right to information. In an age when the fear of AIDS is so pronounced, are there circumstances under which a person's homosexuality should be divulged against that person's wishes? While this case does not directly address this question, the question looms very large.

The most important point which should be emphasized in this case was the minimal knowledge and suspicions upon which Higgins made his observations and judgements about Kelley. While the court followed an elaborate pattern of reasoning to show that no special duty existed, this case rested on very little evidence from its onset. A person talking to people in a park is not evidence of danger, social deviance, or any other type of harmful behavior. This case reflects society's interest in keeping confidential records, specifically those regarding employment. Furthermore, it is evident that a person's name and career can be marked by someone's "suspicions" of behavior which the believer divulges. The court itself stated that "there is a great societal interest in insuring that employment records are kept confidential. It is all too easy to envision a career destroyed by malefic information released by a disgruntled former employee" (p. 5). Sexual preference is a private choice and should be left to the individual.

As social workers, there is no greater a duty to divulge this information than there is to seek it out. The goal in the workplace is to foster equality, fairness, and productivity. This ruling can benefit social workers in their own positions as employees as well as their clients who might be compromised if a social worker were to reveal information regarding their sexuality. Thus, it will be a subjective reasoning test, as a social worker, to use reasonable judgement depending on the specific circumstances.

Ross v. Denver Dept. of Health and Hospitals
883 P.2d 516 (Colo.App. 1994)

FACTS: Plaintiff Mary Ross appealed a judgement from the district court which preempted Ross from receiving sick leave benefits to care for her "same-sex domestic partner." Ross was a social worker with the Department of Health and Hospitals when in 1991 she took three days to care for her partner. Ross was denied sick leave because under the Career Service Authority Rules, a domestic partner did not qualify as a "member of Ross' immediate family," and therefore sick leave benefits were unwarranted.

A hearing officer first heard the case and found that the interpretation of "immediate family" was discriminatory and in violation of the Career Service Authority's anti-discrimination rule. On this finding, the hearing officer found Ross had a right to her family leave sick benefits.

The Department, dissatisfied with this decision, appealed, and the decision was reversed based upon a finding that the interpretation of the Rules was erroneous. Ross sought relief in the district court and review of the Board's decision. The Board's decision was reversed, and the order of the hearing officer was reinstated.

ISSUE: Does the language "immediate family" discriminate against same-sex partners under Colorado's Career Service Authority Rules, when family sick leave benefits are sought?

DECISION: No. Sick leave benefits, under C.S.A. rules 11-32, are provided for as the "necessary care and attendance during sickness . . . of a member of the employee's immediate family" (p. 518). "Immediate family," as defined by the rules includes "husband, wife, son, daughter, mother, father, grandmother, grandfather, brother, sister, son-in-law, daughter-in-law, mother-in-law, father-in-law, brother-in-law, sister-in-law" (p. 518).

REASONING: The issues for the court to decide where whether C.S.A. Rule 19-10(c) superseded the "immediate family" definition and if so, was the denial of sick benefits in and of itself an act of discrimination against Ross because of her sexuality. The court's review of the decision was limited in that "as a general principle, courts defer to the interpretation of an administrative rule or regulation by the agency charged with its administration" (p. 519). The court reasoned that as the board had determined the definition and it administers the CSA rules, it was justified in its determination.

"When interpreting two statutory or regulatory sections, we must attempt to harmonize them in order to give effect to their purposes" (p. 519). The court's threshold test which would invalidate the regulations and rules would be to show they were invalid "beyond a reasonable doubt" (p. 519). The court concluded that the Board's interpretations of the rules were valid and reasonable and chose to use discretionary measures in deferring to the decisions of the board. The court stated further that since the rule applies equally to homosexuals and heterosexuals, no discrimination existed, reasoning that the only possible problem would be the language of "husband or wife" which only differentiated between married and unmarried couples and since Ross was not married she did not fall into this category.

As the court later conceded, Colorado law does not recognize a spousal relationship in same-sex couples. The court resolved this inconsistency by deferring to the legislature's responsibility to legislate on marriage laws, and the court had no obligation to enter into this issue. "If the agency definition is rational and valid, as we determine it is here, we must apply its plainly worded provisions" (p. 521).

In regard to the equal protection and due process issues, the "beyond a reasonable doubt" test was again implemented, and the court determined that since Ross was not treated any differently than anyone not married in a same-sex relationship, she was not discriminated against.

IMPLICATIONS: This case exemplifies legislation that inadvertently adversely affects homosexuals. While a statute may not "discriminate on its face," it certainly has discriminatory effects and may therefore be scrutinized by the courts. This court chose to defer to the legislature. The future effects of legislation such as this support the idea that same-sex relationships do not fall under "family or marriage" definitions.

Colorado law does not distinguish between same-sex couples in terms of commitment, time together, or benefits. This case represents a determination of the legislature and the law to disallow for same-sex couples to have the same benefits which heterosexuals receive.

The decision emphasizes that other cities have adopted rules to apply to "unmarried domestic partners" and are in fact on their way to including all of their citizens in the realm of protections and rights. In fact, a 1991 survey on domestic partners indicates that the number of couples living together is rising and that many cities, some states, and corporations are providing for benefits where legislation does not. This same survey found that 4.2 million households are made up of unmarried couples (Mackey, 1994). With these statistics in mind and the growing number of corporations providing insurance benefits for domestic partnerships, there is reason to believe that the gay community may, in time, receive greater benefits. Nonetheless, the political and economic realities may indicate a counter trend. Tax increases to fund additional health and welfare benefits for domestic partners may be unpopular. And there is concern, although unsupported by hard data, that the cost of domestic partner benefits would be disproportionately higher than costs for spousal benefits.

REFERENCES

Mackey, A. (April 4, 1994). Domestic partners benefits are catching on . . . slowly. *Business and Health, 12*, 73-76.

Belmont v. California State Personnel Board
111 Cal.Rptr. 607 (1974)

FACTS: Josephine Belmont and Glenda Pawsey, two psychiatric social workers employed by the Department of Social Welfare (DSW), filed for review of the department's order suspending them for five days without pay for "willful disobedience" under California law. The department sought to gather data on all its welfare recipients to be entered into a new computer system, for the purpose of streamlining record keeping. The DSW took action against Belmont and Pawsey when they refused to disclose information about mentally and emotionally disturbed persons receiving aid through the department, contending that the agency was breaching their "clients'" right to privacy by requiring that they supply confidential information without their clients' knowledge or consent, that the department's system was unnecessary, and that the information was not properly protected from easy access by those with no right to it. They argued that the department's order requiring them to participate in the invasion of their clients' privacy was contrary to the Fourteenth Amendment, was unlawful, and, therefore, need not be obeyed.

ISSUE: May a department of social welfare lawfully suspend its employees for refusing to obey an order?

DECISION: Yes. The court found that social workers employed by the DSW are legally bound to their employer. Public employees of a DSW may not, at their discretion, determine whether a lawful order is to be, or not to be, obeyed. Welfare recipients' information may be provided for entry into a computerized system. Doing so in no way infringes on a client's privacy rights.

REASONING: The court concluded that although social workers have an ethical duty of loyalty to safeguard their clients' confidential information, this "ethical right" does not constitute the legal right which they claim exists. The "clients" are first and foremost clients of the DSW. Where there is a conflict of interest between the social workers' code of ethics and their duties as employees of the state, the social workers' first duty is to their employers. State law clearly mandates that employees must not disrupt or impair the provision of public services they were hired to be provided [*Morrison v. Board of Education*, 461 P.2d 375 (1969)]. Therefore, it is essential to public service that employees comply with and obey all lawful orders and follow appropriate public policy [*Board of Education v. Swan,* 261 P.2d 261 (1953)].

IMPLICATIONS: Wrongful discharge of an employee is actionable in contract and tort law. In contract law, a party can sue for economic compensation. In tort law, punitive damages and damages for emotional distress may also be sought. In either case, the plaintiffs must show that the employer improperly terminated their employment. While an employer may not discharge an employee for refusing to perform an act that unquestionably violates law of public policy, an employee may not refuse to perform such tasks as are within those parameters. Defining public policy is not easy.

One court recently wrote:

> Jurists to this day have been unable to fashion a truly workable definition of public policy. Not being restricted to the conventional sources of positive law (constitutions, statutes, and judicial decisions), judges are frequently called upon to discern the dictates of sound public policy and human welfare based on nothing more than their own personal experiences and intellectual capacity [*Kessler v. Equity Management Inc.,* 572 A.2d 1144, 1148 (1990)].

A social worker may mistakenly believe that an employer is engaged in improper, unethical, or even illegal behavior. If this leads to the social worker's desire to refuse to do an assigned task, the social worker may be discharged as an employee. Nonetheless, there are "whistleblower" statutes in most states that prohibit an employer from initially taking adverse action against an employee or retaliating against that employee for reporting what was perceived to be improper or illegal activity.

Kilroy v. Lebanon Correctional Institution
575 N.E.2d 903 (Ohio.Ct.Cl. 1991)

FACTS: Social worker Vicki Kilroy was a contract employee for the Lebanon Correctional Institution social service department. Among her responsibilities was interviewing incoming inmates to ascertain what social services they might need. In July 1987, inmate William Wohfcil was assigned to Kilroy. Prison records indicate that Kilroy met with Wohfeil approximately twenty times within a five-month period. Kilroy testified that these visits lasted for 1-2 hours. Other prison employees testified that the visits would be more frequent and would sometimes last for half a day. In fact, employees noted that, in their estimation, Kilroy was spending an excessive amount of time with Wohfeil and that if Wohfeil's problems were so serious, psychiatric counseling should be proposed. After Kilroy's employment was completed, prison officials found pictures of Kilroy and her family and unsigned greeting cards in Wohfeil's cell. There was disagreement as to how these items found their way to Wohfeil's cell. Sometime later, Kilroy sought to do her master's degree research at the prison. The warden told several of his subordinates that he no longer wanted Kilroy at the prison and that he had "lost confidence in plaintiff and that he did not want her around." The warden also testified that he "did not approve of her demeanor with the inmates."

Kilroy filed a lawsuit, claiming that she was slandered.

ISSUE: If it is shown that defamatory remarks about a social worker are true, can a successful legal action be maintained?

DECISION: No. Kilroy alleged that statements made about her were injurious to her in her occupation as a social worker. Kilroy could not prove, by a preponderance of evidence, that her professional reputation had been injured, even if the remarks were defamatory.

REASONING: Ohio law defines "slander" as defamatory if such oral statements "import a charge of an indictable offense involving moral turpitude that subject the offender to infamous punishment, or tends to injure him in his trade, occupation, or profession" [35 *Ohio Jurisprudence 3d* 448 (1982)].

The warden asserted that it was important for prison personnel to not show favoritism to any one inmate. With 1,800 prisoners and only 150 employees, it was a legitimate concern that an excessive amount of time not be unnecessarily given to any one prisoner. Neither the warden nor any other prison officials made any inference that Kilroy was romantically involved with Wohfeil. The court found that:

> . . . plaintiff was spending a comparatively inordinate amount of time with inmate Wohfeil in a prison setting. What may be perfectly normal in an outside setting could be construed as improper in a prison setting. Therefore, truth is a complete defense even if the words could be construed as defamatory (p. 908).

IMPLICATIONS: Defamation lawsuits may be initiated based on wrongful discharge, employment discrimination, or breach of contract. Social workers may find themselves as defendants or plaintiffs in these types of lawsuits. To sustain a valid claim of defamation, several elements must be shown: (1) there was a defamation and false communication made; (2) that the communication asserted a fact regarding the plaintiff; (3) that the communication was published by the defendant; and (4) that the reputation of the plaintiff was damaged. Unless all four elements are proved, the action will be not sustainable. Even if all four elements can be proved, the defendant may have an absolute or qualified privilege to make an otherwise defamatory communication. Examples of absolute privilege include statements made during a trial, a legislative proceeding, or in the course of a client-attorney discussion. An example of qualified privilege includes good faith on the part of the defendant, or the communication was made because the defendant had the duty to do so. Social workers should take great care to ensure that defamatory statements are kept out of written communications such as progress notes, charts, newsletters, memoranda, and client files.

Ginsberg (1992) reports that only 1.4% of NASW members work in the field of corrections. Considering that the population of persons under authority of the corrections system is now over four million (*New York Times*, 1994), it appears that, as a profession, social work has not yet fully embraced the concept of working with criminal offenders. This is especially ironic since the founders of social work were often involved with prisons and prisoners. Brennan et al. (1986) envision the forensic social worker's job "to recognize and integrate the goals of criminal justice and mental health" (p. 342). Is it possible to advocate simultaneously for prisoners, victims, corrections institutions, and society? The role of social worker as advocate within the corrections environment (Severson, 1994) is still in the process of being defined, as are issues of confidentiality (Pollack, 1991), coercive treatment, punishment, overcrowding, etc.

REFERENCES

Brennan, T., Gedrich, A., Jacoby, S., Tardy, M., & Tyson, K. (June 1986). Forensic social work: Practice and vision. *Social Casework*, 340-350.

Ginsberg, L. (1992). *Social work almanac.* Washington D.C.: NASW Press.

NASW. (1994). *Social work speaks.* Washington, D.C.: Author.

New York Times. (October 28, 1994). U.S. prison population crosses one million mark. Al.

Pollack, D. (June 1991). Sharing information without forsaking personal privacy. *Corrections Today*, 30-32.

Severson, M. (1994). Adapting social work values to the corrections environment. *Social Work, 39*(4), 451-456.

Osborn v. Harrison School Dist. No. 2
844 P.2d 1283 (Colo.App. 1992)

FACTS: John Osborn served as a counselor for the Harrison School District since 1976. Requirements of the position of counselor, as set forth by the district, are a master's degree and completion of an approved graduate program in counseling. Similarly, requirements for social workers include a master's degree in social work and completion of an approved graduate-level school social work program. Osborn's salary schedule, based on his 14 years of experience, master's degree, and 48 hours of course work, entitled him to a total salary of $36,590. A social worker with 14 years of experience, a master's degree, and 48 hours of course work receives $39,544, as dictated by the salary schedule for social workers. Without a master's degree in social work, Osborn was not entitled to the comparable social work salary.

Osborn asserts that his salary should be the same as that of a social worker because the assigned duties are identical. Because less money is paid to a counselor than to a social worker with a similar education and level of experience for similar responsibilities, Osborn contends that his contract was breached. The school district moved for summary judgement, claiming that Board of Education statutes and the employment contract supported the salary differential and no breach of contract was involved.

ISSUE: Must mental health professionals performing identical duties receive comparable salaries despite differences in training?

DECISION: No. Rules and regulations may support salary differentiation based on educational requirements.

REASONING: Rules and regulations of the Board of Education provide the following stipulation:

> The board of a school district shall place each teacher in the school district on the salary schedule at least commensurate with, but not limited to, his education, prior experience, and experience in the district as provided in the salary schedule. Section 22-63-105(2), C.R.S. (1988).

The level of education required for a given salary schedule is left to the discretion of a board of education. The law further specifies that school district boards adopt salary schedules which may be by job description and job definition. Accordingly, distinguishing social workers from teachers is permissible.

Though identical duties were performed by counselors and social workers, the different educational requirements are viewed as a reasonable basis for the difference in salary. Also of reasonable determination is payment of a higher salary to a person with a master's degree in social work than to one with a master's degree in another area of study. Not addressed in this case was whether or not one actually needed to be trained as a social worker in order to effectively perform the work assigned.

IMPLICATIONS: This case raises important questions for social workers. In addition to the obvious question of wage discrimination, it highlights the need for professionals in other service disciplines to work jointly to design a viable program which will effectively cope with the large number of problems that children in the public schools currently face.

Public schools are undergoing a major reorganization. Following the lead of major corporations, many administrators have begun to decentralize large districts. As the educational community begins to adjust to changing societal needs, the role of social service personnel in the schools has begun to be examined and questioned as well (Fiske, 1991).

Public schools have been forced to confront a variety of social problems such as drug abuse, teenage pregnancies, delinquency, HIV, and AIDS. Poverty is also a major concern in the schools. As of 1991, more than 14 million children were documented as living in poverty, and of this 14 million, 55% were living in single-parent households. Of the 40 million children enrolled in 82,000 public elementary and secondary schools, 10 million were designated to be "high-risk" (Dryfoos, 1994).

Because of the effects of the cycle of poverty and unemployment, public schools have had to assume a greater degree of responsibility in nonacademic areas such as multiculturalism, special education, connecting schools with the workplace, and providing services for families (Mintzies, 1993). At the same time, budget constraints have placed severe limitations on school administrators, teachers, and support staff.

Budget cuts have forced many school districts to limit support staff and contract out services to community agencies. Consequently, on-site and off-site resource personnel are often not sufficiently linked with one another. Many support workers do not work at the same site each day, and as a result, continuity is severely compromised. Support workers often work alone and rarely receive vital feedback from their colleagues. As a result, opportunities for interaction among professionals are frequently lost, the result being an attitude of competition rather than collaboration (Rosenblum et al., 1995).

Because of the subjective nature of mental health services, there appears to be widespread ignorance about the services that are provided by support staff, and little is known about how the services are implemented (Gibelman, 1995, 1993; Huber & Orlando,1995). Ambiguities regarding service delivery also present significant legal challenges. Wage discrimination (sometimes referred to as "comparable worth") continues to be a controversial issue of civil law and policy. Although this particular case does not deal with gender issues, wage differentials among professionals who are stereotypically "female" have generated a high level of debate among policymakers (Weiler, 1986). For this reason it is important for social workers, as well as psychologists and counselors, to clearly define the parameters of their work.

Employers have also been encouraged to set clear and accurate standards of job evaluation in regard to the setting of wages for employees. A typical evaluation would break down the responsibilities of employees into a small number of common elements such as skill, effort, responsibility, and working conditions (Weiler, 1986). This type of review could help to define the relative worth of each professional and could possibly reduce battles of turf between the professions that have unfortunately become all too common in recent years (Gibelman, 1993; Holley, 1991). Instead, collaborative efforts among social workers, psychologists, and guidance counselors could in many cases lessen the incidence of competition. Similarly, by working as a multidisciplinary team, psychoeducational plans for clients would be more integrated and complete, and unnecessary duplications of services would be avoided (Holley, 1991).

Social workers need to be especially vigilant in protecting their interests both on the local level and at the national level (Gibelman, 1995, 1993; Huber & Orlando, 1995). All too often, decision makers see the role of support services to be superfluous to the educational needs of the children they serve. Most are not aware of the importance of social work interventions for children and families at risk. For these reasons, school social workers who advocate for themselves as well as for their clients must work in harmony with other members of the school staff to have the most desirable impact.

REFERENCES

Dryfoos, J. (1994). *Full service schools.* San Francisco: Jossey-Bass.

Fiske, E. (1991). *Smart schools, smart kids.* New York: Simon and Schuster.

Gibelman, M. (1995). Pay equity in social work: Not! *Social Work, 40*(5), 585-591.

Gibelman, M. (1993). School social workers, counselors, and psychologists in collaboration: A shared agenda. *Social Work in Education 15*(1), 45-53.

Holley, W. (1991). The positive resource team: An interdisciplinary perspective on pupil personnel services. *School Social Work Journal, 17*(2), 47-49.

Huber, R., & Orlando, B. (1995). Persisting gender differences in social workers' incomes: Does the profession really care? *Social Work, 40*(5), 585-591.

Mintzies, P. (1993). The continuing dilemma: Finding a place for the social work profession in the schools. *Social Work in Education, 15*(2), 67 69.

Rosenblum, L., DiCecco, M., Taylor, L., & Adelman, H. (1995). Upgrading school support programs through collaboration: Resource coordinating teams. *Social Work in Education, 17*(2), 117-124.

Weiler, P. (1986). The wages of sex: The uses and limits of comparable worth. *Harvard Law Review, 99*, 1728-1807.

CHAPTER 9
Miscellaneous

Matter of Guardianship of Matejski
419 N.W.2d 576 (Iowa 1988)

FACTS: In 1986, Jan and Tekla Matejski, the legal guardians of their mentally retarded daughter Helen, sought a court order that would allow them to have Helen sterilized. Helen's court-appointed counsel objected, and the matter was eventually appealed to the Supreme Court.

ISSUE: Does a district court have subject-matter jurisdiction to hear a case regarding the sterilization of a mentally retarded adult by her parents?

DECISION: Yes.

REASONING: The court expressed agreement with the Supreme Court of Alaska, which held that jurisdiction should not be confused with "whether or not an order sanctioning the sterilization of a particular incompetent would have been *constitutional* " *[In re C.D.M.*, 627 P.2d 607, 610 (1981)]. As always, a court must remain mindful that it "cannot escape the demands of judging or of making . . . difficult appraisals." [*Haynes v. Washington*, 83 S.Ct. 1336, 1344 (1963)]. Even though the Iowa legislature had recently repealed its mandatory sterilization law, this did not mean that sterilization was prohibited in all circumstances.

IMPLICATIONS: Supreme Court Justice Oliver Wendell Holmes wrote in 1927, "Three generations of imbeciles are enough " [*Buck v. Bell*, 274 U.S. 200 (1927)]. Sterilization laws since then have had a history. While some states passed and then repealed their laws, sterilization *per se* is not unconstitutional, and *Buck v. Bell* has never been overturned.

The reasons behind sterilization are numerous: overly liberal or conservative paternalism; true concern about the impact that becoming a mother or father might have on a person with diminished capacity; a desire to eugenically ensure that society is not financially saddled with another unwanted child; a desire not to deal with more mentally or physically disabled children; a public health concern that promiscuity will lend to the spread of sexually transmitted diseases; and concern about liability of service providers (Parker & Abramson, 1995).

From a public policy and legal perspective, two issues are involved. First, whether an incompetent person has a right to privacy, to not be sterilized, or whether that person is unfairly denied an opportunity to not be sterilized, a right available to all competent persons. Second, whether society's desire to sterilize outweighs the incompetent person's desire not to be sterilized. Courts and professionals have not been of one mind (Ames, 1991; Ragg & Rowe, 1991; Sundram & Stavis, 1994). At issue are such things as the weight to be given to a person's chronological age, experience, and ability to understand the nature and implications of the sexual act, and the ability to consent meaningfully (Hayman, 1990; Kaeser, 1992; Wehmeyer & Metzler, 1995).

REFERENCES

Ames, T. (1991). Guidelines for providing sexually-related services to severely and profoundly retarded individuals: The challenge for the nineteen nineties. *Sexuality and Disability, 9*, 113-122.

Hayman, R., Jr. (1990). Presumptions of justice: Law, politics, and the mentally retarded parent. *Harvard Law Review, 103*, 1202-1271.

Kaeser, F. (1992). Can people with severe mental retardation consent to mutual sex? *Sexuality and Disability, 10*, 33-42.

Parker, T., & Abramson, P. (1995). The law has not been dead: Protecting adults with mental retardation from sexual abuse and violation of their sexual freedom. *Mental Retardation, 33*(4), 257-263.

Ragg, D., & Rowe, W. (1991). The effective use of group sex education with people diagnosed as developmentally disabled. *Sexuality and Disability, 9*, 337-352.

Sundram, C., & Stavis, P. (1994). Sexuality and mental retardation: Unmet challenges. *Mental Retardation, 32*(4), 255-264.

Wehmeyer, M., & Metzler, C. (1995). How self-determined are people with mental retardation? The National Consumer Survey. *Mental Retardation, 33*(2), 111-119.

Wisconsin v. Mitchell
113 S.Ct. 2194 (1993)

FACTS: On October 7, 1989, a group of black men and boys, including Todd Mitchell, were discussing a scene from the movie *Mississippi Burning* in which a black boy was beaten by a white man. The group was asked by Mitchell: "Do you feel hyped up to move on some white people?" Soon thereafter, a white boy walked by. Mitchell said: "You all want to fuck somebody up? There goes a white boy; go get him." They beat the boy so severely that he was in a coma for four days. A jury convicted Mitchell of aggravated battery, an offense that carries a maximum sentence of two years but may be enhanced to seven years when the defendant "intentionally selects the person against whom the crime . . . is committed . . . because of the race, religion, color, disability, sexual orientation, national origin or ancestry of that person . . ." Wis. Stat. § 939.645(1)(b).

Mitchell received a seven-year sentence. He appealed this decision to the U.S. Supreme Court, claiming that a penalty enhancement of this kind violated his First Amendment right of free speech.

ISSUE: Is a "hate crime" statute overbroad because it has a possible chilling effect on a person's First Amendment right to free speech?

DECISION: No. The First Amendment does not prohibit evidentiary use of speech in order to establish motive or intent.

REASONING: A unanimous Supreme Court acknowledged that traditionally judges have taken into account a variety of factors when sentencing a defendant. In addition, the Court gave deference to the Wisconsin legislature's decision to penalize bias-motivated offenses more heavily than other crimes. The "Wisconsin statute singles out for enhancement bias-inspired conduct because this conduct is thought to inflict greater individual and societal harm . . . and are more likely to provoke retaliatory crimes, inflict distinct emotional harm on their victims, and incite community unrest" (p. 2201).

As to Mitchell's assertion that the statute is unconstitutionally overbroad because of its "chilling effect" on free speech, the Court found this argument "attenuated and unlikely." In fact, "evidence of a defendant's previous declarations or statements is commonly admitted in criminal trials subject to evidentiary rules dealing with relevancy, reliability, and the like" (p. 2201).

IMPLICATIONS: There is perhaps no area of law more difficult to understand than the First Amendment. To put any limits on freedom of expression immediately invokes a heightened sense of caution. At issue are the hairline differences between freedom of thought, freedom of speech, the subjective motivation of a defendant, the right to biased or prejudicial feelings, thoughts, or speech, and society's legitimate right to limit any of the foregoing (Barnes & Ephross, 1994; Weiss, 1990). In theory, hate-crime statutes may seem to add greater protection to society and its individual members. Is this protection more symbolic than real? Such laws seem to send a message that bias and prejudice during the commission of a crime will not be overlooked, but one could legitimately ask whether intolerance and hate can really be effectively addressed by legislation rather than education (Resler, 1994).

REFERENCES:

Barnes, A., & Ephross, P. (1994). The impact of hate violence on victims: Emotional and behavioral responses to attacks. *Social Work, 39*(3), 247-251.

Resler, B. (1994). Hate crime—New limits on the scope of First Amendment protection? *Marquette Law Review, 77*, 415-426.

Weiss, J. (1990). Ethnoviolence: Violence motivated by bigotry. In L. Ginsberg et al. (Ed.), *Encyclopedia of social work* (18th ed., 1990 Supp., pp. 307-319). Silver Spring, MD: NASW Press.

GLOSSARY

ABROGATE To annul a previous law.

ABSOLUTE IMMUNITY A total exemption from being sued or from performing duties which other citizens are required to do.

ADJUDICATE a) To settle, pronounce, or award by final judicial decision. b) To act as a judge.

ADVERSARIAL PROCEEDING An action, hearing, or investigation.

AFDC Aid to Families with Dependent Children. Federal/State program designed to provide support for children who are not receiving sufficient financial support from their parents. Financed largely by the federal government and administered by the states. Originally intended for families where one or both natural parents were dead, unable, or unwilling to provide adequate support.

AFFIDAVIT Written statement of fact made voluntarily and under oath (or affirmation).

AFFIRMATION To make a formal declaration of fact or attest to the truth of an affidavit or testimony. Used in place of an oath where religious restrictions prevent oath-taking.

AFFIRMATIVE DEFENSE Facts brought by the defendant in attempt to get excused from a lawsuit, often citing the plaintiff's contributory negligence or the expiration of the statute of limitations.

AGENT A person who acts on behalf or in place of another, generally for business or employment purposes. (Differentiate from Guardian *ad litem*: An agent is authorized by the person who is being represented. A guardian   is appointed by the court to represent a person.)

AGGRIEVED PARTY A party whose legal rights have been violated and who has the right to bring suit against the party who violated those rights.

ALIMONY Payment from one separated or divorced spouse to the other to cover living expenses. (Differentiate from palimony, which awards payment to non-marital parties.)

ANNULMENT A court order invalidating a marriage. (Differentiate from divorce.)

APPELLANT A party who, when dissatisfied with the ruling of a lower court, challenges that judgement by asking for the case to be reviewed by a higher court.

APPELLEE A party who has won a favorable judgement in a lower court proceeding which is being appealed by the appellant. Also called "respondent."

ARBITRATION A way for disputing parties to avoid the formal legal system in which they agree to be bound by the decision of an unbiased, third party.

ARRAIGNMENT Part of a criminal proceeding in which an accused person is brought before the court, is read the indictment, and is asked to plead guilty or not guilty (enter a plea).

BATTERED WOMAN SYNDROME A pattern of constant fear and helplessness exhibited by women who are physically and/or psychologically abused over an extended period of time. Has been used as evidence in cases where battered women retaliate against the alleged batterer.

BATTERY Intentional and wrongful physical contact with another.

BENEFICIARY One who receives or inherits funds, property, or other benefits from another.

BEYOND A REASONABLE DOUBT The standard of guilt which must be met in order to convict a defendant of a crime — overcoming the presumption of innocence until proven guilty.

BRIEF A summary of the facts in a case, applicable law, and supporting evidence written by a lawyer arguing a case in court.

CAUSE OF ACTION A party's grounds for bringing judicial action.

CERTIORARI Latin: To be informed of or to be notified.

CIRCUMSTANTIAL EVIDENCE Indirect evidence that has not been directly witnessed but may be inferred from facts or circumstances demonstrated in a case.

CLASS ACTION A legal action brought on behalf of other people who are similarly situated as is the plaintiff.

CLEAR AND CONVINCING EVIDENCE Evidence which is more believable than "preponderance of evidence" but less than "beyond a reasonable doubt."

COMMON LAW Principles of law derived from community customs and from court decisions recognizing them, but not necessarily from legal statutes.

COMPETENCE The possession of a level of understanding, knowledge, or skill necessary to deem a person qualified to function in certain legal capacities.

COMPLAINT a) Civil case — The first document filed in court by the plaintiff. Contains the cause of action and the demand for compensation for the alleged wrongdoing by the defendant. b) Criminal case — Also called information. A charge in which a person is alleged to have committed a crime. Usually brought by a state prosecutor or other public official and may contain depositions of witnesses to the crime.

CONCURRING OPINION A judge's opinion that agrees with the ruling of the majority of the court but expresses a difference in language, logic, or reasoning for arriving at that conclusion.

CONSENT DECREE A document assented to by opposing parties and agreed to by a court in order to resolve a lawsuit without going through a trial.

CONTINUANCE Court-granted adjournment or postponement of a proceeding to a later date in response to a motion by one of the parties.

CONTRIBUTORY NEGLIGENCE An omission or act by the plaintiff in a case that helped to cause the alleged injury.

COUNTERCLAIM A claim made by one party in answer or opposition to that of the other party.

COURT OPINION The formal, written statement by a court rendering a decision on a case and giving a rationale for its judgement.

CROSS EXAMINATION The questioning of a witness called by the opposing party in a **trial**. (Contrast with direct examination.)

CUSTODIAL PARENT The parent who retains legal responsibility and authority for care, control, and maintenance of a child. Although the non-custodial parent may have a voice in deciding important issues on behalf of the child, ultimate control remains with the custodial parent. (See joint custody.)

DAMAGES Compensation paid to a person who has suffered loss or injury. Damages may be compensatory (amount in measure to actual loss), punitive (punishment), or nominal (awarded in case of general, undetermined, or unproved injury).

DECLARATORY JUDGEMENT A binding determination by a court of the rights and status of litigants in an action without any award of relief.

DEFAMATION Written or oral false communication intended to cause injury to a person's reputation.

DEFAULT a) Intentional failure to perform a duty as agreed. b) Failure to appear in court.

DEFENDANT The person or party being sued or accused.

DEPENDENT A person who relies upon another for support.

DEPOSITION A pretrial discovery device in which testimony is recorded under oath. The testimony may be used as evidence in a trial or to impeach a witness.

DIRECT EXAMINATION The questioning of a witness by the party on whose behalf the witness is testifying in a trial. (Contrast with cross examination.)

DISCOVERY A device used by either party in a trial to obtain information possessed only by the other party and necessary for preparation of the case.

DISSENTING OPINION A written explanation of a judge's or group of judges' reasons for disagreeing with the majority decision. (Differentiate from concurring opinion.)

DIVORCE The ending or dissolution of a valid marriage.

DUE PROCESS CLAUSE The Constitutional guarantee of a fair legal proceeding protecting a person's rights to life, liberty, and property. Appears in both the Fifth and Fourteenth Amendments.

DURABLE POWER OF ATTORNEY A written document authorizing a person to act as another's agent, effective: a) even if the person becomes incapacitated, or b) *only* if the person becomes incapacitated.

EMANCIPATION Parents' surrender of rights and duties concerning the care, custody, control, and earnings of a child. Most often occurs at the age of majority.

EQUAL PROTECTION CLAUSE A clause in the Fourteenth Amendment providing that no person may be denied by a state the same legal protections given to others in similar circumstances.

ESTATE The degree, quantity, nature, and extent of interest or ownership a person has in property.

EX PARTE Latin: An action taken by or on behalf of only one party.

EXPERT WITNESS A person called to testify in a trial because of certain specialized knowledge possessed by that person and not generally possessed by the average layperson. This witness testifies regarding complicated or technical subjects relevant to the case.

FELONY A category of serious crimes including murder, rape, burglary, etc. that are generally punishable by imprisonment of more than one year.

FIDUCIARY A person who willingly accepts the designation or duties of a **trustee,** and who acts solely for the benefit of the person who placed confidence in the fiduciary.

FRAUD Misrepresentation or concealment of fact intended to deceive a person into relying on information which will lead to injury.

GARNISHMENT A procedure by which a plaintiff can obtain money or property of the defendant by collecting it from a third party. For example, collecting money for child support directly from the employer of the person who owes the child support.

GRAND JURY A jury of approximately 12-23 people convened to receive complaints, hear evidence, and determine whether a complaint warrants an indictment.

GUARDIAN *AD LITEM* A person appointed by the court to represent an infant, ward, unborn, or incompetent person in a lawsuit.

GUARDIANSHIP A legal arrangement under which a person has the right and responsibility to care for another or that person's property.

HABEAS CORPUS Latin: Literally, "You have the body." A document which has as its purpose to bring a particular party before a court.

HEARSAY Testimony given by a witness who relates information not known personally. Hearsay evidence is generally inadmissible at trial.

HOLD HARMLESS An arrangement in which one party agrees to hold the other free from responsibility for any liability or damage that may occur within the context of their professional relationship.

HOLDING The legal principle drawn from a judicial decision in a case.

IMMUNITY Freedom from legal responsibility or penalty.

IMPEACH (a witness) To challenge the validity of a witness' testimony to the point of discrediting the witness.

IN CAMERA Latin: In private. In chambers. A proceeding that may be held in a judge's chambers.

INDEMNIFY To compensate a party for loss, expense, or damage.

IN FORMA PAUPERIS Latin: In the form or guise of a poor person. Used to indicate permission granted by the court for an indigent person to initiate a legal action without paying court fees and other legal costs.

INFORMATION A written accusation made by a prosecutor.

INFORMED CONSENT A person's agreement to allow something to happen based on full knowledge of the procedures, risks, and alternatives involved.

INJUNCTION A court order forbidding a person or entity from doing an act or commanding a person or entity to do an act.

IN LOCO PARENTIS Latin: In the place of a parent. A situation in which a person, in the absence of a child's natural parents, accepts responsibility for a child's care and control without formal legal approval.

INTERROGATORY A discovery device consisting of a questionnaire written by one party, submitted to the opposing party, and answered under oath.

INTESTATE To die without leaving a valid will.

ISSUE A disputed fact or question in a court case.

JOINT CUSTODY Arrangement in which both parents retain legal custody of a child as well as sharing responsibility, authority, and physical custody.

JUDICIAL NOTICE Recognition by judge or jury of certain facts as true based on the facts' acceptance as common knowledge and in no need of proof.

JURISDICTION a) The power of a court to hear cases, apply law, render decisions, or enter decrees. b) The extent or range of a court's power, both in legal scope and in geographical area.

LITIGANT Either the plaintiff or the defendant in a lawsuit.

MAJORITY OPINION The opinion of an appellate court to which more than half of its members agree.

MALPRACTICE Professional misconduct, negligence, impropriety, or unreasonable lack of skill resulting in loss or injury to a client.

MISDEMEANOR A category of crimes less serious than felony and punishable by fine and/or less than one year of imprisonment.

MISTRIAL A trial aborted due to an uncorrectable error in procedure, improper jury selection, or a deadlocked jury.

MOTION A formal written or oral request made to the court for an order or ruling.

NEGLECT Finding that a parent or custodian is unable or unwilling to provide proper physical, emotional, or medical care to a child or older person.

OBJECTION A written or oral statement of opposition to a point in a proceeding used to call the court's attention to inappropriate procedure or evidence.

OVERRULE (an objection) A judge's disapproval or disallowance of an objection.

OVERTURN An appellate court's act to reverse a decision made by a lower court.

PARDON An executive official's action to release a person from punishment for a crime.

PARENS PATRIAE Latin: Literally, "Father of his country." Refers to the sovereign power of the government over persons who are incompetent or disabled.

PARENTAL RIGHTS Rights accorded to parents and protected, in varying degrees, by law (e.g., right to discipline or to retain custody of a child). These rights may be assigned by the court to another individual or agency other than the parent.

PAROLE Conditional release of a convicted person prior to having served the full sentence.

PERJURY The crime of lying under oath in a judicial proceeding.

PLEADING A formal statement given by a plaintiff, prosecutor, and defendant listing all claims and defenses by both parties. (See complaint.)

POWER OF ATTORNEY A written document in which a person designates another as an agent to perform specific acts on the person's behalf.

PRECEDENT A previously adjudged case used as guidance for deciding future cases.

PREPONDERANCE OF EVIDENCE The weight of evidence which is greater or more convincing than that of the opposing evidence.

PRESUMPTION An assumption based on law rather than on evidence.

PRIVILEGE AGAINST SELF-INCRIMINATION The privilege afforded by the Fifth Amendment of the U.S. Constitution prohibiting persons from being compelled to testify against themselves.

PROBABLE CAUSE Reasonable ground for believing that a cause of action is valid or that an accused person committed a crime. Necessary for issuing a warrant or making an arrest.

PROBATION A sentence that allows for the release of a convicted person into the community under the supervision of a probation officer.

Often used as a deterrent to help juveniles or first-time offenders avoid imprisonment.

PRO BONO Latin: For the good. Legal work done without pay for the public good.

PROSECUTE To initiate a legal proceeding against a person or entity.

PROTECTIVE ORDER A court order to prevent further harassment of or violence toward a person connected with the proceeding. It may be issued even if there is no trial pending (differentiate from temporary restraining order).

PUBLIC DEFENDER An attorney appointed for the purpose of defending those who cannot afford to pay for legal assistance.

PUNITIVE DAMAGES Damages paid in addition to actual damages as a measure of punishment to the wrongdoer and as a symbolic deterrent to others.

PUTATIVE Alleged, reputed, or supposed (i.e., putative father, putative spouse).

REMAND To send back. Order by a higher court directing a lower court to take action consistent with the higher court's directions.

RES JUDICATA Latin: A thing decided. The principle that determines a court's final judgement to be conclusive, barring any further action between the same parties upon the same claim.

RESPONDENT Person resisting an appeal (see appellee).

RESTITUTION The act of restoring in money or services that of which a person or community has been deprived (see damages).

REVERSE To overthrow, repeal, annul, or revoke a judgement of a lower court.

RULES OF EVIDENCE Rules that govern the appropriate manner of proving facts and the admissibility of these allegations in a trial or hearing.

SANCTION 1) A coercive measure used as a penalty for a violation or as incentive for obedience. 2) To approve, concur, or ratify.

SENTENCE a) Judgement of guilt by a court or judge imposing a punishment to be inflicted. b) The punishment itself (i.e., "serving a sentence").

STANDARD OF PROOF The obligation of litigants to produce sufficient truthful information to win a case. Also called Burden of Proof.

STANDING The right or qualification to initiate or participate in a legal action, established by a party's self-interest in the dispute.

STATUS OFFENSE A type of offense that is considered as such because of the accused person's condition or character (e.g., truancy).

STATUTE OF LIMITATIONS Federal and state law indicating the maximum time period in which to file a lawsuit based on allegation of wrongdoing. After this period has passed, the action may no longer be brought to court.

STIPULATION An agreement made between opposing parties often used to simplify a trial by dispensing with the need to prove uncontested facts.

SUBPOENA A formal document issued by a court ordering a person to appear on a particular date and time and to give testimony before a court.

SUBPOENA DUCES TECUM Latin: A subpoena that directs a person to bring certain documents or other physical evidence to court.

SUMMARY JUDGEMENT A party's motion for quick court judgement, claiming that, since there is no dispute of fact, the moving party is entitled to win the case based on law alone.

SUMMONS A document notifying a defendant of action being brought and commanding the defendant to appear before the court. (Differentiate from subpoena).

SURROGATE MOTHER A woman who agrees to be artificially inseminated with a man's semen, to carry the resulting fetus to term, and to transfer to the man and his wife all rights and obligations to the child.

SUSPECT A person who is believed to have committed a crime.

SUSTAIN (an objection) A judge's approval or affirmation of an objection.

TEMPORARY RESTRAINING ORDER An emergency order of brief duration that is given to prevent damage to one of the parties while waiting for a trial to begin (differentiate from protective order).

TENDER YEARS DOCTRINE (or, Tender Years Presumption) In a custody dispute, automatic award of custody to the mother of a child under the age of thirteen, unless the mother is deemed unfit to care for the child. Recently abolished by many states.

TERMINATION OF PARENTAL RIGHTS A court decision to remove from a parent all rights and responsibilities concerning the child.

TORT Any civil wrong for which a person is liable, causing injury to a person, but not based on breach of contract.

VENUE The appropriate geographic location of a trial. Usually the county or district in which the action arose. (Differentiate from jurisdiction. Both parties may agree to waive a venue but not jurisdiction).

VICARIOUS LIABILITY Indirect legal responsibility for the action of another. Often an employer's responsibility for an employee.

VOIR DIRE French: To speak the truth. a) The process of examining potential jurors for selection. b) A process of inquiring about the admissibility of evidence by questioning a witness out of the jury's presence.

WARD A person, either a minor or incompetent, placed by the court in the care of a guardian or conservator.

WRIT OF CERTIORARI Latin: Order issued by a superior court directing a lower court to send a case record for review.

WRONGFUL BIRTH An action brought by parents of an unwanted child born with defects, claiming damages from the defendant whose negligence caused the unwanted birth.

WRONGFUL DEATH An action brought on behalf of a dead person's beneficiaries, claiming damages from a defendant who willfully or negligently caused the death.

WRONGFUL LIFE An action brought on behalf of an unwanted child born with defects, claiming damages from a defendant whose negligence caused the child's birth.

Recent Bibliography

Alexander, R., Jr. (1993). The legal liability of social workers after DeShaney. *Social Work, 38*, 565-570.

Anderson, D., & Cranston-Gingras, A. (1991). Sensitizing counselors and educators to multicultural issues: An interactive approach. *Journal of Counseling and Development 70*(1), 91-98.

Aubrey, M., & Dougher, M. (1990). Ethical issues in outpatient group therapy with sex offenders. *Journal for Specialists in Group Work, 15*(2), 75-82.

Austin, K., Moline, M., & Williams, G. (1990). *Confronting Malpractice: Legal and Ethical Dilemmas in Psychotherapy.* Newbury Park, CA: Sage.

Beckerman, N. (1995). Suicide in relation to AIDS. *Death Studies, 19*(3), 223-234.

Bednar, R., Bednar, S., Lambert, M., & Whaite, D. (1991). *Psychotherapy with high-risk clients: Legal and professional standards.* Pacific Grove, CA: Brooks/Cole.

Bendor, S. (1991). You are just the patient: A consumer's perspective on preventing medical malpractice suits. *Malpractice Prevention, 6*(3), 6-8.

Bennett, B., Bryant, B., VandenBos, G., & Greenwood, A. (1990). *Professional liability and risk management.* Washington, D.C.: American Psychological Association.

Bennett, C., Blumenfield, S., & Simon, E. (1991). The legal clinic: Helping social workers master the legal environment in health care. *Social Work in Health Care, 16*, 5-17.

Bentley, K. (1993). The right of psychiatric patients to refuse medication: Where should social workers stand? *Social Work, 38*, 101.

Bergin, A. (1991). Values and religious issues in psychotherapy and mental health. *American Psychology, 46*(4), 393-403.

Besharov, D. (1985). *The vulnerable social worker.* Silver Spring, MD: National Association of Social Workers.

Brewer, T., & Faitak, M. (1989). Ethical guidelines for the inpatient psychiatric care of children. *Professional Psychiatry: Research and Practice, 20*(3), 142-147.

Brieland, D., & Lemmon, J. (1985). *Social work and the law.* (2nd ed.). St. Paul, MN: West.

Bullis, R. (1990). Cold comfort from the Supreme Court. Limited liability protection for social workers. *Social Work, 35*(4), 364-366.

Carbino, R. (1992). Policy and practice for response to foster families in the United States facing child abuse allegations: *Child Welfare, 71,* 470-509.

Cayleff, S. (1986). Ethical issues in counseling gender, race, and culturally distinct groups. *Journal of Counseling and Development, 64*(5), 345-347.

Cole, B., & Lewis, R. (1993). Gatekeeping through termination of unsuitable students: Legal issues and guidelines. *Journal of Social Work Education, 29,* 150-159.

Davis, L., & Lieberman, A. (1992). The role of social work in the defense of reproductive rights. *Social Work, 37,* 365-71.

DePauw, M. (1986). Avoiding ethical violations: A timeline perspective for individual counseling, *Journal of Counseling and Development, 64*(5), 303-305.

DeVoe, D. (1990). Feminist and nonsexist counseling: Implications for the male counselor. *Journal of Counseling and Development, 69*(1), 33.

DeWoody, M. (1993). Adoption and disclosure of medical and social history: A review of the law. *Child Welfare, 72,* 195-218.

Frisino, J., & Pollack, D. (1997). HIV testing of adolescents in foster care. *Journal of HIV/AIDS Prevention Education for Children and Adolescents, 1*(1), 53-70.

Garcia, A. (1990). An examination of the social work profession's efforts to achieve legal regulation. *Journal of Counseling and Development, 68*(5), 491-497.

Gelman, S.R. (1990). The practicalities of open access record systems. *The Journal of Social Welfare Law, 4,* 256-269.

Gelman, S.R. (1992). Risk management through client access to case records. *Social Work, 37*(1), 73-79.

Gelman, S.R., Gibelman, M., Pollack, D., & Schnall, D. (1996). Boards of directors on the line: Roles, realities and prospects. *Journal of Jewish Communal Service, 72*(3), 185-194.

Gibelman, M. (1993). School social workers, counselors, and psychologists in collaboration: A shared agenda. *Social Work in Education, 15,* 45-51.

Gibelman, M. (1995). Doing a difficult task "right": Firing employees. *Administration in Social Work, 19*(1), 75-87.

Gibelman, M., & Schervish, P. (1993). The glass ceiling in social work: Is it shatter-proof? *Affilia, 8*(4), 442-455.

Gibelman, M., & Schervish, P. (1993). *Who we are: The social work labor force.* Washington, D.C.: NASW Press.

Grant, L. (1996). Are culturally sophisticated agencies better places for social work staff and administrators? *Social Work, 41*(2), 163-171.

Green, S., & Hansen, J. (1989). Ethical dilemmas faced by family and therapists. *Journal of Marital and Family Therapy, 15*(2), 149-158.

Gustavsson, N., & Kopels, S. (1992). Liability & child welfare. *Child and Adolescent Social Work Journal, 9,* 457-467.

Heinrich, R., Corbine, J., & Thomas, K. (1990). Counseling Native Americans. *Journal of Counseling and Development, 69*(2), 128-133.

Hendrix, D. (1991). Ethics and intrafamily confidentiality in counseling with children. *Journal of Mental Health Counseling, 13*(3), 323-333.

Howing, P., & Wodarski, J. (1992). Legal requisites for social workers in child abuse and neglect situations. *Social Work, 37* (4), 330-360.

Jacobs, C. (1991). Violations of the supervisory relationship: An ethical and educational blind spot. *Social Work, 36*(2), 130-135.

Jones, J.A., & Alcabes, A. (1989). Clients don't sue: The invulnerable social worker. *Social Casework, 70*, 414-420.

Kagel, J., & Kopels, S. (1994). Confidentiality after Tarasoff. *Health and Social Work, 19,* 217-222.

Kopels, S., & Gustavsson, N. (1996). Infusing legal issues into the social work curriculum. *Journal of Social Work Education, 32*(1), 115-125.

Kutchins, H. (1991). The fiduciary relationship: The legal basis for social workers' responsibility to clients. *Social Work*, 36(2), 106-113.

Laury, G. (1992). When women sexually abuse male psychiatric patients under their care. *Journal of Sex Education and Therapy*, *18*(1), 11-16.

Levy, P. (1991). Social work roles in law reform litigation. *Social Work, 36*(5), 434-439.

Linzer, N. (1990). Ethics and human service practice. *Human Service Education, 10*(1), 15-22.

Linzer, N. (1992). The role of values in determining agency policy. *Families in Society: The Journal of Contemporary Human Services, 73*(9), 553-562.

Linzer, N. (1992). Ethical considerations in serving intermarried couples. *Journal of Jewish Communal Service, 69*(1), 92-98.

Melton, G. (1991). Ethical judgements amid uncertainty. *The Counseling Psychologist, 19*(4), 561-565.

Merta, R., & Sisson, J. (1991). The experiential group: An ethical and professional dilemma. *Journal for Specialists in Group Work, 16*(4), 236-245.

Meyers, J. (1994). Expert testimony regarding child sexual abuse. *Child Abuse and Neglect, 17,* 175-185.

Paradise, L., & Kirby, P. (1990). Some perspectives on the legal liability of group counseling in private practice. *Journal for Specialists in Group Work, 15*(2), 114-118.

Pollack, D. (1992). Record retention management: A key element in minimizing agency and worker liability. *Journal of Law and Social Work, 3*(2), 89-95.

Pollack, D. (1993). Liability insurance for foster parents and agencies: The role of commercial insurers. *Journal of Law and Social Work, 4*(1), 33-40.

Pollack, D. (1995). Elder abuse and neglect cases reviewed by appellate courts. *Journal of Family Violence, 10*(4), 413-424.

Pollack, D., & Weiner, A. (1995). Clinical aspects of handling an elder abuse case: The legal and social work perspectives. *Journal of Geropsychology, 1*(4), 271-281.

Reamer, F. (1991). AIDS, social work, and the "duty to protect." *Social Work, 36*(1), 56-60.

Sanders, G., & Nassar, R. (1993). A study of MSW women who have had previous careers. *Journal of Women and Aging, 5*(1), 97-111.

Schnall, D. (1992). Antecedents of social casework in mediating domestic discord. *Journal of Jewish Communal Service, 67*(3), 87-91.

Sobocinski, M. (1990). Ethical principles in the counseling of gay and lesbian adolescents: Issues of autonomy, competence, and confidentiality. *Professional Psychology: Research and Practice, 21*(4), 240-247.

Van Wormer, K. (1992). No wonder social workers feel uncomfortable in court. *Child and Adolescent Social Work Journal. 9,* 117-129.

Wade, K., Stein, E., & Beckerman, N. (1995). Tuberculosis and AIDS: The impact on the hospital social worker. *Social Work in Health Care, 21*(3), 29-42.

Watkins, S. (1990). The double victim: The sexually abused child and the judicial system. *Child and Adolescent Social Work Journal, 7,* 29-42.

Zukansky, T., & Sirles, E. (1993). Ethical and legal issues in field instruction: Shared responsibility and risk. *Journal of Social Work Education, 29,* 338-347.

Index